Chinese Biblical Anthropology

Contrapuntal Readings of the Bible in World Christianity

Series Editors: K. K. Yeo, Melanie Baffes

Just as God knows no boundaries and incarnation happens in shared space, truth does not respect borders and its expression in various contexts is kaleidoscopic. As God's church is birthed forth from local cultures, it is called into a catholic community—namely world Christianity. This series values the twofold identity of biblical interpretations that seek to engage in contextual theology and, at the same time, become part of a global and "many-voiced" conversation for the sake of mutual understanding. By promoting contrapuntal readings that hold contextual and global biblical hermeneutics in tension, this series celebrates interpretations in three movements: (1) those based on the biblical text that honor multiple and interacting worldviews (reading the world biblically/theologically); (2) those that work at the translatability of the biblical text to uphold various dynamic vernaculars and faithful hermeneutics for the world (reading the Bible/theology contextually); and (3) those that respect the cross-cultural and shifting contexts in which faithful communities are embedded, and embody, real-life issues.

International Advisory Board

Walter Brueggemann, William Marcellus McPheeters Professor Emeritus of Old Testament at Columbia Theological Seminary (U.S.)

Adela Yarbro Collins, Buckingham Professor of New Testament Criticism and Interpretation, Yale Divinity School (U.S.)

Kathy Ehrensperger, Research Professor of New Testament in Jewish Perspective, University of Potsdam (Germany)

Justo L. González, Emeritus Professor of Historical Theology, Candler School of Theology, Emory University (U.S.)

Richard A. Horsley, Distinguished Professor of Liberal Arts and the Study of Religion Emeritus, University of Massachusetts— Boston (U.S.)

Robert Jewett, Emeritus Professor of New Testament at Heidelberg University (Germany)

Peter Lampe, Professor of New Testament Theology, Heidelberg University (Germany)

Tremper Longman III, Robert H. Gundry Professor Emeritus of Biblical Studies, Westmont College (U.S.)

Daniel Patte, Professor Emeritus of Religious Studies, New Testament, and Christianity, Vanderbilt University (U.S.)

Volumes in the Series (2018–2019)

Volume 1: *Text and Context: Vernacular Approaches to the Bible in Global Christianity*, edited by Melanie Baffes

Volume 2: *What Has Jerusalem to Do with Beijing? Biblical Interpretation from a Chinese Perspective* (Twentieth Anniversary Edition), K. K. Yeo

Volume 3: *Chinese Biblical Anthropology: Persons and Ideas in the Old Testament and in Modern Chinese Literature*, Cao Jian

Volume 4: *Cross-textual Reading of Ecclesiastes with Analects: In Search of Political Wisdom in a Disordered World*, Elaine Wei-Fun Goh

Chinese Biblical Anthropology

Persons and Ideas in the Old Testament
and in Modern Chinese Literature

Cao Jian

FOREWORD BY
Irene Eber

PICKWICK *Publications* • Eugene, Oregon

CHINESE BIBLICAL ANTHROPOLOGY
Persons and Ideas in the Old Testament and in Modern Chinese Literature

Contrapuntal Readings of the Bible in World Christianity 3

Copyright © 2019 Cao Jian. All rights reserved. Except for brief quotations in critical publications or reviews, no part of this book may be reproduced in any manner without prior written permission from the publisher. Write: Permissions, Wipf and Stock Publishers, 199 W. 8th Ave., Suite 3, Eugene, OR 97401.

Pickwick Publications
An Imprint of Wipf and Stock Publishers
199 W. 8th Ave., Suite 3
Eugene, OR 97401

www.wipfandstock.com

PAPERBACK ISBN: 978-1-5326-5566-1
HARDCOVER ISBN: 978-1-5326-5567-8
EBOOK ISBN: 978-1-5326-5568-5

Cataloguing-in-Publication data:

Names: Cao, Jian, author. | Eber, Irene, 1929–, foreword.

Title: Chinese biblical anthropology : persons and ideas in the Old Testament and in modern Chinese literature / by Cao Jian ; foreword by Irene Eber.

Description: Eugene, OR: Pickwick Publications, 2019. | Contrapuntal Readings of the Bible in World Christianity 3. | Includes bibliographical references and indexes.

Identifiers: ISBN 978-1-5326-5566-1 (paperback). | ISBN 978-1-5326-5567-8 (hardcover). | ISBN 978-1-5326-5568-5 (ebook).

Subjects: LCSH: Bible—Chinese. | Hebrew Bible/Old Testament.

Classification: BS315 J48 2019 (print). | BS315 (ebook).

Scripture quotations marked (NIV) are taken from the Holy Bible, NEW INTERNATIONAL VERSION®, NIV® Copyright © 1973, 1978, 1984, 2011 by Biblica, Inc.® Used by permission. All rights reserved worldwide.

Scripture quotations marked (KJV) are taken from the King James Version (1611). The King James Version is in the public domain.

Manufactured in the U.S.A.   06/14/19

Contents

Foreword by Irene Eber | vii
Acknowledgments | ix
Preface | xi
Abbreviations | xxiv

1. The Old Testament in Chinese Culture: Slow Beginnings in Turbulent Times | 1
2. The Old Testament and New Concerns at the End of the Nineteenth and Beginning of the Twentieth Centuries | 27
3. The Vernacular Old Testament, Education, and the New Literature | 56
4. Monotheism and Chinese Intellectuals in the New Culture Movement | 83
5. Moses, the Prophets, and Chinese Intellectuals | 109
6. Concluding Reflections | 135

Bibliography | 141
Author Index | 167
Subject Index | 173
Scripture Index | 179

Foreword

IN THE EARLY YEARS of the twentieth century, when the new Chinese literature and its writers emerged, the Bible in Chinese translation was part of the new literary trends. To be sure, Bibles already had been translated in the nineteenth century, but a new era began with the Mandarin (*guan hua* 官話) translation of the Episcopal Translating Committee, to be followed by the Union Bible of 1919. To writers and readers of the new literature, the attraction of the Bible—and especially of the Old Testament (OT)—was not only its importance in the West but also its narrative art and its manner of storytelling. Readers were confronted not only by such men as King David with all his advantages and weaknesses, but also with Moses, an outstanding and superior man who was creative and patient as well as inspired to act in a moral way.

Increasingly the appreciation of the OT was enhanced, as shown in this important study, by the development of a commentary tradition. That is, in such journals as *Jiaohui Xinbao* (Church News 教會新報) and *Wanguo Gongbao* (Globe Magazine 萬國公報), Chinese writers gave their readers explanations of how to read and understand the OT in the context of Chinese culture. These initial interpretations are especially significant. By following the actual OT translations, they are the first steps in integrating aspects of the OT into the Chinese context. The OT translation was similarly significant to the movement of writing Chinese as it is spoken (the *bai hua* 白話 movement). Thus, both intellectual change, together with written language change, were significant in this period, and this study reveals how aspects of the OT had a function in those turbulent times.

At the same time, the author is fully aware that monotheism, the importance of the One God, is the central idea in the OT. His discussion of how May-Fourth Chinese intellectuals reconciled monotheism and various ideas of modernity with Chinese thought is singularly perceptive, as is his observation that Chinese thought tends to be inclusive rather than selectively exclusive. This means that ideas we might think contrary to a worldview and which, therefore, need to be rejected, were considered for integration and accommodation within Chinese culture. Thus, aside from Moses who often was shown as exemplary, there were the Hebrew prophets. Despite the ill-fitting Chinese term *xianzhi* (先知; "foreknower"), most Chinese intellectuals were well aware that a *xianzhi* was not someone who merely could know what the future would bring. Rather, he was a man very much concerned with the present, with human life, and the kind of human being a man ought to be. This being the case, OT prophets were not that different from Chinese sages, still revered at the present time.

Attention to the various features of the OT and their appeal to Chinese readers does not mean that the religious content did not speak to new readers as well. Quite the contrary. The Protestant message of Christianity, considering that Protestant translations predominated, was widely heard then, and it continues to be heard to the present day. However, the significant feature of the present work is that it also shows the extent to which Old-Testament content appealed to non-Christian Chinese readers and, as a result, left an imprint on modern Chinese culture.

Professor Irene Eber
The Hebrew University of Jerusalem
January 15, 2018

Acknowledgments

H ERE I WOULD LIKE to express my heartfelt thanks to those who have helped me complete this work. Since this publication is a revised version of my original doctoral dissertation at The Hebrew University of Jerusalem, I would first like to thank Professor Irene Eber. Not only did she serve as my academic instructor but also as spiritual support. Without her supervision and encouragement, this work would not have been possible. My special thanks also go to Professor Roman Malek, former Director of Monumenta Serica Institute, for his extraordinary support during my research visit there. I must mention with gratitude other brilliant scholars who also gave me most valuable advice or instruction, such as Edward Greenstein, Wolfgang Kubin, Maren Niehoff, Tania Notarius, Zvi Werblowsky, to name just a few. In the process of my doctoral research, I benefited from generous grants from Rothberg International School, Katholischer Akademischer Auslaender-Dienst, W. F. Albright Institute of Archaeological Research, the Israel-China Friendship Society, the Institute for Advanced Study in Asian Cultures and Theologies (IASACT), and Raymond Kaplan Scholarship.

Since completing the dissertation in 2009, I have re-worked some sections and expanded them into publishable articles, which can be found in journals or festschrifts. I have been assisted substantially in this endeavor by scholars and editors such as Raoul Findeisen, Marian Galik, Barbara Hoster, Dirk Kuhlmann, Roger L. Omanson, Thomas Tseng, and Billy T. C. Yan.

I am most grateful for Dr. K. K. Yeo's invitation to participate in his new series, *Contrapuntal Readings of the Bible in World Christianity*, and his efficient efforts to facilitate the process. The original title of my dissertation "Men and Ideas of the Old Testament in Modern Chinese Thoughts" has been changed to the present one in order to fit the series better. In editing this version of my dissertation, Dr. Melanie Baffes paid attention to detail and

ACKNOWLEDGMENTS

prepared the manuscript for publication. A special word of thanks also is due to my M.A. students, Yu Zihan and Zhang Haoran, for their most skillful and timely computer help with my last work on the bibliography.

Finally, I wish to thank my mother Ji Qiwen, my father Cao Minglou, and my wife Wu Ying for their unwavering confidence and support all these years. They provide a happy and loving family in which to work and study.

Preface

THE BIBLE, IN VARIOUS ways, has been present in China since at least the seventh century but has witnessed its golden age there only in the last two hundred years. In the Yuan dynasty 元朝 (1271–1368), part of the New Testament (NT) and the Psalms were translated into Mongolian, rather than Chinese, and have disappeared as did other vestiges of the Catholic Church introduced by the Franciscan friars. Neither the Jesuits nor Russian Orthodox Christianity succeeded in translating the Scriptures, despite their encounter with Chinese literati or their uninterrupted presence in the capital.[1] However, when British and American Protestants came to China in the early nineteenth century, it was a different story. They were active in most parts of China—aided by gunboats, merchants, China's weakness, its social unrest, and the pervasive evangelism of their home churches carried out in China. Their remarkable achievement in translating the Bible and introducing it to larger segments of the Chinese population, particularly the educated, is the topic of this writing.[2]

In the nineteenth and twentieth centuries, the introduction of the Bible and the Chinese literary and intellectual reception and appropriation of it, are matters of great importance, for a number of reasons. Christian missionaries came into contact with a highly literate civilization in China. The literary responses to the Bible in Chinese grew remarkably since the

---

1. Nestorian Christians came to China in the seventh century and almost disappeared in the anti-Buddhist sweep between 841 and 845, but they reappeared briefly at the Mongol court centuries later. In 1289, Franciscan friars from Europe initiated mission work in China, which disappeared from 1368, as the Ming dynasty 明朝 (1368–1644) set out to eject foreign influences. In 1582, Jesuits once again instated mission work inside China, but they were finally expelled after 1721 due to a long-running controversy over Chinese customs and names for God. Russian Orthodoxy was introduced in 1715, and Protestants began entering in 1807. For details about Christian groups in China, see Bays, *A New History*.

2. This work is a revised doctoral dissertation I completed in 2009 at The Hebrew University of Jerusalem, supervised by Professor Irene Eber.

1860s. Christians and non-Christians incorporated motifs and themes into their works. They show how nineteenth- and twentieth-century intellectuals have tried to understand the traumatic events of their time by resorting to and interpreting the biblical messages.

In the field of Sino-Western cultural exchange, "The Bible in China" has in the past three decades attracted increasing attention among scholars. Problems concerning introduction, reception, and appropriation of the Bible in China have inspired scholars to raise many questions. Book-long efforts have been made in studying Chinese Bible versions and their literary impact.[3] There are still many questions, while others need rethinking. For example, one result of the prevalent interest in the NT is that the role and impact of the NT or Christian culture often is exaggerated. The lack of research regarding the Old Testament (OT) and Jewish culture in China has been an obstacle to our understanding the history of the Bible and Christianity in China.[4]

Interpreting OT ideas and humanity poses several basic problems. Firstly, there is the question of selection. For what an interpreter will choose is invariably related to specific values, concerns, and even goals of his own period. Secondly, the interpreter's ideological, philosophical, or political point of view is bound to influence the choices he makes. And thirdly, when an interpreter interprets from a literature with whose language he is not familiar—thus using a secondary language—his selection is in fact already pre-selected. Notions gained and views developed regarding other peoples—on the basis of interpretations—are, therefore, sometimes

---

3. Some major works on the Chinese Bible versions include Zhao, *Yijing suyuan* (Tracing the Origin of Bible Translating), 1993; Zetzsche, *Bible in China*, 1999; Xing, *Shengjing guanhua heheben jufa yanjiu* (Syntactic Studies on the Chinese Mandarin Version), 2012; Xu, *Gudai shengjing hanyi* (Chinese Bible Translating in History), 2014 and Liu, *Yuyan de shehuishi* (The Social History of Language), 2015. The impact of the Bible on modern Chinese literature was first studied in Robinson, *Double-edged Sword*, 1986. Some other works are Kinkley, *Odyssey of Shen Congwen*, 1987; Yang, *Kuangye de husheng* (Crying in the Wilderness), 1998; and Wang, *Ershi shiji zhongguo wenxue* (Twentieth-century Chinese Literature), 2000; Guo, *Wusi nüxing zuojia* (The Bible and Women Writers during the May Fourth Period), 2013 and Mak, *Protestant Bible Translation and Mandarin*, 2017. There also are collections of papers such as Eber et al., *Bible in Modern China*, 1999 and Gálik, *Influence, Translation and Parallels*, 2004.

4. Not all impact can be attributed to Christianity and the Christian Bible. For example, Hu Shi (1891–1962) had very close contact with some Jews, including professors and students in America; see Hu, *Hushi koushu zizhuan* (Oral Autobiography of Hu Shi), 33.

distorted. Similarities may be seen where none exist, and differences may be glossed over because they are not properly understood.[5]

Before the 1970s, studies of Christianity in China usually reflected a mission-centered approach.[6] But scholars gradually recognized that they could not study "Christianity in China" without saying anything about the Chinese context and Chinese converts. A "China-centered" approach was advocated by Paul Cohen, when he explained what was happening in modern China. Cohen's point of view is significant, because he argued that concrete historical data comprise not historical events but the personal experiences of individuals, including their thoughts, feelings, and motivations. As a result, Chinese converts too became an important subject. Why did they accept Christianity? Did they respond to missionary preaching? How did they maintain a balance between Chinese culture and Christian ideas? And how did they justify their faith in the face of anti-foreign, revolutionary tides in China?[7] In this writing, these questions are posed also in studying the encounter with the OT.

Modern Chinese intellectuals, whether Christian or not, perceive themselves naturally as the moral, social, and political leaders of their country. The dominant literature of twentieth-century China has therefore been strongly concerned with the problems of intellectuals in China's modernizing society. The terminology and concepts with which writers variously defined their role in society in the early decades of the twentieth century were derived from Western models, including those from the OT, like the prophets.[8]

This work aims to provide a broad picture of the modern history of the OT from the nineteenth century to the twentieth century, showing the ways in which the OT encountered Chinese culture through one of the most difficult, exiting, and confusing periods in China's long history. My major interest is twofold: to study a number of human beings and ideas in the Hebrew Bible and to understand how ideas change when transposed into another cultural context. This raises the question of which OT persons and ideas were important to educated Chinese? What made them

---

5. Eber et al., "Translation Literature in Modern China," 291–311.

6. The mission-centered approach is obvious in such works as Latourette, *History of Christian Missions*, 1929; D'Elia, *Catholic Missions in China*, 1941; Cary-Elwes, *China and the Cross*, 1957, to name just a few.

7. Wang, "Moving toward a Mature, Balanced Stage," 22.

8. McDougall and Louie, *Literature of China*, 4–7.

appealing? How were those OT persons and ideas reinterpreted? In what way did they inspire interested readers? By answering these and other questions, I hope to contribute to a more comprehensive picture of the Bible in modern China.

The growth of a commentary tradition is closely connected with general interest in the OT. The OT in modern Chinese thought can be divided into three major periods reflecting the growth of a commentary tradition. The first period, from the arrival of the Protestants in 1807 to the outbreak of the Sino-Japanese War in 1894, represents the beginning of the OT in China. At this time, foreign missionaries played a decisive role in introducing the OT to Chinese literati. Discussions among both converts and a small number of official scholars ensued as a more broadly-based readership of the OT appeared.

The second period, from 1895 to the 1910s, when the Qing court was replaced by the Republic, was a transitional period. For the first time, diversities and controversies among non-converts appeared. Various perspectives on interpreting the OT became obvious. But due to lack of sufficient knowledge of OT literature, commentary efforts were made only by a small number of interpreters and limited to a very small number of OT motifs.

The third period, dating from the May Fourth Movement to the eve of the establishment of the People's Republic, is a period of the appropriation of OT persons and ideas. Thanks to the successes with vernacular translations and OT education in previous years facilitated by the missionaries, OT commentaries were now much more diverse and extensive using different methods and ideologies. They also covered many more OT persons and ideas, some of these being allusions in the language of the intellectuals despite the non-existence of the referent and reference in the Chinese language.[9]

These periods form the five main chapters of the work. Translation of both the OT and OT studies is considered the first step in the introduction of the OT. The second step concerns its reception, by which I mean the comments by Chinese readers on the OT that represented initial attempts to understand and interpret a text in which new and different ideas were

---

9. An allusion is a direct or indirect reference to a person, place, event, or character, usually well-known in history, literature, legend, mythology, or books like the Bible. In dealing with allusions, we should ask particularly if an allusion adds anything to the meaning or effect of a work. Allusions are deeply rooted in the soil of a particular culture and cannot be easily transplanted into a foreign land and bear the same fruit. Hwang, "Allusions," 14–15.

expressed. It is this reception that led in time to the third step, that of appropriation, when writers and intellectuals integrated OT images, metaphors, symbols and the like into non-religious texts—although the line between reception and appropriation is not always clearly drawn.

A major prerequisite for reception and appropriation is readability. This is the stage in which Chinese translations made their contributions. Two prime examples are the Delegates' Bible in classical Chinese and Schereschewsky's Mandarin translation which, until the appearance of the 1919 Union Bible, was the most widely read version of the OT. Readability is not only clarity of language for understanding the ideas expressed in the text. By readability, I also mean the power to evoke a response, be it a creative act, like writing poetry, or a philosophical inquiry.[10] Reception and appropriation are the very responses evoked by the readability of the Chinese OT. If reception was primarily a function of the new Christian audience, appropriation included non-Christians as well.

The OT in Chinese culture began with its introduction and reception among converts. Persons and ideas of the OT were introduced by Protestant missionary authors like Karl Friedrich A. Gützlaff (1803–1851) and Bible translators like Walter H. Medhurst (1796–1857) and Samuel I. J. Schereschewsky (1831–1906), with the help of their Chinese colleagues. In introducing the Bible, unlike the Catholics, Protestants refer more to story than to dogma, concentrate more on biblical narrative than on creedal formulation.[11] The Bible as story pointed out the specific nature of the biblical presentation of past events: the Bible is more a narrated history than a cause-and-effect reconstruction of the exact course of historic events. It does not primarily reconstruct, but rather interprets.[12]

Moreover, in introducing the OT, Protestant missionaries tended to resort to familiar concepts and paradigms taken from the Chinese Classics. Considering the various translations of the Chinese Bible, none can be considered a literal translation; they can be described only as more or less successful transpositions. To attract Chinese educated readers, the missionary authors and translators also adopted dominant literary devices and

10. Eber et al., "Introduction," 13–26. Initiated by Irene Eber, some most original efforts have been made in recent years in studying the Chinese translation by Schereschewsky; see particularly Eber, *Jewish Bishop*, 1999; Yariv-Laor, "Linguistic Aspects," 101–20; and Cao, "Chinese Mandarin Bible," 122–38. For the study on the 1919 Union Bible, see Zetzsche, *Bible in China*.

11. Marty, "Protestantism," 28.

12. Mascarenhas, "Bible as a Book," 412–13.

styles. As a result, OT persons and ideas indeed aroused interest in the OT and discussions on its motifs among some educated Chinese, first of all, among educated converts.

However, Chinese Christians did not simply follow their missionary leaders, but produced a discourse aimed at forming new terminologies and new theories of understanding biblical doctrines. Although they, like the missionaries, often invoked the Chinese classics to prove a point, most of their essays were explanatory rather than polemical. One example was the attempt to understand the Ten Commandments and to explain them in vocabulary akin to Chinese moral, particularly Neo-Confucian, maxims. In interpreting the Decalogue, instead of stern prohibitions, these initial interpreters chose not only a gentler form such as poetry for conveying OT messages, but attempted also to show that these messages differed little, if at all, from what the Chinese themselves had known and practiced since earlier times.

Chinese non-Christians, especially Confucian literati like reformist thinkers Xu Jiyu 徐继畬 (1795–1873) and Song Yuren 宋育仁 (1857–1931), read the missionary publications and showed an interest in OT motifs. At the time, Protestant missionaries were especially influential in the littoral of China, where most of these reformers were from. While among them the interest was increasingly stimulated, pressure to preserve or redefine their Chinese identities mounted, underscoring the problem of racial difference and Western prejudice. Thus Confucianism, which was after all Chinese, acquired for most of them a new importance and became something to hold onto in their interpretation of OT persons and ideas.

However, once the reformers took control in the littoral, they found themselves in a strategic position to break out of traditional patterns and establish new ones. Through their writings, they transformed what had once been totally strange into something a little less foreign, gradually accustoming people to the newness of the new, making it less conspicuous, more palatable. Broader acceptance was given to ideas that a short time before had been acceptable only to a few. Hinterland change was facilitated by these littoral intellectuals. The reformers before the 1890s were among the first generation of modern Chinese who began the transition to nationalism; therefore, their writings about OT persons and ideas were particularly meaningful.[13]

---

13. My discussion on the role of littoral literati and their impact on the hinterland is based on Cohen, "Littoral and Hinterland," 197–99, 211, and 224–25.

If the Chinese response to the OT until this moment was basically passive and rather limited in scope among non-Christians, after the defeat of China in the 1894 Sino-Japanese War, the response became increasingly more active and pronounced. Together with the growing interest in the OT appeared new interpretative tendencies among educated Chinese like Shan Shili 单士厘 (1858–1945), Tang Caichang 唐才常 (1867–1900), and Kang Youwei 康有为 (1858–1927). These were joined with various political ideals at a time of national crisis. A major phenomenon was the awareness of the Jewish Diaspora. The Jews "culturally constructed/reconstructed" as "other" remained a distant mirror in the construction of the "self" among various social groups in modern China. Thus the definition of "Jew" had both a religious and secular meaning. On the one hand it symbolized tradition, and on the other it invoked modernity.

The Jewish problem became relevant to many of China's revolutionary nationalists, to whom statelessness was the cause of the Jewish tragedy and signaled a powerful warning. Since they found that money could not save the stateless Jews, their criticism also was thus directed toward the modernizing reformers who hoped that the nation's acquisition of wealth might be a solution. By demonstrating that the past glory of the Jews did not save them from their present suffering, revolutionary nationalists also were against the reformist idea of preserving Confucianism and the emperor. To avoid being like the stateless Jews, China must promote nationalism first.[14] During this transitional period, Liang Qichao 梁启超 (1873–1929) showed a keen interest in the OT story of Exodus and Moses in many of his writings. He is, therefore, discussed in more detail with a focus on his creative portrait of a new Moses in accordance with his call for "new citizens" and heroes. Ye Dehui 叶德辉 (1864–1927) the main opponent of Liang among orthodox Confucians and others revealed the impact of the OT motifs in their writings.

During the transitional period, the vernacular movement of Bible translating and the missionary movement of OT education popularized and modernized the reading and study of OT literature among both educated adults and the youth at missionary schools. Without ignoring other reasons for the increasing emphasis on the use of vernacular, clearly Protestant missionaries played a unique and pioneering role in the vernacular movement by means of their constant efforts to produce a unified version

---

14. Zhou, *Chinese Perceptions*, 2, 4, and 52.

of the Chinese Bible and study aids like commentaries and textbooks for Chinese readers.

Vernacularization of Bible translation and reading tremendously enhanced the ever-growing distribution of the OT in China. The sale of the Bible grew fast, even in 1923 and 1924—in spite of and perhaps because of the Anti-Christian Movement.[15] The great number of Scriptures that circulated in China year after year were not without their influence. However, it must be remembered that OT education, together with vernacular Bible translation, augmented the vernacular movement or were part of it.

Missionary schools emerged with the rise of the Yangwu (Foreign Affairs) movement in the second half of the nineteenth century, when the Chinese intellectuals' attitude toward the West changed. These flourished after the Boxer rebellion, when the interest in Christianity grew, and with the establishment of the Republic, which initiated a new epoch for evangelical Christianity in China. During this period, the abolition of the civil-service examinations in 1905 and the end of the Chinese imperial house in 1911 saw the breakdown of the highly integrated traditional political, social, cultural, and moral order.

Administration of the missionary schools was in the hands of the foreign missionaries, and much emphasis was given to Bible study. Courses on OT books were taught at all levels in vernacular. As a result of the joint impact of modern science, Protestant liberal theology, higher criticism in biblical studies, the Student Volunteer Movement for Foreign Missions, the awareness of the Chinese context, and the ambition to take a lead in Chinese reforms, these schools approached OT persons and ideas from not only a theological perspective but also from historical, political, and literary perspectives.

OT education run by missionaries left its mark even on Chinese students abroad. In fact, most students returning to China had been enrolled in Bible classes at some period in their college careers.[16] The Chinese Students' Christian Association was organized in every country where a considerable number of students were present. Bible classes were provided for them. In America, for example, students' summer conferences, where Chinese students were brought in groups to spend ten days with several hundred selected

---

15. For statistic evidence, see Latourette, *History of Christian Missions*, 648 and 788. Also see *China Mission Year Book*, 1923, 116; and 1925, 369–73.

16. Mei, "Returned Student in China," 173.

American students in Bible study, was considered by Arthur Ruth as "the most effective single method of work" for Chinese students.[17]

The introduction and reception of the OT through vernacular Bible reading and school OT education were the major building blocks that facilitated the later entry of OT ideas and imagery into China's wider theological and literary discourse. One immediate result of modern Bible reading and OT education was the interest among Christian intellectuals in the literary significance of the OT. Old-Testament images and imagery often were creatively transformed in their literary works. Although long ignored by scholars, their many discussions on the literary art of the Chinese OT deserve a position in modern Chinese literature. The Chinese OT was a convenient and important source of inspiration to many Chinese authors.

Old-Testament translation into the vernacular, OT education, and literary writings made possible the entrance of OT ideas and imagery into a wider discourse. Even if later theologians, writers, or intellectuals during the following period of the New Culture Movement might not be actually aware of, or had not read these early works, ideas once expressed tended to assume a life and dynamic of their own, spoken of or mentioned perhaps in random conversations. They were transformed into new, or different and more developed, forms by others in another place and at another time. Perhaps they were not a mighty stream, but not a mere trickle either. If these can be taken as signs of the OT text becoming part of the larger cultural context, then we should again remind ourselves that it began with the Bible's readability, progressing from there to interpretability.

Following the transitional period, discussions of OT persons and ideas became abundant and diverse among Chinese intellectuals in an era in which there was a prevalent concern with scientism, Western philosophy, the fate of Chinese culture, and nationalism. The focus of my survey is on the OT ideas of God and monotheism as widely discussed by people of different ideologies. The assumption is that the ideas of God and monotheism, when interpreted in light of scientism, Western philosophy, and traditional Chinese culture, are closely related to the interpreters' ideals of individual and social perfection at the time of suffering and crisis.

The controversy between science and religion in 1921, as well as that between science and life in 1923, were most influential.[18] Christian intellectuals tried hard to reconcile their faith in God with modern science.

---

17. Ruth, "Chinese Students Abroad," 156–57.
18. Lam, *Zhonghua shenxue wushi nian* (Fifty Years of Chinese Theology), 206.

Meanwhile, to counter the challenge of monism of scientism, some non-Christian traditionalists also argued for a value system that originated not in science but in religion, ethics, and aesthetics.[19] There were those who suggested that the contribution of science to national salvation comes neither from blind faith in its omnipotence nor from the extreme views of scientism, but from the scientific spirit, which is similar to religious spirit. In their search for justification in a scriptural text, both theologians and non-Christian intellectuals found the OT a rich and promising source, arguing for the value of Hebrew culture, especially the monotheistic idea of God, at times of cultural and national crises. Preoccupation with social injustice led Chinese interpreters to search for OT persons and ideas that would describe the universality of suffering and oppression.

Chinese liberal Christians considered suffering and oppression as God's punishment but emphasized that punishment was a necessary condition and was rewarded. This is in agreement with authentic Jewish exegesis. According to the latter, eating the forbidden fruit for example is punished, but rewarded too, as knowing good and evil is the essential human ability for moral judgment, which is gained in the same event. This story sets distance or separation between God and man as punishment, on the one hand, and as the motive to enable life and progress, on the other. Punishment in the human world is thus established as a necessary motivation for action and progress.[20]

This agrees well with classical Confucian thought represented by Confucius 孔子 (551–479 BCE) and Mencius 孟子 (371–289 BCE).[21] As a result of their faith in such an agreement, many Chinese Christian intellectuals believed that both the follower of Confucian dao道 (the way) and the follower of God aim for a morally ideal world. In this way, they provided a moral foundation for nationalism and universalism. Since the basic setting of the current anti-Christianity movement was anti-imperialist nationalism, they claimed that nationalism in a broad sense agrees with the principles of monotheism, and monotheism helps accomplish nationalism. Although universalism is the ultimate goal as advocated by the OT prophets, nationalism is the only path one must follow to realize universalism.

19. Kwok, *Zhongguo xiandai sixiang zhong de wei kexue zhuyi* (Scientism in Modern Chinese Thought), 112.

20. Patt-Shamir, "Confucianism and Judaism," 61–64.

21. For relevant discussions of classical Confucian thought, see Lin, "Reflections," 74–99 and Tu, "Rooted in Humanity," 60–65.

Inevitably, for those who believed in national salvation as basically a religious problem of morality, preceding political and social ones, it must start from individual reform, which surely leads to social reforms. Non-Christian intellectuals were occupied equally by the search for a way to perfect personality and a morally ideal world. With a common belief in the aesthetic function of empathy as the key to uniting people, some leading intellectuals like Wang Guowei 王国维 (1877–1927) and Cai Yuanpei 蔡元培 (1868–1940) resorted to aesthetic education. Aesthetics to them refers to more than mere art: it is a more general appreciation of beauty, of harmony and idealization, to which monotheistic sentiment was believed to be particularly helpful.[22]

Among OT men, Moses and the prophets too were noted in this research. They were discussed as religious or political leaders or simply as ideal human beings by converts like Yuan Ding'an 袁定安[23] and Li Rongfang 李荣芳 (1887–1965) but also by others like Sun Yat-sen 孙逸仙 (1866–1925) and Lu Xun 鲁迅 (1881–1936). As mentioned in chapter 5, the meaning and connotation of the word "prophet" in modern Chinese usage is very different from the meaning of the word in the OT. It introduced a new image, which combined the features of a Chinese sage and prophet, though the combination was dependent on the author's ideology. Thus the image of a prophet was very often adjusted to contemporary needs.

Therefore, when observing the cultural encounter between Jewish, Christian, and Confucian traditions and the uses of OT persons and ideas in Chinese intellectual history, it is significant to understand the new meanings added to OT motifs. The OT was part of contemporary intellectual concerns and ideas from one culture interacting with those of another. How those ideas were transposed into the receptor culture is of special interest.

As long as the missionaries supervised their translation and distribution of the Chinese OT, explained them to the Chinese, and adapted their message to Confucian ideology, Christianity remained largely an alien body and failed to take root in Chinese soil. The missionaries could not avoid the bias regarding the superiority of Christian religion and Western philosophy. However, when a Chinese OT commentary tradition developed and when Chinese intellectuals selected, adapted, and integrated the new ideas in the Chinese context, both the OT and the foreign creed became a part of Chinese tradition.

22. Lee, "Aesthetic Education," 19.
23. Hereafter, if dates are not provided, they are unknown.

Contextualization demands pluralism, and intercultural thinking indicates emancipation from all kinds of unitary explanations. With both failures and successes, Chinese OT commentary demonstrated that neither the hermeneutics of total identity—which reduces the other to an echo of oneself and repeats its self-understanding in the name of understanding the other—nor that of radical difference that makes the understanding of the other impossible, is correct. Truth should not be defined in terms of one particular tradition. To put one particular framework in an absolute position is methodologically wrong.[24]

The gap between Jewish monotheism and Confucian non-theistic view is obvious. In Judaism, the *halakha* is given by God and cannot accept human beings as equal creators. The inclination to separation and disharmony are primary motivations for action. The exemplary personality is tested by God and can only follow the way by passing the test. Judaism takes the perspective that human nature had flaw in it (*yetzer hara*), and defines human nature in a dualistic way, as a compound of conflicting tendencies formed in creation.

At great odds is the Confucian vision that stresses the continuity of being between human and cosmic existence. In Confucianism, the general inclination is toward a partnership of the human and dao. It signifies the shared work of co-creation of human beings, earth, and heaven. Hence, unification and harmony are essential motivations for action. The exemplary personality is the full realization of this harmony by means of self-reflection. Early Confucian thought basically defined human nature in a monistic way as a single-minded entity, either in the Mencian case as the good nature to preserve and improve, or, as according to Xun zi 荀子 (313–238 BCE), as a heaven-endowed nature given to us for the work of improvement.[25]

What matters, however, is the fact that despite that obvious gap between the OT and the Confucian views, Chinese intellectuals were still attracted by OT persons and ideas. Even more significantly, they were able to transform them in the new context and made use of them for the purpose of their own agendas. In the process, accommodation was the most fruitful way of action, not only as a strategic method, but as a cultural imperative.

This research is based primarily on the actual writings by Chinese authors. Both well-known and more obscure Chinese figures were important to this research, regardless of their ideologies. As far as their

24. Zürcher, "Aliens and Respected Guests," 91–92.
25. Patt-Shamir, "Confucianism and Judaism," 61–64.

interpretations of OT motifs are concerned, the focus is naturally on the changes the interpreters made of the original OT text. Those differences are significant, because they illustrate more clearly the contextualization of OT persons and ideas in modern China and the meeting points of OT traditions with Chinese culture.

Abbreviations

CFJ	*Caifeng ji* 采风记 (Records of Folk Collection)
CR	*The Chinese Recorder* 教务杂志
CRP	*Chinese Repository* 中国丛报
CYPMYLJ	*Caiyuanpei meiyu lunji* 蔡元培美育论集 (Cai Yuanpei's Works on Aesthetic Education)
CYPQJ	*Caiyuanpei quanji* 蔡元培全集 (Complete Collection of the Works by Cai Yuanpei)
CYPXSQJ	*Caiyuanpei xiansheng quanji* 蔡元培先生全集 (Complete Works by Mr. Cai Yuanpei)
JDJYWX	*Jidujiao yu wenxue* 基督教与文学 (Christianity and Literature)
JHXB	*Jiaohui xinbao* 教会新报 (Church News)
JYRWZ	*Jiuyue renwu zhi* 旧约人物志 (Personalities of the OT)
LXQJ	*Luxun quanji* 鲁迅全集 (Complete Works of Lu Xun)
NT	New Testament
OT	Old Testament (Hebrew Bible)
SB	*Shenbao* 申报 (Shanghai Daily)
SJB	*Shengjing bao* 圣经报 (The Bible Newspaper)
SM	*Shengming* 生命 (Life)
SXZ	*Shenxue zhi* 神学志 (Theological Quarterly)
WGGB	*Wanguo gongbao* 万国公报 (Globe Magazine)
WMCYWB-S	*Wanmu caotang yigao waibian-shang* 万木草堂遗稿外编（上）(Additional Manuscripts of Wanmu Grass Hall)
XY	*Xiwang yuekan* 希望月刊 (Christian Hope)
YBSHJ-WJ	*Yinbing shi heji-wenji* 饮冰室合集-文集 (Collected Works and Essays of the Ice Drinker's Studio-Essays)

YBSHJ-ZJ	*Yinbing shi heji-zhuangji* 饮冰室合集-专集 (Collected Works and Essays of the Ice Drinker's Studio-Works)
YHZL	*Yinghuan zhilue* 瀛寰志略 (Brief Description of the World)
YJCB	*Yijiao congbian* 翼教丛编 (Collected Writings for Upholding Orthodoxy)
ZG	*Zhenguang* 真光 (True Light)
ZGZZ	*Zhenguang zazhi* 真光杂志 (True Light Review)
ZJ	*Zijing* 紫晶 (The Amethyst)
ZLYSM	*Zhenli yu shengming* 真理与生命 (Truth and Life)

1

The Old Testament in Chinese Culture

Slow Beginnings in Turbulent Times

Introduction of Western Learning Together with the Old Testament in the Nineteenth Century

IN THE WEST, THE nineteenth century was called the "scientific age," and it was known as a time when knowledge of the natural world grew rapidly. The entire conception of the natural universe was changed by the recognition that human beings are subject to the same physical laws and processes as the natural world. The scientific methods of observation, induction, deduction, and experiment apply not only to the subject matter of pure science but also to nearly all the many and varied fields of human thought and activity.[1] As a response to the challenge of the scientific age, nineteenth-century Christianity established so-called "natural theology." The knowledge of the natural world and recognition of the natural universe were introduced to newly opened China primarily by Protestant missionaries by means of translators, who believed that spreading science also meant spreading the natural theology of Christianity. Despite his ignorance of the Chinese translators' role, Young John Allen (1836–1907) was basically right to say that, without the missionaries' work of translation, the Chinese would have known nothing of Western learning.[2]

Missionaries, in particular, drew from their contact with the Chinese state and society a profound impression of China's ethnocentrism.[3] Already in the first half of the nineteenth century, Protestant missionaries who went to China from the West had made their missions "in larger part a matter of print."[4] The religious tract, which was a principal feature of mission

---

1. Dampier, *A History of Science*, 200.
2. Allen, *Zhongxi guanxi luelun* (On Sino-Western Relationships), 17.
3. Fairbank, "Introduction: The Many Faces," 15.
4. Fairbank, "Introduction: The Place," 6.

work, was soon found inadequate for such a setting. Narrowly religious and devotional in content, it held no interest because of the vast cultural and historical differences between China and the West. What was needed instead were materials that would show that the West was a highly developed civilization equal to China, that its Christian religious tradition was worthy of respect, and that missionaries were scholar-teachers similar to those found in the Chinese tradition.[5] Therefore, dramatic changes in the tract literature of the early Protestant missionary movement included an emphasis on secular learning and the integration of religious ideas into written materials more broadly historical and cultural in nature and intended for use in non-church settings.[6]

This was more the case in the second half of the nineteenth century, when among Chinese readers the missionaries soon sensed a demand for global knowledge of the world and when the Western worldview was largely composed of the Newtonian universe and the Darwinian world of humanity.[7] Isaac Newton, however, provided a materialistic picture of humanity and the universe without denying God in the creation of the cosmos. Nature was a mechanical system functioning automatically and independently, and it was the primary source for human beings to know the will of God, the designer. Western liberalism was the theological response to the new view of humanity and God's world that developed along with Darwinism and the rise of sciences.[8] Liberals called themselves "modernists" in the conviction that the adjustment of religion to contemporary culture was both an admirable and an inevitable process. The nature of the theology preached helped to determine which audience the missionary would reach—which segments or social strata in the recipient society would be most heavily influenced by this particular form of Westernization.[9]

To eliminate the threat of Darwinism to Christianity and to reconcile the two, missionaries tried hard to find a point of agreement between Christianity and the theory of evolution—with the goal of establishing evolutionary theism. After describing the evolution of the earth on the

---

5. Leonard, "W. H. Medhurst," 50–51 and 53; and Fairbank, "Introduction: The Place," 13.

6. Leonard, "W. H. Medhurst," 47–48.

7. Kwok, *Zhongguo xiandai sixiang zhong de wei kexue zhuyi* (Scientism in Modern Chinese Thought), 28.

8. Fairbank, "Introduction: The Many Faces," 8–9.

9. Hutchison, "Modernism and Missions," 111–12.

basis of modern scientific discoveries, Alexander Williamson (1829–1890) attributed the natural process to God's wisdom and compared God to a garden designer.[10] John Gulick (1832–1923) stated that, in contrast to other scientific theories, evolution helps a person understand the magnificent adaptability of the physical and spiritual activities of humankind with the natural order. No matter where they were, surviving living beings managed to adapt themselves to circumstances, because God was with them in these circumstances. Therefore, evidence of evolution demonstrated that rational human beings needed religious faith in God.[11]

Combining secular knowledge with sacred faith, natural theology legitimized the spread of both secular civilization and Christianity. Moreover, natural theology emphasized the intimate relationship between the two. First, the missionaries spoke highly of the role religion played in the development of modern science. They declared that, in both theory and practice, modern Christian civilization in its essence was closely connected with scientific progress and that science grew from within Christianity and could never be separated from it.[12] Timothy Richard (1845–1919) wrote: "The wonderful reforms of Western civilization are enormous; but still these are, comparatively speaking, only branches. Christianity is the greatest source of blessing, producing powerful effects for good in the material, intellectual, political, social, moral and spiritual department of life. True Christianity is never final; the Holy Spirit is given to guide into *all truth* and to perfect us in love."[13]

Second, the missionaries realized that science and religion were mutually beneficial and complementary. Science provided support for the Mosaic account, while God's revelation offered moral vitality to science. The missionaries believed that, together with faith in Jesus, secular knowledge would make the world whole.[14] Among highly rational Chinese people, the missionaries came to realize that interest in Christianity was best supported with arguments of natural theology.[15]

10. Williamson, "Jizhi diqiu kezhi shangdi zhi zhuzai" (God's Dominance Can Be Known from [the Evolution of] the Earth), 339a.

11. Gulick, "Theory of Evolution," 295–97.

12. Mateer, "What is the Best Course?," 52.

13. Richard, "Historical Evidences of Christianity," 498 (Richard's emphasis).

14. Liu Shijing, "Xiangzheng tiandao qi" (Evidence for the Revelation of the Heavenly Way), 50a–b.

15. Hu, "Jindai laihua chuanjiaoshi de kexueguan" (Attitudes toward Science among the Missionaries in Modern China), 248.

The Old Testament was part of Western learning because of its importance to Christianity, world history, and Western civilization. According to William Ashmore (1824–1909), we should study it

> because the OT is a key to the history of humankind, a key to the origin of nations and the starting point for all human research; . . . because it is of transcendent importance to have a historical basis for a Dogmatic Faith; . . . because a thorough understanding of all the circumstances attending the giving of the fiery law is an indispensable prerequisite to an understanding of the whole scheme of grace. . . . We call them Jewish and local, but they form a sure foundation for all just jurisprudence; and justice is to be recognized before grace can come in at all.[16]

The relevance of the OT to Western learning also is reflected in the new perspectives and methods adopted in OT studies, as well as in the trend toward treating OT study as one discipline of academic or scientific research. Sacred geography was studied with all possible archaeological or geological findings and scientific aids like indexes, calendars, maps and tables.[17] Research concerning biblical animals, reptiles, birds, and plants was carried out as if people were studying biology.[18] OT history was much studied,[19] and OT studies were connected with what was happening in the world at the time.[20] Much effort was invested in reconciling modern science and the OT biblical texts.[21] The method of comparative mythology popular in nineteenth-century Western studies was applied to some approaches of Genesis stories,[22] while higher criticism on the biblical text was

---

16. Ashmore, "Why We Should Study the Old Testament," 249–55.

17. See Owen, "Mosaic Account of the Creation," 1–17; McIlvaine, "The Garden of Eden," 344–62; and Review of *Youtai dili zeyao* (An Essential Geography of Judea), 152–62, to name only a few works.

18. See Graves for studies on these subjects in *CR* 10 (March–April 1879), 124–28; *CR* 14 (November–December 1883), 479–85; *CR* 22 (April 1891), 157–61; *CR* 22 (June 1891), 253–55; and *CR* 23 (April 1892), 158–62.

19. See "Note on *Shengshi ji*" (An Account of Sacred History [in the Old and New Testaments]), 287 and "Review of *Wansuo shengshi*" (Studies on the Sacred History [in the OT] by Earnest Faber), 90–91.

20. See McClatchie, "Jewish Nation," 81–85.

21. See B. C. C., "Review of *Beginnings of History*," 152–62; "Review of *Scriptures in the Light of Modern Discovery*," 158–60; and "Review of *Harmony of the Bible with Science*," 245.

22. See Query, "Noah—Nüwa," 297. In Chinese mythology, Nüwa 女娲 is a mythological female character best known for creating and reproducing people after a great calamity.

adopted elsewhere.[23] These were published in China for both a missionary audience and a Chinese one.

The Bible remained for many missionaries the source of truth and the touchstone for determining truth. To Elijah C. Bridgman (1801–1861), the sons of Noah had possessed religious truth when they came to China; it had been lost later when the forces of evil had been allowed to prevail in the great Manichean controversy embroiling China for centuries. He reasoned that Chinese paganism might be rejected summarily once the ancient religious truths found in China's classical literature could be persuasively linked to the truths of the modern Bible.[24] To influence the Chinese literati to recognize that link and the existence of Western civilization, many missionaries tailored the comparative approach to suit that purpose.[25]

For example, the missionary magazine *Dongxiyang kao meiyue tongji zhuan* 东西洋考每月统计传 (Eastern and Western monthly magazine, known in the West as the *Chinese Magazine*), whose major editors were W. H. Medhurst and F. A. Gützlaff, recognized the Chinese respect for history. This resulted in an effort, using several pages of each issue for a year, to equate the antiquity of the West with the ancient Chinese experience. The result was a chronological comparison of Chinese and Western history, on the Chinese side from Pangu 盘古 to the Song dynasty 宋朝 (960–1279) and, on the Western, from Adam to the Roman Empire and finally to the kings of England.[26] Likewise, OT stories were cited as a way to explain Chinese origins, so that the ancient Chinese were related to the tale of the Tower of Babel and the confusion of tongues.[27] The method of chronological comparison was adopted by contemporary and later Chinese intellectuals, as will be discussed in the following chapter. The magazine was in literary Chinese, and its readers included not only Christian converts but also

---

23. See "Shengshu jiuyue yizheng" (Dating of the Five Books of Moses), 210a–11b.

24. Drake, "Protestant Geography in China," 93.

25. See McIlvaine, "Cushite Ethnology," 344–62; "Noah in China," 251–59; and Crawford, "Ancient Dynasties of Berosus and China," 411–29. In these essays, the authors tried to establish the conformity of OT records to extant Chinese literature and language.

26. Medhurst, "Dongxi shiji hehe" (A Comparative Study of Eastern and Western History), in the issues of *Dongxiyang kao meiyue tongji zhuan* from July 1833 until June 1834. Pangu was the first living being and creation began with him. For Medhurst's justification of the publication, see Medhurst, *China*, 278.

27. See *Dongxiyang kao meiyue tongji zhuan*, 4a–b.

educated non-Christian literati and even Buddhist practitioners.[28] Hence, Chinese readers inevitably learned about OT persons and ideas.

Particularly interesting is the attention paid to the art of OT narrative in characterization and storytelling. Gützlaff composed and published biographical accounts of the OT patriarchs and Moses early in the 1830s.[29] For Gützlaff, history was the working out of God's will and a means of moral instruction. Ethics was intertwined with politics.[30] Not surprisingly, the life stories of these OT persons were retold by Gützlaff in the shadow of God's sovereignty. Moses, for example, was a sage established by God and bestowed by God with courage, talent, and wisdom. Nevertheless, the image of patriarchs and Moses were remarkably shaped by the Confucian concept of sage. United with God, Moses had all the virtues of Confucian sagehood, thus becoming both ruler and teacher to his people. With heaven's decree, he extended the great dao under the heaven by means of laws.[31]

Other authors seemed to be well aware of the important principle in discussing the OT narrative—"God, in the Bible, does not profess to give us every fact . . . nor the whole of every occurrence. In the Bible we find only what is essential for the end for which the Bible was given."[32] Ashmore, for example, explained why the OT should be studied from a literary perspective:

> Because its types and symbols also have not yet exhausted their significance. Deeper meaning and wider sweep of application disclose themselves as the ages wear on. . . . because it contains descriptions or practical definitions of the theological terms used in the New Testament. . . . In the New Testament we have the words . . . in the Old Testament we have the process pictured out. . . .

28. Letter of Gützlaff, July 14, 1828, in Tomlin, *Missionary Journals and Letters*, 218; also 149–50, 188–89, 219, and 329.

29. Gützlaff, *Moxi yanxing quanzhuan* (Complete Biography of Moses' Words and Action), 1836; and Gützlaff, *Shengshu liezu quanzhuan* (Complete Biographies of the Patriarchs in the Holy Bible), 1838. The former is a memoir of Moses as a great legislator, commencing with the genealogy and birth, and detailing the principal leading and collateral events in the life of Moses, the Decalogue, and various laws and institutions introduced by him. The latter is a history of Abraham, Isaac, and Jacob. For a later example of missionaries' attention to OT narration and storytelling, see "Review of *The Representative Men of the Bible*," 513–14.

30. Gützlaff, "Literary Notice," 186–87 and "Remarks," 119 and 27.

31. Gützlaff, *Moxi yanxing quanzhuan* (Complete Biography of Moses' Words and Action), vol. 1, 1 and 8; vol. 5, 48–49; and vol. 7, 63.

32. Collins, "On Some Early Scriptural Traditions," 101.

because in the Old Testament we have such minute and powerful delineations of human nature acting itself out under every conceivable variety of moral condition; all presented unerringly without flaw and without partiality. The number of these delineations and touches of character run up into the thousand, so that if one were to be only a student of human nature, the Old Testament would be worth to him more than a hundred Shakespeares . . . because in the Old Testament we see exhibited so clearly the mode of cooperation of the divine and the human in the affairs of every-day life. . . . The ministry of angels, taken as an understood thing in the New Testament, is illustrated more in detail in the old; a ladder to heaven, with angels ascending and descending is only one of the pictures. . . . because the old book is . . . a portrait gallery of heroes whom we are to imitate.[33]

In fact, an increasing number of missionaries at the time became interested in using literature as a tool for evangelical work. Young J. Allen even warned that, if the missionaries disregarded secular literature, another Dark Age would occur.[34] OT commentators among the missionaries tended to emphasize the literal rather than the "hortatory or homiletic" sense of the OT text.[35] They usually commented especially on the language and style of OT translations and aids for OT studies. An easy and simple language style was preferred. For example, *Jiuyue kelue* 旧约课略 (Lessons from the OT), a translation from a successful textbook by Michael George Glazebrook (1853–1926) in England, is an OT history in the language of Scripture, whose translation was taken from Schereschewsky's Mandarin version of the OT. In the introduction, Bishop John S. Burdon (1826–1907) wrote: "Nothing can equal the vividness, the simplicity, the beauty of the original of the OT, even when rendered into other languages. We wish to familiarize the Chinese Christians with the form in which the Bible tells its own story."[36]

In the nineteenth century, OT works were basically in an easy *wenli* 文理 (literary style), hoping both to reach a broader audience and to win respect among educated readers.[37] At the turn of the century, however,

---

33. Ashmore, "Why We Should Study the Old Testament," 252–54.

34. *Records of the General Conference*, 239–40. Also see Allen, "Wenxue xinguo ce xu" (A Preface for *Literature Helps China*), 3b–6a.

35. J. J., Review of *Shipian shiyi* (A Commentary on the Psalms), 361.

36. See Burdon's quotation in "Review of *Jiuyue kelue*" (Lessons from the OT), 140.

37. The advantage of *wenli* was clearly expressed in the review of *Jiuyue shipian* (Ou

increasingly more works were written in spoken style to meet the call for Mandarin writings.[38] The result was that, as the missionaries had hoped, their painstaking efforts with printed matter not only helped to spread progressive secular knowledge among Chinese literati but also helped to introduce Christianity and the OT to a wider audience, thus contributing to a "new and less reassuring Chinese sense of identity."[39]

Nineteenth-Century Protestant Bible Translations

The encounter of the Chinese people with the OT is closely connected with its translations into the Chinese language. All religions entering China had to accommodate their message to the Chinese context. Accommodation began in the very act of translation into Chinese written characters, for certain characters and not others, together with their burden of accumulated connotations, had to be chosen to convey the foreigner's ideas. Thus began the interaction between the China missionaries and their far-from-passive Chinese environment.[40]

Unlike their Catholic counterparts,[41] Protestant missionaries emphasized the significance of Bible translation from the very beginning of their arrival in China in the early nineteenth century. To evangelists, translation and distribution of the Bible were integral parts of their missionary endeavor. Moreover, the highly literate Chinese civilization attached great importance to the written word. Missionaries realized that the Christian message could not remain verbal and conveyed solely in preaching; it had

---

the Book of Psalms) and *Jiuyue zhenyan* (On the Book of Proverbs): "It is that the whole order of the educated Chinese mind at least is formed and based on the higher literary style everywhere prevalent. Such a style attracts the scholar, and he can hardly tolerate anything else . . . it is beautiful, terse and expressive, allowing a few words to do duty for what would otherwise be a lengthy passage which the intelligent reader dislike." See W. M., "Review of *Jiuyue shipian jiuyue zhenyan*" (Old Testament books of Psalms and Proverbs), 301.

38. "Review of *Notes on Genesis*," 365.
39. Fairbank, "Introduction: The Place," 14.
40. Fairbank, "Introduction: The Many Faces," 10.
41. Catholics did not translate a complete Chinese Bible until 1953. For the reasons, see Standaert, "Bible in Seventeenth Century China," 64–86. For details of the Catholic partial versions, see Garnier, *Chinese Versions of the Bible*, 2–14; Zetzsche, *Bible in China*, 25–31 and 418–22; and Camps, "Father Gabriele M. Allegra," 55–76.

to be reinforced by a written text.⁴² In fact, by the end of the nineteenth century, they had produced eight complete translations of the Bible and dozens of partial versions.⁴³

The first complete Chinese Bible appeared in 1822 at Serampore, India, translated by two Baptists, Joshua Marshman (1768–1837) and Joannes Lassar (1781–?). The translators had no Chinese-language material whatsoever in the first few years of their translation work and, due to the Chinese assistant's lack of scholarship—according to John Wherry—Marshman and Lassar's version was awkward, narrow in its vocabulary, ungrammatical, and stylistically crude.⁴⁴ The second complete Chinese Bible, but the first in China, was by Robert Morrison (1782–1834) and William Milne (1785–1822) and was published in 1823. Morrison, the main translator, had been the first Protestant missionary in China. Living in Canton (Guangzhou), he was exposed to the Cantonese dialect, which differed significantly from other dialects, including Mandarin. He only gradually developed the concept of different styles of Chinese.⁴⁵ Morrison and Milne's version was published hurriedly, and both had insufficient recourse to Chinese assistants. Although Morrison believed that a Chinese Bible must follow the Chinese mode of writing,⁴⁶ the work did not represent a big step forward. Despite its positive reputation in Britain, American writers tended to be much more critical of Morrison and Milne's work, and the version was not honored by the Chinese either for stylistic reasons.

Since neither Marshman's nor Morrison's versions were satisfactory, Medhurst, Gützlaff, Bridgman, and Morrison's son, John Robert Morrison (1814–1844), prepared another Chinese translation of the Bible at the end of the 1830s. This translation became the chief one in use during the 1840s. Medhurst advocated for a Bible translation that was not bound to the letter of the original text, but rather to its meaning in a non-Christian

---

42. Eber et al., "Introduction," 14.

43. Fairly comprehensive lists of translations are: Spillett, *Catalogue of Scriptures*, 1975; Wylie, *Catalogue of the Chinese Imperial Maritime Customs Collection*, 1876; and Wylie, *Catalogue of Publications*, 1876. Besides the complete translations, there were also many partial translations of portions of the Bible, among which were some made by Chinese readers, some in dialects, some in speeches to ethnic peoples, and even some in romanized alphabets. Since all these translations were rather limited in use and distribution, they will not be discussed in this paper.

44. Wherry, "Historical Summary," 50–52.

45. Zetzsche, *Bible in China*, 20.

46. Zetzsche, *Bible in China*, 64 for Morrison's argument.

culture.⁴⁷ Nonetheless, the NT section was criticized by the British for being stylistically unsatisfactory and not sufficiently idiomatic; whereas the OT section, mainly the work of Gützlaff, was considered careless and lacking in good judgment.⁴⁸

After the First Treaty Settlement, the missionaries and their societies urgently pressed for a joint effort and better cooperation in Bible translation projects, which led to the First General Missionary Conference in 1843 in Hong Kong. The missionary delegates decided that a Chinese Bible should be "in exact conformity to the Hebrew and Greek originals in sense, in style, and in manner so far as the idiom of the Chinese language will allow."⁴⁹ For the first time, questions concerning how to translate terms like "God," "gods," and "Spirit" were raised, albeit not without much controversy. Unwilling to compromise on the translation of "baptism," the Baptists withdrew and, in 1868, Josiah Goddard (1813–1854), William Dean (1807–1895), and Edward C. Lord (1817–1887) produced their own complete translation. Because translations by the three Baptists were not mainstream Protestant versions, they were unknown to most missionaries and hardly ever employed by later translators.⁵⁰

The other delegates remained but were again split into two groups. From the first group, Medhurst, John Stronach (1810–1888), Milne, and James Legge (1815–1897) finished the OT in 1854.⁵¹ It was bound together with the NT completed two years earlier primarily by Medhurst, Bridgman, and Milne, and was called the "Delegates' Version." Stylistically, the Delegate's Version was an improvement over the previous translations, and it was widely used for many years. However, since it was primarily intended for highly educated readers, it was considered by many critics to be too classical and too difficult. Moreover, some argued that it was not sufficiently faithful to the original text and that it employed a terminology more suited to Chinese philosophy.⁵² In comparison, the version (the NT in 1859 and the OT in 1862) by Bridgman and Michael S. Culbertson (1819–1862)

---

47. Ibid., 20 for Medhurst's argument.

48. See the comments from the letters Medhurst wrote to the London Missionary Society on June 30, 1849 and October 8, 1849 in Zetzsche, *Bible in China*, 70–71.

49. Zetzsche, *Bible in China*, 79, and for other decisions made by the delegates. The First Treaty Settlement is the collective term of the treaties signed after the First Opium War or the First Anglo-Chinese War (1839–1842).

50. Ibid., 120.

51. This is called the *London Mission Version OT*.

52. Zetzsche, *Bible in China*, 103.

of the second group was more faithful to the original and proved a valuable aid to theology students and pastors. Nonetheless, stylistically, it was considered inferior, obscure, and harsh.[53] Adopted by the American Bible Society, it was used primarily by the American missionaries.

In order to win respect from and gain influence among Chinese literati and government officials, all complete Bible translations employed classical literary Chinese. However, missionaries were increasingly in need of a Bible in the colloquial style. In response to the advice from the Shanghai corresponding committee of the British and Foreign Bible Society that the Bible should be prepared in Mandarin, the Beijing Translation Committee was constituted in 1864 on Schereschewsky's initiative.[54] The committee consisted of Henry Blodget (1825–1903), J. S. Burdon, Joseph Edkins (1823–1905), W. A. P. Martin (1827–1916), and Schereschewsky. In contrast to previous translation teams, they worked with a tolerant spirit and in close collaboration. The committee also employed well-educated Chinese co-workers in the hope that the assistance of these Chinese scholars would make it possible to develop a written text in idiomatic Chinese that was neither too classical nor too colloquial.[55] After ten years, the complete Bible in Mandarin was published in 1874. It immediately enjoyed great success. In 1899, the 1874 version was revised to take into consideration linguistic changes that had occurred over time.

From this general survey, we can see that the Protestant missionaries, who repeatedly translated the Scriptures, increasingly paid attention to style, terminology, and translation mode. To some extent, all the Bible versions in Chinese were joint products between the missionaries and their Chinese co-workers. When missionaries used more Chinese co-workers, their translations enjoyed better style, were therefore easier to use, and had wider distribution. In fact, as early as the eighteenth century, Carlo Horatii (1673–1759) had opposed independent Bible translating by Catholic missionaries, insisting that rendering the Bible into Chinese should be done primarily by Chinese co-workers aided by European missionaries, so that the translation would be "literal, elegant, and solemn."[56]

---

53. Ibid., 106–7.

54. Eber, *Jewish Bishop*, 146.

55. Ibid., 109–10. For more details regarding the committee, see also Eber, "The Peking Translation Committee," in *Jewish Bishop*, 107–23.

56. Willeke, "Das Werden der Chinesischen Katholischen Bibel," 285. Willeke found it in the letter from Francesco Jovino (1677–1737) to Horatii dated February 13, 1726.

After remarking on the qualifications of Bible translators, including "a much greater degree of acquaintance with the original tongues, with the form and composition of the sacred books, with the Jewish antiquities, sacred geography, and biblical criticism in general," an article in the *Chinese Repository* discussed the great challenges of translating the ancient foreign books of the Bible into a newly acquired and difficult foreign language like Chinese. Elegant translations can hardly be expected from the pens of foreigners.[57] J. K. Fairbank, who believed that the participation of Chinese personnel and the use of Chinese terms were two necessary steps in the sinification of Protestant Christianity,[58] has given us a lively description of how a missionary translator might have cooperated with his Chinese co-worker:

> The early missionaries began without libraries and indeed almost without dictionaries.... Knowledge of the language consequently had to be gained mainly from Chinese teachers through long hours of application out of sight of the suspicious Chinese public. Over the years, sessions with their teachers as walking dictionaries became an integral part of most missionaries' daily routines. As the ambitious evangelist acquired his religious vocabulary and sought to compose tracts or translate scripture, his teacher-partner became indispensable, not only to draft in easy classical *wen-yen* style what was first discussed in vernacular *pai-hua*, but also, in the process, to be on the outlook for obscurities due to poor usage or unconventional phraseology, and especially for unintended puns that could trip up any writer of Chinese and induce in readers a sly smile if not an outright guffaw that would vitiate his purpose.[59]

Let us read a report by a missionary translator himself and consider how intimately the Chinese co-worker might be involved in the preparation of a piece of translation work:

> I then read it over with another Chinese assistant who is ignorant of English. He suggests such alterations as may seem necessary to render the language perfectly clear. It is then corrected, and a clean proof given.... This done, I sit down alone and read it.... Having written in the margin of the sheet every alternation my

---

57. "The Bible: Its Adaptation," 299–304.
58. Fairbank, "Introduction: The Place," 9.
59. Ibid.," 7. *Wen-yen* means higher *wenli* or classical literary style, whereas *pai-hua* literally means "plain speech."

mind suggests, and everything that seems a discrepancy, I then consult Mr. Lassar and the Chinese assistant together, sitting with them till every query be solved and every discrepancy adjusted. This done, another clean proof is given, which, when read, I give to my son John that he may examine for himself, as his knowledge of the Chinese idiom is perhaps greater than my own. When he has satisfied himself respecting it, another clean proof is given, and then I give one to my Chinese assistant, to read alone, and one to Mr. Lassar, that they may each point out separately whatever they dislike.... I then in another clean proof, desire the Chinese assistant to add the stops according to his idea of the meaning; these I then examine, and if his idea of the stops agree with mine send it to the press. When on the press, a clean proof is brought to me, which I first give to the Chinese assistant to see if all be right, then to Mr. Lassar, and lastly read it myself, and order it to be struck off.... It must be remembered, however, that these frequent revisions involved the judgment of four different persons—Mr. Lassar, the Chinese assistant, myself, and my son; each of whom judges independently of the other three.[60]

The Chinese co-workers also frequently participated in discussions concerning questions of terminology. The missionaries were "glad to learn and state the opinions of Chinese scholars,"[61] who based their criticism on such classical dictionaries as *Peiwen yunfu* 配文韵府 (Rhyme Storehouse of Esteemed Phrases).[62]

As can be seen from the above quotations, Bible translations into Chinese and the involvement of Chinese co-workers were significant for several reasons. First, biblical exegesis and interpretation was carried out both by the missionaries and their Chinese co-workers. Second, the translation process explained very well the need for contextual exegesis and interpretation. Third, Bible translations into Chinese made Scripture more accessible to Chinese readers, invited discussions among the Chinese audience, and finally paved the way for the beginning and development of a Chinese Biblical commentary tradition.[63]

60. "Chinese Version of the Bible," 254.

61. "Chinese Version of the Holy Scriptures," 109.

62. "Revision of the Chinese Version," 163. *Peiwen yunfu* is a 1711 Chinese rhyme dictionary of literary allusions and poetic dictions. Collated by tone and rhyme, the dictionary serves the composition of poetry. It was compiled under the patronage of the Kangxi Emperor (1654–1723).

63. Doing Bible translating with Chinese co-workers is a great model speaking to

The Beginning of the Chinese Old-Testament Commentary Tradition

When Chinese Christians in the early nineteenth century wrote evangelical tracts, they generally used OT motifs in their commentaries. A good example is Liang Fa 梁发 or Liang A-fa 梁阿发 (1789–1855) from Guangdong and his *Quanshi liangyan* 劝世良言 (often translated as *Good Words to Admonish the Age* or *Quest for Moral Power*),[64] which includes ten excerpts from eleven chapters of the Morrison-Milne translation (1823) of Genesis, Ecclesiastes, and Isaiah. Many of these are accompanied by Liang Fa's commentaries on OT concepts such as God, monotheism, and morality.

Liang Fa especially was taken by the OT concept that monotheism is a focus of filial respect and moral seriousness.[65] He insisted that the backbone of God's morality was filial devotion. After all, to honor father and mother is an OT commandment. However, ritualistic piety as existed in Chinese society, especially offering sacrifices to the dead, is not only idolatrous, according to Liang Fa, but also hypocritical and incapable of engendering an interior morality. God was both the Creator and the "heavenly Father" who loves mankind as a parent loves his children. To show filial gratitude, everyone must revere and worship him. Liang Fa denounced Chinese image-worship as lacking a filial commitment to God and attributed that lack to the existence of evil in China. The human spirit was endowed with God's pure nature when God created humankind and, for some time, man lived in perfect harmony with God. But man was seduced into rebellion against God. For the original sin of "unfiliality," God banished man from paradise and all people have lived in moral turpitude ever since.[66]

Gadamar's "fusion of horizons" theory. By receiving information from their Chinese co-worker, the totality of all that could be realized or thought about by the missionary at a given time in history and in a particular culture widened and enriched, and *vice versa*. See Gadamar's definition of "horizon" in Gadamar, *Truth and Method*, 302. This "fusion of horizons" means "an event in which a world opens itself to him." See Palmer, *Hermeneutics*, 209.

64. The book was first published in Guangzhou in 1832 with the help of Robert Morrison in colloquial Chinese and included nine volumes. Frequently reprinted and widely distributed by the missionaries, it was most popular and used into the twentieth century. The author once helped William Milne with *Cha shisu meiyue tongji zhuan* (known in the West as the *Chinese Monthly Magazine*) and was baptized by Milne in 1816. Ordained by Robert Morrison in 1821, Liang was the first Chinese Protestant minister and evangelist.

65. Bohr, "Liang Fa's Quest," 36.

66. Liang, *Quanshi liangyan*, 7, 12–13, 39–41, 52, 83, 109, 111, 124, 128, and 146.

Liang Fa, furthermore, wrote that China's classics elucidated a monotheistic God. Human beings are endowed with the capacity to comply with God's moral commandments and are able to choose correct ways or achieve sincerity (诚). Each person has a God-given soul, which is the means of linking the individual to God's moral power. Because human nature was derived from matter (气), Liang Fa believed, it was not inclined toward goodness. Rather, it was malleable and weak. But, since the soul also was composed of God's principle (理), it could draw upon moral purity so that the self could be perfected. Liang acknowledged that the soul shares with Confucianism the "five constant virtues," which include benevolence, a sense of righteousness, propriety, rationality, and good faith. These virtues have moral power only because they flow from Christian monotheism rather than from Confucian humanism. It is particularly lamentable that the Chinese were ignorant of God and persisted in praising Confucius' skepticism about religious matters.[67]

Good Words to Admonish the Age presents a blueprint for the redemption of society, as well as the individual, through monotheism. Liang Fa did not criticize China's political order but suggested that the Confucian virtues of propriety and righteousness underlying the political order must be broadened to include filiality on a cosmic scale through devotion to God. Monotheism would endow significance to the relationships, which Liang saw as anchored in both family and monarchy.[68] Clearly, Liang Fa turned to the OT not to repudiate the ideals of his own Chinese moral tradition but to reaffirm them. For him, the OT complements Confucianism.[69]

Due to unfavorable conditions for evangelical work, Protestant missionaries were mainly limited to Bible translation, and Christian converts like Liang Fa were rather few. The First Treaty Settlement ended the heterodox status of Christianity in China and brought missionary establishments to the five treaty ports. The Second Treaty Settlement extended to the missionaries the privileges of erecting churches, preaching, converting, and traveling for free in the Chinese interior. It also enabled missionaries to come north, including to the capital Beijing. During this period, missionary work developed significantly, and Chinese Christian reading matter became increasingly available.[70] The development of missionary work also initiated responses

---

67. Liang Fa, *Quanshi liangyan*, 40–41, 64, 100–101, and 116.
68. Ibid., 4, 105, and 146.
69. Bohr, "Liang Fa's Quest," 36.
70. Alexander Wylie listed the 338 missionaries who had arrived in China by 1867,

to the Bible and Christianity among Chinese converts.[71] Together with increased proselytism,[72] missionaries were met with suspicion and hostility from the Chinese literati, especially Confucian scholars.[73] Fully aware of the importance of the Confucian elites in Chinese society, missionaries turned their attention from the masses to the educated Chinese.

They were fully supported in that endeavor by educated Chinese Christians. Zhang Gengsheng 张更生, a convert from Yangzhou, wrote to *Jiaohui xinbao* 教会新报 (*Church News*, henceforth *JHXB*), suggesting that "Christianity be testified in Confucian books" (以儒书证圣教) and explaining:

> After several decades . . . the non-believers are still countless. Let's analyze the reason. Scholars are highly respected in China. They rigidly adhere to Confucian books. . . . In these Confucian books, records about human affairs are abundant, while those about the heavenly dao are relatively neglected. However, if one reads them carefully, one will find places that elucidate and complement Christianity. . . . I earnestly request that talented converts would find those expressions and analyze them. When more are assembled, they should be published in *JHXB* to convince Confucian scholars of the true origin of the dao. When Confucian scholars are convinced, so will be the masses.[74]

As a direct result of the change in evangelical work, Protestant missionary newspapers, magazines, and journals proliferated, and contributions from Chinese converts increased. Since a major interaction between the missionaries and their Chinese audience was reading the Bible, human beings and ideas of the OT became regular topics for Chinese contributors. If Liang Fa's interpretation of OT motifs was a very rare instance at this time, Chinese contributors who discussed OT persons and ideas now were

---

whose Chinese publications totaled about 787 items. See Fairbank, "Introduction: The Place," 1. The Second Treaty Settlement is the collective term of the treaties signed after the Second Opium War or the Second Anglo-Chinese War (1856–1860).

71. Eber, *Jewish Bishop*, 116–18. According to Fairbank, "the Protestant mission to the Chinese became in larger part a matter of print." Fairbank, "Introduction: The Place," 6.

72. Fairbank, "Introduction: The Place," 7 and 10; and Fairbank, "Introduction: The Many Faces," 10.

73. Cohen, *China and Christianity*, 1963.

74. See the quoted letter in Yao, "Jidulun yu yangming xinxue" (Christology and Wang Yangming's Doctrine of Heart-Mind), 357–65 (my translation; the other translations from Chinese also are mine unless specially indicated).

no longer isolated cases. At last, with their engagement, the Chinese OT commentary tradition began to take shape.

That tradition shows that, by converting to Christianity, Chinese Christians did not cease to define themselves as Chinese, and, moreover, they understood the biblical message through the prism of Chinese cultural norms. Once the OT was translated into Chinese and circulated in print, its interpretation and appropriation by Chinese Christians was largely no longer controlled by missionaries, who had expected the converts to adhere to the meaning of the OT text or its relevance to the NT as they interpreted it. A good platform for a survey of the Chinese OT commentary tradition is *JHXB*, which was from September 1874 on named *Wanguo gongbao* 万国公报 (*Globe Magazine*, henceforth *WGGB*), because the magazine reflected the concerns of the first generation of Christian converts after the opening of the treaty ports.

In the beginning, Protestant missionaries played a major initiating and sponsoring role. Especially in its first two years, *JHXB* invited readers to discuss the comparative merits of Christianity and China's ideological heritage, especially Confucianism. An essential question that missionaries urged Chinese converts to consider was: What kind of book was the OT? Some converts compared the OT with Chinese classics, while others considered the OT in relation to the NT. In both cases, converts regarded the OT, together with the NT, superior to all other books in the world as well as helpful, as argued by Cai Hongzhang 蔡鸿璋, a convert from Ningbo, and He Yuquan 何玉泉, a convert in Hong Kong.[75]

According to Huang Pinsan 黄品三 (1823–1890), a convert from Shanghai, the OT is a mirror for everything in the world, including religious rituals, Scriptures and classics, customs, and even the Chinese language. Therefore, the Ten Precepts in Buddhism are analogous to the Ten Commandments.[76] Such Chinese traditional classics as the *Book of Changes* (易经), the *Book of Rites* (礼记), the *Book of History* (书经), the *Book of Songs* (

---

75. Cai, "Quandu shengjing wen" (Exhorting People to Read the Bible), 310b–11b; and He, "Shengshu lun-qier" (On the Bible II), 553a–54a.

76. The Ten Precepts of Buddhism are: first, refrain from killing living things; second, refrain from stealing; third, refrain from unchastity (sensuality, sexuality, and lust); fourth, refrain from lying; fifth, refrain from taking intoxicants; sixth, refrain from taking food at inappropriate times; seventh, refrain from singing, dancing, playing music or attending entertainments programs; eighth, refrain from wearing perfume, costumes and garland; ninth, refrain from sitting on high chairs and sleeping on luxurious, soft beds; tenth, refrain from accepting money.

诗经), the *Spring and Autumn* (春秋), the *Zuo Commentary* (左传), *Daodejing* (道德经), *Zhuang zi* (庄子), and "The cawing ospreys" (关雎) are comparable to the prophetic literature and the books of Leviticus, Deuteronomy, Psalms, Joshua, Kings, Proverbs, and Song of Songs. Mythical records about the creation of the world and the flood, idiomatic terms like "*chaiwang*" 柴望 (the general term for offering sacrifices to gods and ancestors), fixed expressions like "*renming guantian*" 人命关天 (human life is related to heaven) in the Chinese tradition are related to Gen 1–2, the flood, Sabbath, burnt offerings, and Cain killing Abel.[77]

Missionaries played a major organizing and guiding role, which can be seen by their frequent efforts to solicit contributions of essays from converts to the magazine. With a special interest in the OT and a healthy respect for Chinese culture, the soliciting efforts proved fruitful. In the following paragraphs, some notices and responding contributions in *JHXB* and *WGGB* will be studied in order to show how missionaries and Chinese Christians together supported the growth of the Chinese OT commentary tradition in its initial stages.

When foreign missionaries were compelled to use Chinese terms and the classics to meet the needs of educated Chinese and the new evangelical context in China, Chinese Christians helped voluntarily from the very beginning. Where missionaries were guarded in consulting Chinese classics and tried their best to retain the meaning of the OT text as they understood it, Chinese Christians felt unrestrained in using Chinese classics and often expressed their views unreservedly. Inevitably, among Chinese Christians, the OT text was often interpreted in their own ways. However, too much misinterpretation in random OT commentary was definitely not what Protestant missionaries hoped to see. Aiming to put the Chinese biblical commentary on the expected track and making converts adhere more closely to the Christian line, in the summer of 1870, Young J. Allen solicited contributions from Chinese readers to *JHXB* under the title of "Who Do You Say I Am?" (Matt 16:15, NIV). Twenty prize essays would be chosen, and the top five would be awarded bonuses.

---

77. Huang, "Daoying leibian xiaolu" (Brief Measuring by the Standards of the *Dao*), 575b–78a. Irene Eber pointed out in a discussion with me that the concept of *renming guantian* is significant because it implies sanctity of human life. Namely, life is not just matter, it is also related to the transcendental. Similar ideas were already raised in such classics as the *Lunyu* (Analects), *Meng zi* (Mencius), and *Hanshu* (A historical account of Han dynasty).

The result was not quite as Allen had expected. In deciding on the order of the top five, Chinese appraiser Chiping sou 持平叟, from the Shanghai Methodist Episcopal Church, disagreed with the missionary appraisers, Allen and William Muirhead (1822–1900). Holding Confucian as well as Christian ethical values and being well-versed in Chinese literature,[78] Chiping Sou paid much attention to the prize essays' style and use of Confucian classics. Consequently, the top five he chose were by Qianbao zi 潜抱子, Haishang shanren 海上山人, Lianxi yishi 莲溪逸史, Zuijing sheng 醉经生, and Lianfeng jushi 莲峰居士. Allen, in contrast, emphasized first of all the essays' adherence to Christian theology, and paid only secondary attention to the style and references to Confucian classics. As a result, his top five choices were different from those of Chiping sou.[79] He argued that Qianbao zi's essay should not win the first prize "because, although its language and structure are the best, it strays from the subject in the middle part and fails to elucidate the practical meaning of following the holy virtues of Jesus." In the end, Allen published only three of the five in *JHXB*.[80]

Chinese readers, however, sided more with Chiping Sou. Bangu yongren 半瞽庸人, a convert from Jinling, Jiangsu, who had read all five essays, suggested to Allen that the other "excellent" essays be published as well because of their "convincing" use of Confucian classics and elegant language. He also praised them as "understanding thoroughly the ideas of the Bible" and as being "very helpful for preaching Christianity." He explained, "While Westerners and veteran converts may like reading essays with supporting materials from the Bible, Chinese readers, especially the non-Christians, prefer those supported by Confucian classics."[81]

At the end of his prize essay, Haishang shanren expressed views similar to those of Bangu yongren, "To achieve clarity and lucidity, one should interpret biblical ideas with the help of Chinese classics so as to meet the taste of the Chinese readers for classical literature, stimulate their imagination,

---

78. For evidence, see Chiping sou, "Jinchang bian" (On Prohibition of Prostitutes), 1–2; and "Nü tanci xiaozhi" (A Brief Biographical Note of a Female Storyteller), 2–3.

79. See *JHXB* 3 (November 12, 1870), 53a–b. Allen's top five were respectively Lianfeng jushi, Lianxi yishi, Qianbao zi, Haishang shanren, and Zuijing sheng. It is impossible to identify the original names of Chiping sou and the prize winners since they did not use their real names. It is the same with Bangu yongren, Jieyu zi, Juemeng jushi, Yili shi, and Buwang below.

80. They were Lianfeng jushi, Lianxi yushi, and Qianbao zi.

81. Bangu yongren, "Qing meiguo linmushi" (A Letter Requesting the American Pastor Allen), 52a–b.

and encourage their further study of the biblical text." He agreed with Jieyu zi 劫余子, a Confucian, who complained that insufficient traditional learning of most Chinese converts had invited the contempt of the Confucian literati. At the end of the essay, Haishang shanren added, "I make full use of the Chinese literary language and Confucian thoughts in my essay because only in this way can I possibly reveal the two principles of the Ten Commandments of the OT, namely, to love God and to love mankind, and the relationship between them."[82]

Magnanimous enough, editor Young J. Allen published both Bangu Yongren's letter and the two essays by Haishang shanren and Zuijing Sheng, although in another place, he criticized them as he did Qianbao zi's.[83] Allen's criticisms of these essays, which were favored by Chinese readers, were not unreasonable. The authors, although converted to the Christian faith, interpreted OT ideas in terms of Chinese culture. Although their essays were expected to discuss Jesus the Son of God, they were nevertheless more interested in the OT notion of God the Creator and the Confucian dao that, in their eyes, supplement and complement each other. The NT quotation, "Who do you say that I am?," suggests that Jesus is the Messiah. Yet according to Haishang shanren, a person can understand dao within himself because dao, which is omnipresent, is with mankind. Human conscience and nature reflect dao. Since dao is with God and dao is God, if I know who I am, I will know dao. Throughout the essay, by emphasizing nature (性), heart-mind (心), and soul (灵) in ontology and epistemology, the author referred to Neo-Confucian thinkers of the Song and Ming (1368–1644) dynasties, such as Li Yanping 李延平 (1093–1163), Zhu Xi 朱熹 (1130–1200), and Wang Yangming 王阳明 (1472–1528).[84] Jesus was only meaningful to the author because of his moral perfection, which resulted from his unity with God. In short, the emphasis was on the unity of man and dao.

In the winter of 1879, Timothy Richard also solicited essays from Chinese readers for *WGGB*. He called for commentaries on Psalms and required that the contributions be traditional verses or rhapsodies in concise and simple language so that they would be easily understood and enjoyed by the less educated. Again, there would be a competition and the

---

82. Haishang shanren, "Wei er yan wo wei shui" (Who Do You Say that I Am?), 52b–3b. See Jieyu zi's complaint in Jieyu zi, "Yesu jiaotiao yi" (Some Comments on Jesus' Doctrines), 201b–2a.

83. See Allen's criticism quoted in Yao, "Jidulun yu yangming xinxue."

84. Haishang shanren, "Wei er yan wo wei shui," 52a–53a.

prize essays would be awarded attractive bonuses.[85] Richard also solicited contributions for his evangelical summer mission to Mount Wutai, a holy place and a propitious time for Buddhist pilgrimages. Trying to win over Buddhist devotees, Richard encouraged Chinese Christians to write on Christianity and the Bible, taking into consideration Buddhist Scriptures and classics like the *Jingang jing* 金刚经 (Diamond Sutra). Richard advised authors not to violate Buddhist customs and not to criticize or condemn Buddhism. Together with this notice, Richard published another to invite contributions, this time with references to Confucian classics, for a planned evangelical visit to the upcoming provincial examination triennially held for Confucian scholars.[86] The fact that Chinese Christians welcomed and warmly responded to these efforts to solicit OT commentaries is significant, and in 1881, for example, there were more than one hundred contributions. Richard prepared fixed titles, the first two being "God the Unique Creator Deserves Our Obedience" and "A Commentary on the Ten Commandments."[87]

Gradually, Chinese Christians also participated in soliciting OT commentaries. Zheng Yuren 郑雨人, a convert from Jinling, wrote a notice inviting Christian writings from Chinese readers. Again, Zheng believed that biblical ideas should be discussed together with Chinese classics. When Chinese classics are in agreement with the Bible, so far so good; when conflicts are found, the argument must be developed in gentle, fair, and reasonable ways in order not to antagonize readers. Zheng determined the topics for discussion, one of which was "God is neither matter (气) nor principle (理)."[88] Topics like this made converts think over the differences between the OT idea of God and Confucian concepts of matter and principle. One convert wrote, "We Chinese know *shangdi* 上帝 (Supreme God) exists, but do not know who *shangdi* is.... Neither matter nor principle are *shangdi* because they both were created by *shangdi*."[89]

85. Richard, "Yingguo jiaoshi qingzuo sheng dawei shipian shici qi" (A Notice Inviting Poetic Contributions), 161b.

86. Richard, "Qingzuo shengshu liangqi" (Two Notices Inviting Contributions), 207a. Christian tracts like *Tiandao mingjing* (A Mirror of the Heavenly *Dao*) and *Shengdao dayuan* (The Origin of the Holy *Dao*) would also be distributed to Confucian scholars who attended the triennial provincial examination.

87. "Pingfen jiayi" (The Appraisal), 265a–b.

88. Zheng, "Qingzuo shengshu gaobai" (A Notice Inviting Contributions on the Bible), 171a.

89. Juemeng jushi, "Shangdi bushi qi yu li" (God is Neither Matter nor Principle),

In addition to the idea of God, the Ten Commandments were noted in particular. In fact, God, monotheism, and the Ten Commandments were the OT concepts that converts discussed most extensively. If the monotheist God in the OT often was understood by converts as a counterpart of dao in Confucianism, the Ten Commandments often were thought of as the reinforcement and perfection of Confucian ethics. In a poem on the Ten Commandments, where they are also called the "Holy Commandments" (圣诫) and the "Heavenly Commandments" (天条), Chen Shenxiu 陈慎修 from Changle, Fujian, introduced the term "*xin*" 心 (heart-mind) and referred to it eight times in his commentary. According to Chen, one must be pure-hearted (洁心) and single-hearted (一心) in worshiping God, so that God in heaven can always dwell in one's heart (天上有神心上勘) and so that all human beings can be of a common heart (同心), in order to follow God, to avoid having a killer's heart (诛心), easily tempted in the heart (心迷), guilty in the heart (心亏), and greedy in the heart (贪心). With such a heart of sincerity (诚), one will surely obtain goodness (善) and eventually achieve happiness (福).[90]

Liu Changxing 刘常惺, from Henan, wrote an essay arguing that the Ten Commandments conform to the teachings of Confucianism. According to Liu, the Ten Commandments that God gave to Moses on Mount Sinai correspond to the doctrines in the Four Books (四书) and the Five Scriptures (五经) of Confucianism.[91] Using the method of the Confucian scholar Zhang Zhongcheng 张仲诚 (1630–1712), he stated that the Ten Commandments can be grouped into two groups of four and six. Those in the former group are about fundamental principles (体) such as worship of God (敬神), sincerity within (诚中), great root (大本), benevolent heart (仁人心), attaining knowledge (致知), loyalty (忠), and essence (惟精). Those in the latter group are about practical application (用), such as love of mankind (爱人), external propriety (形外), prosperous way (达道), righteous path (义人路), investigation of things (格物), forbearance (恕), and consistency (惟一). Realizing these correspondences, Liu assumed,

---

49b–50a.

90. Chen, "Shangdi shijie shi" (A Poem of God's Ten Commandments), 79b–80a.

91. The Four Books are the *Analects*, *Mencius*, the *Great Learning*, and the *Book of the Mean*, while the Five Scriptures are the *Books of Songs*, *History*, *Rites*, *Changes*, and the *Spring and Autumn Annals*.

enables the reader to understand both Confucian and OT books without confusion or conflict.⁹²

Besides Neo-Confucian concepts, Buddhist assumptions also left their impact on converts' commentaries on the Ten Commandments. The seventh commandment against lewdness, according to Tao Chengqi 陶澄祺, from Qujiang, repeats the Buddha's saying that lewdness is the worst of all vices (万恶淫为首) and Shen Xiu's 神秀 (606–706) poem, "The body is a tree of Awakening, / The mind is like a clear mirror; / At all times we must strive to polish it, / And must not let the dust collect" (身是菩提树, 心如明镜台; 时时勤拂拭, 勿使惹尘埃).⁹³ Shen Xiu, representative of the northern school of Chan Buddhism, took the positivistic approach, asserting that there is a pure substance within us that is called "Buddha nature" (如来臧), which one should maintain by keeping away defilements. Such an approach agrees with the liberal theology of Christianity and Neo-Confucianism, which consider ethics vital and think of individual salvation largely as a function of good works.⁹⁴

Since filial piety was a primary ethical value for the Chinese, the fifth of the Ten Commandments was especially attractive, as it had been to Liang Fa. Yang Jiantang 杨鉴堂 emphasized the comprehensiveness (全) of filial piety. One should show filial respect not only to parents but also to the monarch and the elders.⁹⁵ Like Liang Fa, Yili shi 一蠡氏 insisted that true filial feeling must be expressed during the lifetime of the parents. Moreover, as the Creator, the True God deserves a debt of gratitude from each worshiper, as does a father who similarly deserves filial respect from the child.⁹⁶ Tao Chengqi interpreted the fifth commandment in this way: if a person repays his parents for their giving birth to his body, he can expect blessings from the True God for good health.⁹⁷

Finally, one must not neglect converts' love of using poetry and storytelling devices in their commentaries. Many converts wrote poems on

---

92. Liu, "Moxi shijie" (The Ten Commandments of Moses), 405a. For a similar discussion, see Yang, "Shangdi shijie jie" (A Commentary on God's Ten Commandments), 177b–78a.

93. Tao, "Shijie shi" (Some Verses about the Ten Commandments), 117b–18b. The translation of Shen Xiu is by Philip B. Yampolsky; see Yampolsky, *Platform Sutra*.

94. In contrast, Hui Neng (638–713), representative of the southern school of Chan Buddhism, argued that pure nature is empty.

95. Yang, "Shangdi shijie jie", 177b–78a.

96. Yili shi, "Shangdi shijie shi" (A Poem on God's Ten Commandments), 76b–77b.

97. Tao, "Shijie shi," 117b.

OT motifs, and there were exchanges of poems, such as one person writing a poem and another writing one in reply. For example, in *WGGB*, Jiang Lianyuan蔣连元, from Jiujiang, composed eleven poems on the Ten Commandments in reply to similar poems he had read in *WGGB* by another convert from Hankou, using the same rhyme sequences.⁹⁸ Tao Chengqi wrote ten poems on the Ten Commandments and confessed that he was inspired by the touching poems he had read in *WGGB*.⁹⁹

Aware of and interested in the OT art of narrative and storytelling, Pan Wenhe 潘文鹤, from Ningbo, recounted events from the book of Genesis in eight poems. All the poems are in the classical form of *qilü* 七律 (an eight-line poem with seven characters to a line and a strict tonal pattern and rhyme scheme). From the many Genesis events, the author selected Adam and Eve's transgression in the garden of Eden; the flood; Abraham being tested; Isaac marrying Rebekah; Esau selling his birthright; Jacob working for Laban and marrying his daughters; Joseph being sold by his brothers; and Joseph extending relief grain and making himself known to his brothers. In Pan's poems, the role of God is rarely mentioned. When it is, the reference is usually indirect and obscure.¹⁰⁰

Interest in storytelling was confined not only to poetry but also to prose narration. Below is the story of Jacob and Esau (Gen 25:29–34) as retold by a convert:

> Esau and Jacob were twins, but Esau was considered the eldest son because he was born first. They had different dispositions: Jacob was refined, while Esau was crude and rash. As the eldest son, Esau often took advantage of his superior status and bullied Jacob. Jacob thought, "He does not treat me as a brother but as a slave. He and I are twins, how come he is the eldest son while I am not!" Besides, Isaac the father was partial to Esau, while Rebecca the mother favored Jacob, which made relations between Esau and Jacob even more strained. And that is an ill omen. One evening, Esau came back from afar empty-handed, exhausted, and terribly hungry after a whole day of hunting.... When he got home, Jacob had just cooked some red soup (汤). Esau, who could not bear the hunger any more, asked Jacob for the soup. Jacob thought, "Esau

---

98. Jiang, "He hankou jiaoyou" (Poems on the Ten Commandments as a Response), 369b, continued in *WGGB* 13 (June 1881) 387 b and *WGGB* 13 (July 1881) 396b.

99. Tao, "Shijie shi," 108b.

100. Pan, "Ningbo panwenhe jiaoyou jiuyue qilü bashou" (Eight Poems by Pan Wenhe), 162a–b.

is always putting on airs and bullying me. This time I must make a fool of him." So he said to Esau, "As the eldest son with such an honorable and powerful status, how come you are short of a bowl of red soup?! And how come you beg me?! Well, I won't give it to you unless you sell your inheritance right to me." Though Esau knew Jacob was making a fool of him, he thought, "Although I am the eldest son, I can dominate nobody but Jacob and what the status will be in the future is indefinite and unreliable. Even if it is promising, distant water won't quench present thirst." Although he felt wronged, to Jacob's surprise, he cast rashly aside his status of eldest son, saying, "What is the use of status if I have nothing in my stomach and starve to death now? In that case I might as well exchange it for a bowl of red bean soup. Why don't I?" Jacob, who was only joking, now took it seriously and thought, "Though he promises now, he probably will not keep it tomorrow." So he insisted that Esau swear. Esau who became impatient with Jacob swore as Jacob demanded. How stupid Esau was to underestimate the status of eldest son and how clever of Jacob to value it![101]

Imaginatively and by means of personal commentary, Buwang 补网 revealed Esau's and Jacob's minds through their conversation. But Buwang did more than retell the story; he also supplied an allegorical interpretation, saying to his readers, "The status of the eldest son is valuable, let alone the status of morality; a temporary inheritance should not be lost, let alone an eternal one! Never try to save a little only to lose a lot."[102]

Clearly, many OT commentaries, contrary to missionaries' expectations, were not undertaken in relation to the NT and Jesus; they concentrated more on mundane concerns than on transcendental matters. Still, missionary editors did not reject such commentaries because of their Neo-Confucian or Buddhist doctrines; instead, they encouraged their publication. An important reason is that these commentaries also basically confirmed the liberal theology of Christianity, which became popular in the second half of the nineteenth century among American missionaries like Allen and Richard. In affirmative liberal theology, the central point was God's incarnation in man through Christ; on that foundation, asserted liberals, rests the innate goodness of man and the bright prospects for human society.[103] This did not mean that all of humanity

101. Buwang, "Kongyou xingyin wangru yisao" (See that No One is Sexually Immoral), 370a–b.
102. Ibid., 371a.
103. Hutchison, "Modernism and Missions," 111–12 and 116.

would be saved, but it indicated that all would have the chance to be saved. God is in all men, and human sinfulness therefore involves a betrayal of what is most natural in man.[104]

Throughout the nineteenth century, Protestant missionaries followed two basic strategies for introducing the OT to educated Chinese. Together with the introduction of Western learning, they conveyed the impression that the OT was an important part of Western learning. But it was their repetitive efforts in translating the OT into Chinese, aided by Chinese co-workers, that demonstrated the beginning of OT ideas and human beings being interpreted and transformed in the context of Chinese culture. Since the mid-nineteenth century, with the development of the publishing enterprise, especially journals like *JHXB* and *WGGB*, missionaries sponsored and organized Chinese OT commentary activities on a larger scale among Chinese readers and contributors. In the process, a Chinese OT commentary tradition slowly took shape, and contributors interpreted the OT text often in conformity with the Neo-Confucian concepts with which they were familiar. There also was increasingly an interest in the art of the OT narrative. Indeed, OT commentaries in this first stage were basically advanced by converts. However, missionary journals were fairly widely distributed and were read by non-Christian literati. They inevitably exerted an impact on the latter, especially when times became ever more turbulent toward the end of the nineteenth century.

---

104. Smyth, "Christianity and Missions," 186, 155, and 153–90.

2

The Old Testament and New Concerns at the End of the Nineteenth and Beginning of the Twentieth Centuries

DAVID POLLARD CORRECTLY WROTE that "foreign literature in translation [in early modern China] was more of an inspiration than the native literature and played a positive role in shaping minds, creating expectations, setting goals and delineating role models."[1] Undoubtedly, "inspiration" and the "positive role in shaping minds" were reflected by human beings of various persuasions and exerted an impact on readers of various backgrounds. In this chapter, I show how foreign literature, including the OT in translation, inspired non-Christians, especially the Confucian literati.

After the First Opium War (1840–1842), the OT came to be recognized by reformist thinkers as a source of history for Western civilization and, therefore, worth reading. Many did not consider Christianity and the Bible a major threat to Confucianism, although their commitment to Confucianism was undergoing changes. However, as hostility toward Christianity among the Chinese literati grew, the OT began to be seen as a potential danger and was attacked as heretical; at the same time, presumably the impact of Chinese culture on Moses was used to show the Chinese origin of world civilization.

With the development of newspapers, contemporary Jews were introduced to Chinese readers, who naturally related their suffering in exile to historic events in the OT. After 1894, the stateless Jews offered a perfect mirror for China about what might happen if there were no reforms. The Jewish "other" was viewed from different perspectives by conservatives, reformists, and radicals. The involvement of ultraconservatives was meaningful because it demonstrated that the OT had exerted an impact on a wider area. Liang Qichao 梁启超 (1873–1929) was important because he

---

1. Pollard, "Introduction," 5.

not only discussed the OT in more articles and more systematically than others, but also he integrated his democratic ideals of the hero and new citizen in his portraits of Moses.

Old Testament and Reformist Thinkers before 1894

Before 1894, it was Xu Jiyu 徐继畬 (1795–1873), the author of the famous world geography *Yinghuan zhilue* 瀛寰志略 (Brief Description of the World, henceforth *YHZL*), who discussed the Jews.[2] The *YHZL* proved very influential on many leading thinkers and activists in modern China. To name just a few examples: in 1852, a volume entitled "Xiyindu zhi Rudeyaguo yan'ge 西印度之如得亚国沿革" (A History of Judea to the West of India) discussed the geography and history of ancient Israel, which was based on *YHZL*, and was inserted by Wei Yuan 魏源 (1794–1857) in his *Haiguo tuzhi* 海国图志 (Illustrated Gazette of Maritime Countries); Zeng Guofan 曾国藩 (1811–1872) frequently used Xu's geography; Kang Youwei 康有为 (1858–1927) read it twice, once in 1874 and again in 1879 or 1880; and Liang Qichao read it in 1890, the year considered by Liang himself very important in his worldview.[3]

Xu Jiyu used much Western material, mainly of Protestant missionary origin, in composing the *YHZL*. Protestant missionaries did not attract serious attention from the Confucian literati with their publications until after the First Opium War. Though the Confucian literati generally resented the missionaries' presence and rejected their religion, some admitted that China's ignorance of the outside world could not be condoned and had been one of the causes of recent disasters.[4] They began to realize that knowledge about

---

2. The first edition of *YHZL* appeared in 1848, the second in 1850, the third in 1859, and the fourth in 1861. It was reprinted again by *zongli yamen* (the Ministry of Foreign Affairs) in 1866 and became a manual for the Tongzhi Restoration (ca.1860–1874) leaders. A final nineteenth century edition was published in Shanghai in 1873 for popular consumption, much reduced in size so it could be easily carried.

3. For Zeng's use, see Teng and Fairbank, *China's Response to the West* 62; for Kang's, see Kang, "Kangnanhai zibian nianpu" (Chronological Biography of Kang Youwei), 115; for Liang's, see Levenson, *Liang Ch'i-ch'ao*, 17.

4. Some Christian converts were also aware of that at Xu's times. For example, Liang Fa insisted that China was merely part of a larger universe of moral virtue. The Chinese must abandon the attitude of cultural superiority that had blinded them to Christian truth. Implicit in his universalistic argument was a denial of China's self-identity as center of the world. Liang, *Quanshi liangyan*, 37 and 105.

the outside world could be gained from missionary writings. Xu and others were most likely influenced by the prevalent school of evidential research (考证学), and the early Qing scholar Gu Yanwu 顾炎武 (1613–1682), who had condemned Ming Neo-Confucian scholarship for restricting Chinese thought—thereby reducing Chinese awareness of political realities and opening China to the Manchu invaders.[5]

Predictably, missionary writings provided the Confucian literati with some knowledge about Jews and Judaism, although often with a Christian bias that was unrealistic; missionaries referred only to what was portrayed or prophesied in the Bible, and Jews were used to illustrate God's divine plan. Xu Jiyu read both Catholic and Protestant literature in Chinese, but he preferred the latter because of its "sincerity" and "indisputably reliable facts of the rise and fall of states."[6] One indication that Protestant literature was acceptable to him is the fact that many selections from Bridgman's and Gützlaff's works about world geography and history were incorporated into YHZL.[7] In Gützlaff's works, Jews like Abraham, Moses, David, and Elisha were "good" because they obeyed God, and God therefore blessed them. Those who turned against Jesus, however, were punished, hence Jerusalem was seized and destroyed by the Roman army. The Jewish people were either slaughtered or sold as slaves all over the world.[8] Also, the method of tracing the history of ancient Israel and the West in accordance with traditional Chinese chronology was adopted by Medhurst in "Dongxi shiji hehe 东西史记和合" (A Comparative Study of Eastern and Western History). It no doubt stimulated an open-minded evidential research scholar like Xu Jiyu to become interested in the history of the Jews; Jewish history was, as Gützlaff demonstrated, the antiquity of the West, and its culture was as great and old as the Chinese.[9]

Xu had learned from the Englishman George T. Lay (1800–1845), whom Xu found respectful and conciliatory, more about the Jewish people:[10]

5. Drake, *China Charts the World*, 53.
6. Xu, "Fanli" (Guide to the Use of the Book), 2b.
7. For evidence, see Xu, *YHZL* 2, 31b–32. On the basis of Medhurst's "Dongxi shiji hehe," Gützlaff compiled in 1840 a work entitled *Wanguo dili quantu ji* (An Illustrated World Geography). It soon became one of the main sources for Chinese scholars and was widely cited.
8. Gützlaff quoted by Zhou Xun in Zhou, *Chinese Perceptions*, 19.
9. Ibid., 17.
10. Xu, *YHZL* 6, 16a–b. For Xu's attitude to Lay, see Wen, *Chouban yiwu shimo*

The various kinds of books in Western states are interpreted by Jews and the record of their own state is particularly detailed. European scholars often go to study in Greece and Judea probably because they are districts of European culture. It is also said that Jewish women are beautiful and entrancing; they are quiet and perceptive by nature. They are completely different from women of other areas. If one marries a Jewish girl, she will bring dignity to his home.[11]

As a holder of the *jinshi* 进士 degree and an admirer of graceful women,[12] Xu Jiyu would naturally be interested in a people that possessed literary talent and that produced good wives and mothers. He would be furthermore interested in their classics such as the OT that Protestant missionaries had translated and used together with the NT.

Xu Jiyu very likely had a copy of the OT at hand, together with other Western materials in Chinese, when he was writing the YHZL. He had, moreover, good personal relationships with the missionaries. In accordance with the principles of the school of evidential research in gathering and organizing material, Xu must have frequently consulted the OT when he came across references to the OT in Western materials and when he attempted to incorporate selections from them into his own work. It is, therefore, useful to consider how he reinterpreted OT humanity and ideas in the YHZL.

In addition to bringing to China a more accurate picture of the location of the world's states, Xu's account stressed the ancient heritage on which Western civilization was based.[13] He included a section on the history and geography of ancient Israel, which was more or less a repetition of OT information.[14] He dated the events according to Chinese dynastic periods and found the earliest stage of Western civilization coinciding with the most ancient era of Chinese culture, an age of mythical sovereigns and cultural heroes known to Chinese scholars as the Xia dynasty 夏朝 (ca. 2000–1600 BCE). In earliest times, after the great flood, Noah of

---

(Complete Account of Management of Barbarian Affairs), 72:12 and 73:39b. Original publication date unknown. As an example of Lay's comparatively moderate attitude to China and the Chinese, see Lay, *Chinese as They Are*, 1843.

11. Xu, *YHZL* 6, 16a–b.

12. See Xu's deep love for his wife and attitudes to women in Drake, *China Charts the World*, 42–43.

13. Ibid., 67–68.

14. Xu, "Yindu yixi huibu siguo" (Four Countries to the West of India), 30.

Mesopotamia, along with his sons Shem, Ham, and Japheth, was "the ancient ancestor [of the peoples] of the various Western states."[15] Ham's son, Mizraim, during the Xia dynasty, founded Egypt in North Africa. Here he taught the people to build dwellings; he established a government with officials and devised a system of writing. Several generations later came Abraham, who saved his people from enemies; from that time on, they learned methods of military preparation. Despite inaccuracies and even mistakes, the *YHZL* introduced OT characters such as Abraham, Jacob, Joseph, Moses, Joshua, and David when it described the development of Israel from the tribes to the united monarchy.[16]

Like many Christian converts, Xu was also interested in the Ten Commandments. He compared them with Jesus' and Confucius' teachings. Moses, "whose scholarship was superior," led his people out of Egypt to Canaan. There he became their king and proclaimed ten precepts in order to instruct the people:

> [These precepts] taught [the people] to serve their *shentian* 神天 (divine heaven), to respect their parents, not to kill, not to commit adultery, not to steal, not to lie, not to desire the belongings of others, and to worship every seven days. This was the beginning of the West's religion.[17]

Xu noted the continuities from Judaism to Christianity by tracing the development from Moses, to Abraham, to David, and finally to Jesus Christ:[18]

> Although the ten precepts of Moses were shallow, they were just and without defect. Jesus provided an inspiring example and exhorted men to be good. In this he did not go beyond the basic ideas of Moses.[19]

Obviously, ancient Israelite history and religion were interesting to Xu because he understood them as part of Christian history and Christian civilization, and as part of Western history and Western civilization. European power was based on ancient developments. Xu's motivation to examine

---

15. Drake, *China Charts the World*, 118.
16. Xu, *YHZL* 13, 10b, 13, 19, and *YHZL* 8, 4b.
17. Xu, *YHZL* 6, 9a–b and 10b. Drake's translation in *China Charts the World*, 119. Also see Xu, *YHZL* 3, 35–38b and *YHZL* 6, 14–15.
18. Xu, *YHZL* 6, 37b–38.
19. Xu, *YHZL* 3, 40b–41. Drake's translation in *China Charts the World*, 107.

the development of Western civilization was to answer a basic question: How had the ancient West emerged from barbarism? His examination led him to conclude that the West's development did not radically differ from that of China. First were intelligent men, cultural heroes like Mizraim and Abraham, who taught the people aspects of civilization. On the basis of their achievements, ancient states like Judea and Babylon arose. The states competed with each other, just as in the time of the Warring States (403–221 BCE) in China. Religions like Judaism developed, urging people to be good. Then came the Roman Empire which, like the Qin Empire 秦王朝 (221–207 BC), expanded its control over large areas and brought its civilization and Christianity, based on Judaism, to Europe.[20]

Xu Jiyu's primary message in *YHZL* was that China now competed for survival in a world of states that looked not to morality or virtue for legitimacy, but rather to industrial and military power.[21] However, he never doubted the validity and final triumph of Confucian morality and virtues in the new world. On the one hand, he was aware of the secular power and appeal of Western civilization; on the other, he did not think that Western civilization, especially Christianity, constituted the primary threat to China.[22] In fact, Xu called the authenticity and efficacy of Christianity into question. He implied that the reason European leaders had passed on the story of Moses at Mount Sinai was merely to deceive the people and gain their respect.[23] The laws of Moses were untrue, so the Christian teachings were not true either. He mocked, "Jesus established his teachings to save the world. But the various states have been destroying and killing each other due to divisions in religion. If Jesus knew that, what would he say?"[24]

But still, the greatest intellectual contribution of the *YHZL* was its clear demonstration of the fact that other worldviews, such as monotheistic religions, were possible. It revealed a pluralism of cultures and civilizations, all of which had developed semi-independently according to individual patterns, but always with cross-cultural influences. Xu admitted the legitimacy of these non-Chinese civilizations, although they lacked the truths of Confucius and Confucians.[25] As non-Confucian values began to be taken

20. Drake, *China Charts the World*, 117 and 192.
21. Ibid., 58–59.
22. Ibid., 231n30.
23. Ibid., 119. See Xu, *YHZL* 6, 13.
24. Xu, *YHZL* 6, 39a–b.
25. Drake, *China Charts the World*, 191. Xu even mentioned Moses and Jesus parallel

seriously, the ecumenical pretensions of Confucianism became more difficult to sustain. Thus, even when Confucians like Xu kept their commitment to Confucianism, the nature of the commitment underwent subtle changes.[26] In that way, important steps toward modernity were taken.

In the meantime, Christian missionary activities developed rapidly, and the Bible was translated and distributed, especially among China's educated elites. Christian missionaries by their calling often were in conflict with the established order in China because they sought to change Chinese minds and hearts. They penetrated Chinese everyday life and became most deeply involved in the local scene,[27] which resulted in increasing hostility among the Confucian literati. Despite being open-minded diplomats and reformers, Zeng Jize 曾纪泽 (1839–1890) described the OT as "ludicrous."[28] Xue Fucheng 薛福成 (1838–1894), in turn, regarded the Bible as "a bunch of fiction stories; even Chinese classic novels, such as *The Investiture of the Gods* (封神演义), *Journey to the West* (西游记), and the like, were not as superficial [as the Bible]. Even a three feet tall child knows that the Bible stories are not true."[29]

However, hostility toward Christianity and the Bible did not prevent Confucian scholar-officials from advocating closer study of the OT. Song Yuren 宋育仁 (1857–1931), another famous diplomat and reformer, not only read the OT but also strongly suggested to other scholar-officials that they read it, since "The religion [of Christianity] stems totally from the books [of the OT]."[30] He criticized those who would not read or study the OT thoroughly:

> In our dynasty, scholar-officials did not read the books [of the OT], and thought they were not worth observing carefully. Yang

---

to Duke Zhou of the Western Zhou dynasty 周朝 (ca.1066–771 BCE) and Confucius. "The ideas of Duke Zhou and Confucius were not translated into their [Western] languages. Intelligent and outstanding men of other lands arose, instructed people in their customs, and urged them to do good. Their intentions were no more wrong than China's. Therefore, it was not necessary for them to grasp the rule of Confucius." Xu, *YHZL* 3, 40b–41. Drake's translation in *China Charts the World*, 107.

26. Cohen, "Littoral and Hinterland," 224.
27. Fairbank, "Introduction: The Place," 2.
28. Zeng, *Chushi ying fa e riji* (Diaries of Missions), 873.
29. Xue, *Chushi ying fa yi bi siguo riji: 1890–1894* (Diaries of Missions to Four Countries), 792–93. Both *The Investiture of the Gods* and *Journey to the West* are widely read sixteenth-century novels.
30. Song, "Religion," 2a.

Guangxian 杨光先 (1597–1669) refuted the heretical ideas and Wei Yuan wrote a study on Catholicism that touches upon the gist [of the OT]. However, the book by Guangxian has not analyzed the origin [of the OT], whereas the book by Wei Yuan does not scratch where it itches. During my stay in the Western countries, I obtained the books of the OT. In the study by Wei Yuan, only the books of the NT are listed.[31]

Obviously, like Xu Jiyu, Song was interested in the OT because of its relevance and importance to Christianity. The reason the OT should be read carefully was its potential danger to China. Since Christianity was "heretical" to Song Yuren, the OT was equally so. He wrote:

> The OT and the NT . . . appear to be speaking the truth, but actually tell lies. Yet their principles are simple and easy to follow. Even though the missionaries have not the heart to incite rebellion, they have the ambition to change China. . . . Their doctrine that [the world] originated from *tian* is directed especially against Confucianism. Since the minds of people will be easily harmed [by Christianity], its lies should be discerned carefully.[32]

To Song, the heresy of the OT is best understood in light of Confucian doctrines. Therefore, "If a Lord who created the earth and the heavens is to be believed, there will be no need to respect *tian* 天 (heaven) and *di* 地 (Earth); besides, it will be useless to distinguish *yin* 阴 and *yang* 阳."[33] Even when particularly interested in the story of Samson while introducing the book of Judges, Song did not forget to remind his audience at the end, "If a ruffian [like Samson] could enjoy divine favor, then the book is truly a wild and fanciful one."[34] He paid special attention to the "lies" of the Book of Genesis:

> The chronology of the book of Genesis is totally in conflict with Chinese historical records. Its language is careless, absurd, and irrational. . . . The reason for Moses' authorship is that [the leaders

---

31. Ibid.
32. Song, "School," 9a.
33. Song, "Secular Custom," 7b. Yin and yang are two opposing but interrelated active forces in the world. The yang force is positive, bright and dry, and is an attribute of the sun and of males reflecting the dominant position of males in Chinese society and their importance in the perpetuation of the family line. Yin and yang are defined in relation to one another, and each contains within itself the generating germ of the other. Eliade, *Encyclopedia of Religion* 3:290.
34. Song, "Religion," 7a.

of the Israelites] wanted to use a religion to unite the people in the competition with others and did not entertain the high hope that their religion would spread widely to other countries on earth.[35]

More importantly, in Song's interpretation, Moses was a deceitful politician:

> What Moses did was actually using unusual tricks for personal ambitions and about ill-treating other peoples. . . . With the help of strange tricks, Moses . . . rose up from the wilderness and wanted to rejuvenate his people. . . . [He] relied upon God and claimed to be the servant of God in order to transmit orders. The Ten Commandments . . . were actually an artifice for uniting the tribes and a stratagem that ensured success in contending for supremacy. Like those who do not live by honest labor, Moses, with extraordinary wisdom and ambition, was not aiming at missionary ends but taking advantage of religion to cultivate people's good will. Therefore, whenever he transmitted orders in God's name, he always said, "I brought you here from Egypt where you were enslaved." That is in fact Moses' personal utterance to win over his people. . . . That Moses made the Levites kill three thousand people who worshiped the calf . . . was nothing but a trick to wipe out the dissidents.[36]

The other reason the OT should be read was its importance for understanding the origin of Western religion and development. As a reformer who admired Western power and wealth and a diplomat who spent years in Western countries, Song Yuren, similar to Xu Jiyu, was interested in the source of Western civilization. He stated that:

> The source of Western learning all comes from its religion. . . . In England, I met a parliament member of the Upper House, Duke Wellington. When speaking of the principles of personal moral cultivation and national administration for Western countries, Duke Wellington said they were all based on the Ten Commandments of Moses, four of which are about cultivation of one's moral character and six about management of state affairs. [The Ten Commandments of Moses] are the basis for all laws and moral standards. Therefore, Western countries all turn to the religion in them for principles.[37]

---

35. Ibid., 2a–4a.
36. Ibid., 4a–5b.
37. Song, "Public Law," 1b. Song added at the end, "[The Western Governments] adhere to the Ten Commandments of Moses so as to cheat the public." Ibid., 2a.

Aside from the Ten Commandments, the other laws of Moses were for the administration of the tribes. Roman law was also based on Mosaic law but eliminated the divine aspect. According to Song, secular tribal laws, as well as the Ten Commandments of Moses, had established the foundation for Western religion, its legal system, and government politics. He argued that Moses laid the foundation for Western religion and statehood when he transmitted the commandments, set up alters and tabernacles, divided his people into twelve tribes, created rituals, and appointed Aaron the High Priest.[38]

As a typical reformer who legitimized borrowing from the West by declaring that much of Western knowledge had been derived from China in the past,[39] Song Yuren believed the OT books to have eastern roots. He found the book of Job close to the *Daodejing*, whereas the book of Ecclesiastes resembled Buddhist literature.[40] But Song's focus was on Moses and his achievements as related in the book of Exodus. If the Chinese impact on Moses could be substantiated, there would be no need to show the Chinese origin of world civilization. "Before Moses, his people were originally barbarians. Even Moses himself, despite his extraordinary talent and wisdom, was like a brigand with natural instincts to rob and kill. He united the tribes in the wilderness and gave priorities to worship and ethics, for which there must be a source." For Song Yuren, that source was Chinese shamanism. In remote ages, Zhuan Xu 颛顼, grandson of the Yellow Emperor 黄帝, killed the tribal-alliance in the south (九黎), and Shun 舜 expelled the tribal-alliance in the east (三苗) from China. As a result, "Their shamanistic religion spread to the western barbarians from the near to the distant. . . . Their scriptures were translated several times. There are some records identical with [Chinese] ancient books, which clearly show that [shamanistic] religion originated in China." To support that, Song listed fifteen examples from the OT text, showing that the OT inherited Chinese shamanism.[41]

---

38. Song, "Religion," 4a–5b.

39. For supporting details, see Song, "Secular Custom," 6b–7a. For similar cases with other reformers, see Drake, *China Charts the World*, 195.

40. Song, "Religion," 8a.

41. Ibid., 10b–11a. Song also wrote, "Moses lived in the middle of the Xia dynasty. Qi, son of Yu and founder of Xia dynasty . . . believed in shamans. The principles of Xia upheld piety but lost by worshipping ghosts. Mo zi 墨子 (ca.490–403 BCE) recounted the principles of Xia, thus advocating . . . the notion of heavenly ghosts. In the Shang dynasty 商朝 (ca.1600–ca.1046 BCE) . . . shaman officials were appointed in charge of the services to the divine. Those were not far from the times of Moses." Ibid. Yu's grandfather

In Song's view, because of its Chinese origin, the religion of Moses was still upright without many deceitful ideas. However, after a long time of migration, heretical ideas flourished, while authentic ideas withered. The ignorant Western barbarians acted recklessly by changing laws. Since Jesus, Christian laws have become increasingly wild and inferior to the laws of Moses. He concluded that Western wisdom has been exhausted, and nothing in the West is more progressive than the Ten Commandments of Moses.[42]

In summary, reformist thinkers' discussions of OT persons and ideas are particularly significant in the history of Chinese OT commentary tradition. For the first time, the OT and its motifs merited serious attention from non-Christian official scholars. Although their interpretations were limited still to a small number of scholars and were undertaken often in parallel to Chinese traditional culture as was done by converted literati, reformist thinkers' perspectives were different because of their absolute confidence in Confucianism and strong commitment to it in regard to the Western challenges.

New Tendencies in Old-Testament Discussions at the Turn of the Twentieth Century

Before the 1894–1895 Sino-Japanese War, missionary periodicals and newspapers had already begun to report and discuss current Chinese affairs. They, like *JHXB* and *WGGB*, brought contemporary Jews to the attention of Chinese readers. For the Chinese who could only learn about Jews from either the OT or from accounts based on the OT, news reports in journals informed them that the Jews were not merely ancient people in history, but also real and living today.[43] Their lack of a state and their exile today was due to historic events in the past. For example:

> In the war with the Roman Empire two thousand years ago, Judea was defeated, and the people left their country under compulsion and lived scattered among other states. In recent times,

---

was Zhuan Xu. Both Zhuan Xu and Shun were among the mythical Five Emperors four thousand years ago and legendary leaders of ancient China.

42. Song, "Religion," 10b–11a and Song, "Public Law," 1b–2b.
43. Zhou, *Chinese Perceptions*, 21.

descendants of Judea who live and do well in Germany have been donating money to help Jews return to their native land."⁴⁴

When the relationship between past and present was pointed out, the OT, which was believed to have recorded the history of ancient Jews, became less obscure to the Chinese literati, who had always emphasized the importance of history to a nation. Similar to Chinese historical literature, the OT, on the one hand, established for contemporary Jews the foundation of collective memory and identity; on the other, it afforded readers of later generations useful lessons.

Aside from Protestant journals, books of world history and geography also began to mention Jews in exile. In the popular Chinese translation of Okamoto Kansuke's 冈本监辅 (1839–1904) world history, the narrator, when talking about the ancient Israelites, introduced heroes of the OT. He wrote, "When Moses was brought up and educated, he saw the Hebrews' hardship and could never forget it in his heart, saying, 'The Hebrews are my brothers, so I will save them.'" He selected the story of Samson, retold it, and even added to the OT narration, "Though treated like an animal, Samson did not give up during his term of imprisonment, but determined to wear his hair long in order to avenge himself." Furthermore, Okamoto introduced the Israelites' history of sufferings. He told his readers about the Roman destruction of Judea, about Emperor Hadrian (ca.117–138) expelling the Jews, and about the start of Jewish exile.⁴⁵

The reason for the interest in the suffering Israelites in exile and their heroes can be found in the prefaces for the Chinese translation of Okamoto's book. Two Japanese scholars and sinologists wrote for the benefit of Chinese readers:

> Principles of prosperity and decline, waxing and waning, are present in change, whereas signs of good and ill luck, fortune and misfortune, are in the histories.⁴⁶

---

44. "Youtai guoren si guiguo" (Jews Wish to Return to their State), 149b. Xu Jiyu mentioned earlier also described the destruction of Jerusalem, the exile, and the Diaspora of the Jewish people who were keen to preserve their Jewish identity in ancient times, but without any reference to contemporary Jewry. See Xu, *YHZL* 6, 7.

45. Okamoto Kansuke, *Wanguo shiji* (Historical Records of Ten Thousand Countries), 8a, 9b, and 15b. The book was first translated by the author into Chinese in 1878. It was reprinted in 1895 and 1902.

46. Nakamura Masanao, "Preface," 4a.

> [China] claims to be the center of other countries, though her power was in the past. She still regards others as either barbarians or vassals. She is neither concerned about their political gains and losses, nor is she interested in their strong and weak points. . . . China is one of many countries in the world, big or small. . . . The famous Wei Yuan is intelligent and well-informed, but he continues in habitual ways of thinking . . . and does not examine his own [country].[47]

However, before 1894, responses of Chinese readership to the reports of the Jewish loss of state in the Diaspora were not many, and the Chinese educated elite, who were still fully confident and optimistic of their tradition and empire—as already shown above in the cases of Xu Jiyu and Song Yuren—seemed to have not much interest in small and vanquished states like Judea and the fate of their inhabitants. The prevalent self-assuredness of the Chinese literati did not change until after the Sino-Japanese War 1894–1895, when China was crushingly defeated by Japan, and the Chinese elite experienced a profound psychological shock. A large empire like China defeated by a small country from across the sea! Dismemberment of the Chinese state and enslavement by the imperialist powers became a real threat. The literati began turning to aspects of Western learning like religion, politics, and laws—as opposed to technology—for keys to Western wealth and power.[48]

To be able to do so, translation became of paramount concern. Together with this, the publishing industry developed rapidly. In the last decades of the nineteenth century, the number and range of Western works multiplied.[49] Between 1902 and 1907, published translations for the first time exceeded original works, with a large proportion of works on humanities and social sciences.[50] The term "New Learning" (新学) was

---

47. Shigeno Yasutsune, "Preface," 2a.

48. Those Chinese familiar with Western learning broadly comprised four classes. The first were specialists active in translation and publishing agencies. In the second class were those who had studied abroad and had gone abroad as diplomatic emissaries. The third class included products of modern schools. The fourth class only had a smattering of foreign languages but had a very strong interest in Western learning. Xiong, "Degrees of Familiarity," 30–31.

49. Xiong, "Degrees of Familiarity," 30.

50. Tarumoto Teruo, "Statistical Survey," 37–42. As more recent translation studies and theories suggest, translation is a purposeful activity. When translators decide to pick up a certain piece of work to translate, they wish the translation to serve a certain purpose, be it political, economic, educational or aesthetic. See Nord, *Translating as a*

used alongside "Western Learning" (西学) and eventually was preferred by Chinese intellectuals who came to regard the distinction between Chinese and Western as unnecessary, because knowledge was a universal inheritance that knew no geographical boundaries.[51] With a desire to see Chinese affairs in a worldwide context, Chinese intellectuals, by wanting China to be in and a part of the world, necessarily stressed the importance of translating from New Learning. Moreover, with the introduction and acceptance of the Darwinian theory of evolution, "new" became associated with the fitness for survival.[52]

The word "new" symbolized a turning of the tide; it also meant new interests, new ways of interpretation, and new values. Chen Juemin 陈觉民 loosely translated Rosswell Hobart Graves' book on Jewish geography in Chinese in 1902. He defended his adoption of new material, new style, and a new perspective:

> The author of a foreign history is not necessarily a professional historian and the translator does not always follow the style of a [Chinese] historical book; yet the lessons in it about gains and losses, order and chaos, are all too clear. The ancient sages drew lessons from the history of past dynasties. Today, let us use the experience of the myriad countries.[53]

Clearly, Chen's purpose was not to present a felicitous translation, and he did not restrain himself from putting into the text what was not there. In *Xishi tongzhi* (A General Account of Western History), in which Chen's *Youtai dili zeyao* (Essence of Jewish Geography) was included, there was a detailed and independent discussion of Moses as presumably transmitted by the OT text. Here, Moses was not only "a sage," "a great master," and "an initiator" of religion and state, but also he was highlighted as "a great hero" and "a great man" for his people.

> When he was young in Egypt, one day he walked out of the palace and saw by accident an Egyptian killing a Hebrew without reason. . . . Later, he further witnessed the Hebrews of his race subjected to all kinds of cruel maltreatment in Egypt. Disregarding dangers, he personally led two million people out of Egypt. Isn't that a move that can only be made by a great hero?! . . .

Purposeful Activity, 1997 and Álvarez and Vidal, *Translation, Power, Subversion*, 1996.

51. Xiong, "Degrees of Familiarity," 35.

52. Ibid., 35.

53. Graves, *Youtai dili zeyao* (Essence of Jewish Geography), 35.

Moses is widely regarded as a modest gentleman, a great man who was persevering, independent, hardworking, and unafraid of hardships.... Moses founded a new dynasty and originated a new way of abdicating in favor of the most qualified. Therefore, he did not designate his son [as heir] but transferred power to Joshua a virtuous and talented person in his tribe.... Throughout the forty years [of wandering], Moses never regretted [his actions].... It is all the more difficult for Moses to lead the masses into exodus.... However, Moses did not hold a grudge against the ignorant and obstinate people, but kept leading his compatriots to the land of happiness.[54]

To the narrator, a national hero and political leader who could deliver his people from bondage was just what China badly needed at the time of the crisis after the 1894–1895 Sino-Japanese War. Since Confucianism was suspected of lacking validity and China was experiencing a change she had never had before, a gentleman (君子) not of Confucian style but of Moses' type, would be able to deliver the Chinese people.

After 1894, the Chinese literati, furthermore, paid attention to world affairs.[55] If discussions before 1894 about the world outside China were undertaken mainly to help scholar-officials of the Qing Empire gather information about the "barbarians," those after 1894 showed much more clearly that China struggled along with others for survival. Reformers realized that it was not enough to specify what should be pursued by following the examples of Western powers; one also had to know what must be avoided, namely, what might happen if there were no reforms.

Naturally, special attention was paid to the fate of oppressed peoples in dismembered or conquered states like Finland, Poland, Greece, Egypt, India, and Judea,[56] with the implication that the Chinese people might similarly suffer oppressions because their state was in danger of being dismembered. Among these, Judea and the stateless Jews often were singled out and reports about the Jewish Diaspora, translated from Western sourc-

54. "Moses," 1–2. The Chinese term for "Hebrews" was *xibolai ren*, and the term for "Israelites" was *yiselie ren*. They might be used synonymously for Jews at ancient times, but only the latter was used for modern Jews.

55. The sudden growth of interest in world affairs was reflected in journals and newspapers, which developed quickly after 1894. For example, the circulation of *WGGB* rose from 1,000 in 1889 to 38,400 in 1898 and 54,000 in 1903, during which time it reached reformist Chinese intellectuals. Pollard, "Introduction," 7.

56. For the attention to oppressed peoples and the role of the press in bringing about this attention, see Eber et al., *Voices from Afar*, 3–5.

es, but often mixed with comments by Chinese editors, were published.⁵⁷ Undoubtedly, the Jewish people offered a perfect mirror for the Chinese. For example, Shan Shili 单士厘 (1858–1945) urged her countrymen to think over the suffering of the Jewish people because "in a hundred years, we could end up like them."⁵⁸

The Jewish "other" was seen from various perspectives, including the ethnic. Shan Shili wrote that anti-Semitism was not religious but ethnic (种族) hatred.⁵⁹ Tang Caichang 唐才常 (1867–1900) also understood the conflicts between Jews, Christians, and Muslims as "ethnic turmoil." He even took the clashes between Turks and Europeans like the English and the Russians as "continuation of the Jewish ethnic turmoil of thousands of years."⁶⁰ Zhou Weihan 周维翰 based his argument on the book of Genesis and traced the origins of the Eastern ethnic groups back to the migrations of Cain's descendants and the Western ones back to migrations after Babel.⁶¹

Radicals who supported ethnic independence and called for ethnic revolutions received a different kind of inspiration from the OT. Wang Jingwei 汪精卫 (1883–1944) urged his audience to resort to "universal principles" (公理) and to seek "China's position" in the world in light of these principles. One "universal principle," as shown by the exodus of Israelites out of Egypt, is that a conquered ethnic group can rise with force and spirit for ethnic independence and prosperity when the time comes.⁶² Zhang Taiyan 章太炎 (1869–1936) emphasized the importance of territory to an ethnic group and illustrated it with the example of the ancient Israelites.⁶³ He believed the book of Exodus actually to be nationalism (民族主义).⁶⁴

---

57. For an example, see "Eren jiongqu youtairen" (Russians Expel Jews), 10b–11a. There was also the new interest in the achievements by Jews in the Diaspora. For an example, see "Youtai mingshi zhuanlue" (Biographical Notes of Famous Jews), 5a–6b.

58. Shan, "Moxijiao liuxing Zhongguo ji" (Note on Moses' Religion in China), 196–203.

59. Ibid., 204.

60. Tang, "Xiao yaxiya zhonglei kao" (A Study of Ethnic Groups in Asia Minor) 11a–b, n.d.

61. Zhou, *Xishi gangmu* (Outline of Western History), vol. 2, 35a–b.

62. Wang, "Minzu de guomin" (National Citizens), 4. According to his definition, "universal principles" were "principles and standards obtained through deduction and induction for the coming generations to follow in the constantly changing world." Ibid.

63. Zhang, "Shehui tongquan shangdui" (A Discussion on General Sociology), 8.

64. Zhang, "Bo shenwo xianzheng shuo" (Refuting the Idea of Constitutionalism), 10.

There were, of course, those who hoped the royal court and the emperor of the Qing dynasty 清朝 (1616–1912) would oppose ethnic revolution. On the one hand, they belittled the value of the religious faith of the subjects who rebelled against their monarch. Although Zhou Weihan consulted many reference works when composing a history of ancient Israel,[65] he developed his own comments on some OT ideas and men. He called into question the omnipotence of Yahweh. Except for some Israelites, most people did not believe in Yahweh. Yahweh even failed to rescue the Israelites in the exodus: they wandered for forty years, and 600,000 died—a fate worse than the mistreatment in Egypt. Yahweh could not stop all practices of idolatry, nor could he attract all the Israelites, which shows that his virtues were insufficient to touch human beings to the depths of their souls.[66]

On the other hand, Zhou emphasized the importance of the monarch. About the destruction of Judea and the prophets, he wrote:

> Rise and decline of a state is a matter of course in the world. If anyone should be responsible, it is the monarch with his chief ministers, not the subjects. . . . At the time of Zedekiah, Judea had accumulated weakness to the utmost, whereas Nebuchadnezzar king of Babylon was of matchless martial bearing. Being all-conquering, Nebuchadnezzar was ambitious to unite Asia Minor. Then how was Zedekiah able to defend himself?! . . . To make it worse, he did not form an alliance with a powerful neighbor but with distant Egypt, which landed him in a hopeless situation. . . . Therefore, not the Judeans, but Zedekiah alone, should be held responsible for the destruction of the state. The prophets in Judea attributed it to the Judean people who did not worship Yahweh but idols. Such [an explanation] . . . can only make fools of the Jews. Isn't it too superficial to deceive the whole world?![67]

Kang Youwei, who advocated establishing Confucianism as the national religion, brought the OT interpretations into line with his utopian

---

65. They include Xu, *YHZL*; Wei, *Haiguo tuzhi* (Illustrated Gazette of the Maritime Countries); Shan, *Guiqian ji* (Diary of Italy); Okamoto Kansuke, *Wanguo shiji* (Historical Records of Ten Thousand Countries); the two testaments; Williamson, *Eryue shiyi* (A Commentary on the Two Testaments); *Wanguo tongjian* (A General Record of Ten Thousand Countries); *Wanguo tongshi* (A General History of Ten Thousand Countries); *Youtai dizhi* (Geography of Judea); *Youtai liewang zhuan* (Biographies of the Kings of Judea); and *Yiselie liewang zhuan* (Biographies of the Kings of Israel); Zhou, *Xishi gangmu* (Outline of Western History), bibliography.

66. Zhou, *Xishi gangmu*, vol. 5, 21b–22a.

67. Zhou, *Xishi gangmu*, vol. 8, 29a.

blueprint for China. Not surprisingly, when speaking of the OT and Moses, he declared that the Bible became pervasive when China was broken and in turmoil, and that nothing but the religion of Confucianism could resist either.⁶⁸ Kang saw nothing special about Moses and Judea. He wrote that the Ten Commandments are identical to the Buddhist precepts, whereas Judean as well as Greek civilizations, similar to the learning of evidential research in China, does not benefit nature (性), principle (理), and the great administering of the state (国之大政).⁶⁹

When speaking of the survival of Jews in the light of the dismemberment danger that China faced after 1894, his tone changed: "Since [the traditions of Jewish] etiquette, custom, religion, and education have never been dead, the lofty spirit of the Jewish nation does not die even though their land has been destroyed."⁷⁰ His confidence in the function of tradition was impressively consistent. Even on February 20, 1913, after the 1911 Revolution and downfall of Qing court, Kang Youwei published "Thoughts on Jews wailing under the wall at noon in Jerusalem."⁷¹ Two years later he wrote:

> Oh, my compatriots! If you worry about China and want to save her, do it today! . . . The word "Judea" (犹太国) seems to mean "no dying." My explanation is: The Jewish state was destroyed, but the Jewish nation has not perished because their ancient religion has been strictly observed. . . . In their homeland, at noon each day, righteous descendants of the [Jewish] state gathered and wailed under the Wall of David and Solomon. In such ways they have been urging themselves on very hard. No wonder they can survive till today!⁷²

To Kang, when the OT threatened Confucianism, everything about it was negative and should be rejected; but when it could help explain the contribution of religion to a state's survival, it was positive and should set an example for China to follow the religion of Confucianism. Kang Youwei's discussions regarding the OT and Jews were mainly confined to his ambition to save China with Confucianism as a native religion.

68. Kang, "Zhi Zhurongsheng shu" (A Letter to Zhu Rongsheng), 808.
69. Kang, "Fu Kangchangru xiaolian" (A Reply to Kang Changru), 831–34.
70. Kang, Untitled Essay, 347.
71. Kang, "Yelusaleng riwu nanfu kucheng" (Thoughts on Jews Wailing Under the Wall), 9–11.
72. Kang, "Da zhongguoren si" (A Fourth Message to the Chinese), 103–6.

As both a reformer and a scholar steeped in traditional learning, Liang Qichao wrote many articles interpreting non-Chinese ideas, including those of the OT, intending to stimulate the Chinese people to build a new China. In his writings, he argued that China should use the teachings of Confucianism differently from the orthodox, while also learning from the successes of Westerners, for whom, he believed, the OT was an important source. Liang discussed Moses while in Changsha, the capital of Hunan, before the 1898 reform movement. Those discussions were undertaken in the framework of his reformation ideals and invited fierce attacks from local literati, particularly Ye Dehui 叶德辉 (1864–1927). Even Zhang Zhidong 张之洞 (1837–1909), who had previously supported Liang, now decided to stop Liang and wrote to Xu Renzhu 徐仁铸 (1868–1900):

> I have found recently more strange comments by Liang [Qichao] in *Xiangxue bao* 湘学报 (Hunan journal). Liang holds Moses in esteem, advocates civil rights, and misinterprets Confucius' *Spring and Autumn*. . . . Those annoying comments should not be spread.[73]

According to Zhang Zhidong, the Western doctrine of civil rights (民权说) referred to the right of people to express their opinions through the system of parliament. It did not mean that the people should enjoy political power. It was even more absurd to understand it as advocating that every person has the power to make his own decision. According to the OT, God bestowed a soul on human beings so that each of them has his own will. It was a big mistake to relate this to the individual power to make one's own decision. However, Zhang believed that the Ten Commandments were the basis for ethical human relations.[74] Therefore, Zhang was not always against OT ideas. What bothered him was Liang Qichao's application of OT ideas to their "dissenting views."

The widespread distribution of Christian literature in the second half of the nineteenth century aggravated the hostility the literati felt toward Christianity. In the late 1880s, much literature distribution by the Central China Religious Tract Society took place in Hunan province, where foreign missionaries had not yet secured a permanent foothold.[75] In response, an upsurge of anti-Christian literature appeared in the early 1890s. Though an

---

73. See Zhang's "Letter to Xu Renzhu," in *Zhangwenxiang gong quanji* (Complete Works of Zhang Zhidong), 21a–b.

74. Zhang, *Quanxue pian* (Exhortations to Study), 13–14 and 22–23.

75. Bays, "Christian Tracts," 21.

ultraconservative Confucian scholar, Ye Dehui read the works about the world, including the ones by Wei Yuan and Song Yuren. He also read the OT carefully.[76] He commented that:

> The religion of the West is not sufficiently studied by Wei Yuan in *Haiguo tuzhi* (Illustrated Gazette of the Maritime Countries). Besides, the OT is not covered, which also shows that it is not comprehensive. In *Caifeng ji* (Records of Folk Collection) Song Yuren refutes the religion of the West without ignoring either the OT or the NT, thus defending Confucianism validly . . . The religion of the heavenly Lord (天主) took the root in [the Ten Commandments of] Moses. Although the Ten Commandments of Moses still did not go against the Great Way (大道), [the religion of] the heavenly Lord strayed from the principle of it and added illusions. As a result, there exists much absurdity in the OT. . . . If it is superficial of some Chinese scholars to think that the Westerners have no ethics, it is scoundrel-like to think that their religion is superior to Confucian teachings.[77]

Ye reasoned:

> The teachings of [Confucian] sages give first priority to human relations and hold the way of gods as supplement. By contrast, the religion of Jesus first cowed people into submission with [ideas of] ghosts and spirits, then offered sacrifices to the one God and checked ethics as secondary, all of which are clearly revealed in the story of Creation.[78]

In contrast to Liang Qichao, who "praised Moses highly" and advocated "civil rights" (民权),[79] Ye believed that, not a Western-style democratic system but a strong sovereign was the only guarantee for the victory of Confucianism over Christianity. According to Ye, the doctrine of equity (平等说) originated in both Buddhist literature and the OT.[80] Without read-

---

76. Ye even noticed the different versions of the Chinese OT. In his opinion, there appeared different translations of the OT because the evangelic aims of the missionaries were changing. See Ye, "Yehuanbin (dehui) libu mingjiao" (Ye Dehui Expounding Confucianism), 163.

77. Ibid., 163 and 166–67. See Song's similar criticism about Wei Yuan in Song, "Religion," 2.

78. Ye, "Yelibu yu nanxuehui pilumen xiaolian shu" (Ye's Letter to Pi Lumen), 418.

79. Ye, "Xiangsheng xueyue" (Study Regulations for Hunan Province), 367–76.

80. Ye, "Yelibu *Changxing Xueji* boyi" (Ye Dehui's Criticism on *Research Records Made in Changxing*), 241–300. Kang, *Changxing Xueji*, 1896. Kang discusses in this book

ing the Old and the New Testaments, one would not understand well the attempt of Kang Youwei and Liang Qichao. Moreover, he considered the emphasis on the sovereign as a unique feature of Confucianism that was lacking in the foundation of Western religions, namely, the Ten Commandments of Moses, though both advocated worship of *tian*, filial obedience to parents, and universal love.[81]

Therefore, Ye warned that if the teachings of Confucius would be preached in Kang Youwei and Liang Qichao's way, Confucius would become another Moses.[82]

> Today's learning is very much in disorder. In the period of Warring States, the cause of ruin was Yang Zhu 杨朱 and Mo zi; but Meng zi 孟子 (372–289 BCE) refuted them. Since the Han dynasty 汉朝 (206 BCE–220), the root of trouble was the Buddha, Lao zi 老子 (600–470 BCE), and Han Fei 韩非 (280–233 BCE); but Zhu Xi refuted them. Today, Moses is the bane; but nobody refutes him. Instead, people follow him and agree with him. As a result, absurd remarks are running wild, while both integrity, sense of honor, and dao are perishing.[83]

Such discussions on the OT in a stronghold of Confucianism in the hinterland were particularly meaningful because they demonstrated that OT ideas and persons had exerted an impact on a wider area and a larger population of gentry.

The Old Testament and Liang Qichao

Liang Qichao had published the majority of his discussions on the Jews and OT personages, Moses in particular, during his exile in Japan (1898–1912) and the years in the 1920s. They are contained in *Yinbingshi heji* 饮冰室合集 (Collected Works and Essays of the Ice-Drinker's Studio, henceforth *YBSHJ-ZJ* for works and *YBSHJ-WJ* for Essays) and cover the two periods.

---

research method, self cultivation, and the doctrine of equality. Liang Qichao made it a required reading when lecturing in Changsha.

81. Ye, "Yelibu yu yukeshi guancha shu" (Ye's Observatory Letter to Yu Keshi), 441–46. In Ye's view, Confucius also respected heaven, though it did not refer to the heavenly Lord.

82. Miluo xiangren (Ye), "Miluo xiangren xueyue jiumiu" (A Person from Miluo Redressing Errors), 333–39.

83. Ye, "Yelibu yu daixuanqiao jiaoguan shu" (Ye's Letter to Dai Xuanqiao), 431–34.

He had three basic concerns: citizenship, leadership, and culture. For Jewish history and what happened to Jews, he provided both a Chinese and a general historical context and never approached the human beings and ideas of the OT independently. Instead, he nearly always invoked the authority of the Chinese classics when discussing aspects of the OT, and he interpreted OT motifs in parallel with Chinese ones, trying to make the OT relevant to a new context and his personal agenda.

Liang's knowledge of the OT came from at least two sources. First, he read intensively authors like Xu Jiyu, who introduced the geography and history of the ancient Israelites in their works.[84] His second source was Protestant missionary publications, especially those published by the Society for the Diffusion of Christian and General Knowledge in Shanghai.[85] For example, in his *Xixue shumubiao* 西学书目表 (Book List of Western Learning), Liang lists *Eryue shiyi congshu* 二约释义丛书 (Collected Writings on the Two Testaments) edited by Alexander Williamson.[86] He also read *WGGB* and had personal contacts with missionaries like Y. J. Allen and T. Richard. The missionaries had their influence on especially the first stage of Liang's intellectual development.[87]

Liang paid attention to the Jews because of China's national crisis. The lesson in the history of the Jews was meaningful because Liang saw the Jews both as winners and losers. And he, furthermore, perceived similarities and differences between the Chinese and Jews. The image of Jews as winners can be seen in their lasting cohesion in the Diaspora and their material wealth in modern times. When in the United States, Liang was amazed by the wealth and power of Jewish immigrants. He noted their distinguishing capacity to unite, which no other people could match. He sighed:

---

84. Liang failed the metropolitan examination in 1890. On his way home, he purchased *YHZL* by Xu. See Chen, "Liang Ch'i-ch'ao's 'Missionary Education,'" 78.

85. One method of the society was to have the missionaries of the various societies in the provincial capitals distribute free copies of its publications to all the students who assembled there every three years to compete for their *juren* 举人 degree.

86. Liang listed it because it "contained certain historical records of the Western nations," which included the ancients Israelites. Liang, *Xixue shumubiao* (Book List of Western Learning), 3b.

87. See Chen, "Liang Ch'i-ch'ao's 'Missionary Education,'" 86–87 and 102–3. Liang was particularly influenced by Richard. He served as Richard's Chinese secretary from about October 17, 1895, to February 24, 1896. See Richard, *Forty-five Years in China*, 255.

"Alas! A people that have lost its homeland for thousands of years can still stand steadfastly as a cohesive group and be a great power in the world. However, we Chinese still fight and kill each other at home. In contrast to the Jews, how shameful we are!" [88]

The positive image of Jews as winners also was evident in their role in furthering progress of world civilization. According to Liang, peoples around the world can be divided into two principle varieties: the historical (历史的) and the unhistorical (非历史的). The former category referred to those who formed cohesive groups and hence developed capacities to play an important role in human history. The latter are those who did not form cohesive groups and who were often subjugated by others. Among peoples, only the white and the yellow can be called historical. Measured by this standard, both Jews and Chinese were winners for being historical.[89]

Historical peoples could be further divided into two categories: the world-historical (世界史的) and the non-world-historical (非世界史的). The former designation refers to those who have the capacity to expand outside the territory of their origin and to have a world-wide impact by promoting human progress. The latter refers to those who cannot play such a role in human history. Jews, as a leading Semitic people, or "head" of the Semites in Liang's words, had contributed to ancient European civilization. Besides, there was a direct connection between Jews and world civilization. Jews served as a link between the past and the future in classical European history. Jews established Judaism, which preceded Christianity and Islam. Jews also produced Moses and Jesus, two religious founders whose influence has penetrated every corner of Europe. Liang concluded that the Semites dominated the second stage of world history. Therefore, Jews were winners for being world-historical. But the Chinese, being non-world-historical, were losers.[90] The lesson for Chinese was obvious: they would

---

88. Liang, "Xindalu youji jielu" (Selected Records of the Journey to the New Continent), 35–36.

89. Liang, "Xin shixue" (New historiography), 13–14. In support of Darwinism and the German theory of state, Liang praised jungle law and colonists. Moses became Liang's hero of colonization. Liang told the stories of the eight Chinese who rose up, opened territories, and proclaimed themselves kings of southeastern China in the Ming and Qing dynasties. He expressed much admiration for their great pioneering work of colonization. He compared them to Moses and some famous colonists in European history, calling them great men who won honor for the history of their nations. Liang, "Zhongguo zhimin bada weiren zhuan" (Biographies of Eight Great Chinese of Colonization), 4.

90. Liang, "Xin shixue," 15–16.

have to take part in world competition if they wanted to survive as a group in human history.

However, Liang quickly noted that the victory of Jews was limited because they retreated from the stage of modern European civilization, which was the sole creation of Aryans. Liang saw it as a result of the inescapable working of the law of natural evolution. Hamites, who dominated the first stage of world history, were succeeded by Semites at the second stage because Hamites did not know how to disseminate their culture. Semites were replaced by Aryans in the third stage because Semites did not know how to imitate. Liang's view of world order was one in which inter-group conflicts were inherent and resulted in a tendency toward domination of the weaker by the stronger.[91] Here we see the image of Jews as losers. But the negative image of Jews as losers was mainly due to their exile. In some of his early articles written in Japan, Liang described the Jews as an oppressed people without a homeland. He warned the 400 million Chinese of a potential Diaspora.[92] He even used the adjective "Jewish" as a verb in *youtai wo zhonghua* 犹太我中华, literally meaning "to 'jewish' the Chinese" or literally "to make the Chinese suffer like the Jews."[93]

Liang pointed out that, although Jews were famous in world history, they never achieved political cohesion. In contrast, the Chinese, despite a population of hundreds of millions, can unite into a political organization, namely a state, and stand firm in the world for thousands of years. At all times and in all lands, there has been no parallel to the Chinese. Without a unique and deep-rooted national character, the Chinese would have never achieved that.[94] Now the Chinese are winners, while the Jews are losers.

91. Ibid.
92. Liang, "Lun bu bianfa zhi hai" (On the Harmfulness of No Reforms), 6–15.
93. Liang, "Lun hequn" (On Group Cohesion), 80.
94. Liang, "Zhongguo qiantu zhi xiwang" (The Promising Future of China), 8–9. Liang analysed why the Jews could not rise after being subdued by foreign peoples. The Jews knew they must be whole, but they did not realize that they must also be citizens of a state. Being whole means national unity and uniqueness, while state citizenry refers to political independence. It is commonplace in history for one people to be conquered by another. Whether the conquered can stand up or not depends on the sense of national consciousness, which means first being citizens of a state that cannot be disunited and eliminated. The reason for China's longevity is her power to unite. Since antiquity Chinese have always believed that they are like brothers of the same clan, who cannot be separated. They also have the national spirit of independence and would never yield to the pressure of foreign power. Liang, "Xinhai geming zhi yiyi" (The Significance of the 1911 Revolution), 1–3.

Liang's admiration for Jewish cohesion of identity and successful accumulation of wealth was so strong that he even spoke in defense of Jews against anti-Semitic views. He did not refute the prevalent prejudice that Jews are moral to each other on the one hand, but immoral to non-Jews on the other. However, Jews should not be blamed because the same is true for others as well. To be moral means exactly to love one's own kind and benefit one's own group.[95]

To Liang, outstanding leaders of a nation are heroes. Heroes are produced by the times (时势所造的), and heroes produce their times (造时势的). While the first kind knows how to take advantage of their times, it is the second kind who are creators in this world.[96] Whereas in Chinese history, many ordinary heroes took advantage of their times, there has never been a hero who produced the times. That is why Chinese history is always following a set routine and cannot blossom in radiant splendor.[97] China must have a hero to put an end to the old times and introduce the new. But the questions to Liang were: first, who would be an ideal model? Second, what characteristics should a hero have to produce the times? To both questions, Liang's answer was Moses.

A hero who produces the times lives undoubtedly in a transitional period (过渡时代), which was the boundary between decline and prosperity, slavery and freedom, destruction and survival. Even a minor mistake by the leader in making choices or taking measures could invite defeat or destruction. Liang introduced Moses because, in his view, Moses was a hero neither of a new world nor of an old one, but a hero of a transitional period, a link between the past and future.[98] According to the Book of Exodus, Moses was brought up by an Egyptian princess, well trained in Egyptian religions and learning, and nourished with Egyptian wisdom and knowledge. After that, however, Moses led his people and initiated Hebrew culture.[99]

A hero like Moses had three indispensable virtues: he boldly took chances, he was patient, and he was creative. Of the three, patience or the power to endure (忍耐) was most necessary in the middle phase of the transitional period. In the exodus out of Egypt and the march to Canaan, Moses at the head of the Jews wandered in the desert for forty years, when he had

95. Liang, "Xindalu youji jielu," 36.
96. Liang, "Ziyou shu" (Notes on Freedom), 9.
97. Liang, *Lun Li Hongzhang* (On Li Hongzhang), 4.
98. Liang, "Guodu shidai lun" (On the Transitional Period), 27–32.
99. Liang, "Xin shixue," 15–16.

to struggle with a harsh climate, beasts, and barbarians. The journey was exhausting, and life was tough without a moment's peace. He also had to endure the complaint and resentment of his people. At the time, moreover, Moses was already at an advanced age. Therefore, one who is called upon to lead the people of his nation through a transitional period must excel in patience; otherwise, he is bound to give up before the end.[100]

Liang highlighted Moses' strong will power (毅力) and called him the greatest man of ancient times. At first, the Jews were reluctant to follow him. After ten years when he made them move at last, the Egyptians obstructed his aim. No sooner had he left than he lost his way, thus followed forty years of wandering. If Moses had been discouraged by the stubbornness of the Jews at the early stage, or if he had been frightened by the fierce and hostile Egyptians at the middle stage, or if he grew desperate trying to find Canaan, the land of happiness, at the final stage, Moses would undoubtedly have been doomed to failure. Liang cited Zeng zi 曾子 (505–436 BC), "A gentleman must be strong and resolute, for his burden is heavy and the road is long. He takes benevolence as his burden. Is that not heavy? Only with death does the road come to an end. Is that not long?" Without will power, a man can achieve nothing even if he has a lofty goal and distinctive talents. Living is like sailing against the current. This is not only true of an individual but also of a nation and even of the whole world, wrote Liang.[101]

But in spite of all the dangers and difficulties, a transitional period also suggests hope. Without transitions, there would be no progress. Liang declared joyfully that after stagnancy for thousands of years, China ushered in at last a transitional period.[102] Liang probably considered his own exile in Japan, after the failure of the 1898 reform movement, a transitional period in his life. It was in the hope of reaching Canaan, the land of happiness, that Moses led the stubborn and impetuous Jewish people. When a hero of this kind sets out on a long journey, he is helping the world evolve day by day, wrote Liang, thus joining hope to the idea of evolution.[103] Liang considered

---

100. Liang, "Guodu shidai lun," 27–32.

101. Liang, "Xinmin shuo" (On New Citizens), 96–97. The Chinese original of the quotation is "shi bukebu hongyi renzhong er daoyuan yiwei jiren buyi zhonghu sier houyi buyi yuanhu" (*Lunyu* 8:7) and its English translation is from Confucius, *The Analects*, 71.

102. Liang, "Guodu shidai lun," 27–32.

103. Liang, "Xinmin shuo," 7 and 26.

hope the raw material that produces a hero who is the guide for world evolution. The loftier the hope, the more advanced the evolution of society.[104]

However, hope requires that a person take risks and forge ahead.[105] For Liang, the courage to do that comes from strong and lofty desire (欲望). Echoing Tokutomi Soho 德富苏峰 (1863–1957), Liang wrote that everyone has desires, but also should know which is the loftiest and sacrifice all others for it. This he called "complete sincerity" (至诚). The reason Moses abandoned the comfort of a high official and instead chose the life of a wanderer is that he had a strong and lofty desire.[106]

But how was it that Moses had the right desire, hope, will power, and courage? To Liang, these derived from inspiration (烟士披里纯). Leading Jews to wander in the desert, Moses was obviously moved and prompted by inspiration. For the same reason, he could not stop until his goal was attained. In fact, he could have done nothing if he had not been inspired. Liang described inspiration as happening suddenly and mystically to a person,[107] regardless of his will and causing him to become forgetful of self. The inspiration that made Moses a unique hero in history was unlike politics or patterns that can be learned or imitated. When a person is inspired, he cannot reject the inspiration.

Although inspiration is beyond description and cannot be learned or imitated, it can still be obtained if one is completely sincere, which means being single-mindedly devoted to the goal. Complete sincerity is man's true attribute, so everyone can be completely sincere through his own efforts. In the state of complete sincerity, the true feature (真面目) of a man establishes a link with *shenming* 神明 (the miraculous). Instantly, the weak becomes strong, the dull wise, and the incompetent competent. That is why Moses was able to lead thousands of Israelites out of Egypt. Liang cited Mencius, "There has never been a man totally true to himself who fails to move others. On the other hand, there has never been one not true to himself who is capable of doing so."[108]

---

104. Liang, "Shuo xiwang" (On Hope), 18–20.

105. Liang, "Xinmin shuo," 7 and 26.

106. Liang, "Ziyou shu," 73–74. For the reference of complete sincerity in the *Book of the Mean*, see 104n1.

107. This is reminiscent of the Chan Buddhist idea of sudden enlightenment.

108. Liang, "Ziyou shu," 70–73. See the Chinese of the quotation in *Mencius* 4A:12 and its English translation in Mencius, *Mencius*, 161.

But the question is: What kind of goal should one be loyal to and single-mindedly pursue? To answer this, Liang resorted to the idea of natural law (自然法). Natural law is the loftiest criterion to follow so that things are managed properly and function normally. Without bothering himself with the differences, Liang declared that the Confucian ideas of nature (性), the Way (道), benevolence (仁), righteousness (义), propriety (礼), and wisdom (智) were all identical with the natural law because they are universal (普遍性) principles in the human world.[109]

In Liang's view, one who is loyal to natural law, namely the universal principles in the human world, is a sage (圣人). He differentiated two kinds of sages: those appointed by heaven and those who know heaven (知天). Moses was a sage directly appointed by heaven. Besides, that Moses' law code was handed down from *tian* or the Creator (造化生) was not a phenomenon unique to the Israelites but also was prevalent among many other primitive peoples. It may be also found in Confucian classics, such as in the *Book of History* and in the *Book of Songs*.[110]

Since the sages directly appointed by heaven were very few in history, there appeared the sages who have enough knowledge to know heaven. Although the latter are of lower rank, they are also united with heaven (与天同体). To know heaven means to know the Way of change and heaven's will. Only complete sincerity makes it possible for one to know heaven. Liang quoted the *Book of the Mean* (中庸), "Only that one in the world who is completely sincere is able to give full development to his nature;" and "It is characteristic of the complete sincerity to be able to foreknow.... Therefore the individual possessed of complete sincerity is like a transcendental being." Only with complete sincerity were the great classics written and the great foundation was laid. In other words, only the sages can make laws because they are like transcendental beings. As incarnation of heaven, organ for the natural law, and the appointed sage by heaven, Moses composed the Five Books or Torah because his will was heaven's will, his word was heaven's word, and his laws were the code of heaven's law.[111]

---

109. Liang, "Zhongguo falixue fadashi lun" (History of the Development of Law Studies in China), 54–69. Liang and T. Richard held similar views about the natural law. Typical of a Protestant missionary, Richard felt that the advantage of Western civilization was "the fact that it sought to discover the working of God in Nature, and to apply the natural law for the service of mankind." Richard, *Forty-Five Years in China*, 158.

110. Liang, "Zhongguo falixue fadashi lun," 54–69.

111. Ibid., 54–69. See the Chinese of the quotations in Chapters 22 and 24, the *Book of the Mean*. According to Liang, Moses was a prophetic hero, which ranks as the first of

Liang's foremost agenda was his call for unity among the Chinese in both a national and political sense. On the one hand, the Jews were winners because of their unity. This was a unity in a national sense and the strong national identity was brought about by their strong religious consciousness. On the other hand, the Jews were losers because they lacked unity in a political sense. Again, the reason for the lack of political unity was their steadfast religious passion. National unity had made the Jews a whole nation despite the long exile; while the lack of political unity had made them suffer oppression from others during the exile. Both facts can teach the Chinese a valuable lesson. The re-interpretation of Moses was Liang's call for heroes. This was obviously a call for the new citizen (新民) or renovation of his people. However, with an ambiguous use of terms like "great man," "hero," and "sage," this was also a call for great historical figures in the transitional period to lead the people out of crisis to a new world.

If reformist thinkers before 1894 began to pay serious attention to the OT as origin of Western religion and to guard Confucianism against its heresy, the Chinese literati after 1894 related the historic events in the OT to stateless contemporary Jews in the Diaspora and saw in the mirror of the Jews for the Chinese a lesson about what would happen to them if they did not change. However, no matter from what perspective they interpreted Jewish history in the OT, their focus was upon the ruling class and social elite. Liang Qichao took a large step forward by introducing democratic ideals of the new citizen and transitional heroes in his interpretation of Moses. These were new elements in interpreting the OT that would develop further as a result of vernacular Bible translating and the vernacular movement, which is discussed in the next chapter.

---

six kinds of heroes. The other five are: poetic hero, religious hero, literary hero, political hero, and military hero. Liang, "Xin yingguo juren kelinweier zhuan" (Biography of the British Giant Cromwell), 2.

3

The Vernacular Old Testament, Education, and the New Literature

ANY DISCUSSION OF THE origin of the vernacular movement in the 1910s and 1920s must be related to the political propaganda of the early radicals, commercial success of the newspaper business, the educational reform launched after the Hundred Day Reform (1898), and even the tradition of vernacular drama and fiction. At the same time, the impact of the vernacular OT and modern OT education conducted by missionaries must be considered. Moreover, the vernacular OT and OT education were generally interwoven with the above factors. Hence I will discuss in this chapter the missionaries' views of a vernacular Bible and demonstrate how those views contributed to the use of vernacular as a literary vehicle and one Chinese language for the entire nation.

By means of OT education, Protestant missionaries led young people to read the Scriptures extensively and tried to guide OT study in line with their aims in meeting the challenges of the times. As a result, the OT played a role in the mass educational movement for national enlightenment. Without considering the impact of OT education on students at an earlier age, it would be hard to explain their knowledge of the OT in later years during the New Culture Movement. The Protestant missionary journal *The Chinese Recorder and Missionary Journal* (CR) is a major source for supporting these assumptions.[1]

---

1. *The Missionary Recorder* was launched at Fuzhou in 1867 and replaced by *The Chinese Recorder and Missionary Journal* (CR) in 1868. The monthly journal was published by the Protestant missionary community in China and was the only English language publication for seventy-two years until 1941. It served as a link between the various missions that were part of the rise and heyday of the Western effort to Christianize China. Therefore, it is a particularly valuable source for studying the missionary movement and the effects the missions had on shaping Western perceptions of and relations with China.

Finally, the new interest in the OT's literary significance will be discussed, showing the relevance of the vernacular OT translation and education in the birth of a new literature. Since the relevance of Christianity and the Bible to modern Chinese literature has been partially explored by a number of Western and Chinese scholars, my survey will focus on the OT, Christian authors, and Christian journals, neither of which has been explored sufficiently.[2]

Missionary Discussions about Language Change in Old Testament Translating

It is frequently stated that in modern China, Huang Zunxian 黄遵宪 (1848–1905) was the first to advocate the unity of writing and speaking (言文合一).[3] The idea was strongly supported by Liang Qichao who, at the turn of the twentieth century, called for a literary revolution (文界革命), a new literary style (新文体), and a literature written in colloquial style for the enlightenment of the masses and national salvation.[4] Finally, Qiu Tingliang 裘廷梁 (1857–1943) was the first to formally advocate the replacement of the classical literary style with vernacular.[5]

---

2. The leading journals to be used in this chapter include *Anzhong zhiguang* (Light in Darkness), *Chenguang* (Morning Light Magazine), *Daofeng* (Spirit of the Way), "Jidu hao" (Christ) attached to *Daguang bao* (Great Light Newspaper), *Lingguang* (Spiritual Light), *Shenxue zhi* (Theological Quarterly) and the later *Jinling shenxue zhi* (Nanking Theological Seminary Quarterly), *Shengjing bao* (Bible Magazine), *Xiwang yuekan* (Christian Hope), *Zhenguang* (True Light) and the later *Zhenguang zazhi* (True Light Review), *Shengming* (Life), *Zhenli yu shengming* (Truth and Life), and *Zijing* (Amethyst). The editorial staff of Christian journals consisted of Chinese Christians. They were usually not sponsored by churches but financed by advertisements and donations. Published in major cities, they were read by both converts and non-Christians. They could be fundamentalist, semi-conservative, or liberal, as well as mixed, and usually advocated the use of vernacular. Most contributors were Christians.

3. Huang, *Ribenguo zhi* (Introduction to Japan), 2005. The book was written in 1887 and first published between 1890 and 1895.

4. Liang, "Lun youxue" (On Children's Education), 44–60; "Shenshi yinshu xu" (Preface to Mr. Shen's Book on Phonetics), 56–76; "Mengxue bao yanyi bao hexu" (A preface for the enlightenment school and the historic romance newspapers), 56 and "Lun jinbu" (On Progress), 67–8. For the new literary style advocated by Liang Qichao, see his *Qingdai xueshu gailun* (General Introduction to the Learning of Qing Dynasty), 1920.

5. Qiu, "Lun baihua wei weixin zhi ben" (Vernacular as the Basis for Reforms), 176–80. In this essay, Qiu argued strongly for the natural beauty of vernacular in order to justify its aesthetic value and importance in literary activities.

However, the controversy about linguistic style broke out first not among the Chinese but among the missionaries. Years before Huang Zunxian, Liang Qichao, and Qiu Tingliang, some missionaries were already advocating the vernacular language as the style for the Chinese Bible. The controversy about the style for the Chinese Bible contributed much to the vernacular movement. P. F. Price once remarked that, in the intellectual awakening of modern China, marked by widespread propaganda, modern educational methods, scientific inquiry, and freedom of thought and speech, the pioneer propagandist was the Christian missionary, together with the mission press and the vernacular Bible.[6] Price did not exclude the role of the Chinese in the vernacular movement, but he was correct in stating that the missionary, the mission press, and the Bible are an important component of the picture and should not be ignored.

As mentioned earlier, Protestant missionaries at first believed that the Chinese Bible had to appear in classical literary style to win over Chinese literati and officials. After the two treaty settlements, contact with the population at large led to the realization among missionaries, however, that translations in literary style did not reach the lower strata of society and necessitated translation of the Bible into local vernaculars. At the same time, the idea that "the Chinese are a reading people,"[7] held for long by missionaries, began to be challenged by some because they became aware of the illiteracy of the masses,[8] to whom the Bible had to be read.[9] Consequently, Bible translations in such southern dialects as *min* 闽, *wu* 吴, *yue* 粤, *ke* 客, and *gan* 赣 began to appear from the late 1840s on. Those vernacular renderings were primarily in Chinese characters but also were transliterated phonetically.[10] Due to the circumscribed use of local dialects, vernacular

---

6. Price, "The Present Intellectual Awakening," 411–13.

7. Wylie, "The Bible in China," 121; originally read at the Quarterly Missionary Meeting in Union Chapel, Shanghai, April 1968.

8. For an example, see Knowlton, "Bible Distribution in China," 209.

9. Joseph Edkins, inaugural sermon of his presidency to the Chinese Religious Tract Society in Union Church, Shanghai, 1891, quoted in an editorial comment in *Twelfth Annual Report of the Chinese Religious Tract Society, 1890*, 234. In the same sermon, Edkins emphasized Chinese readers' special love for colloquial novels, which should be "a sphere for a Tract Society."

10. Roman and other phonetic characters are systems of phonetic shorthand script, which is easily learnt by illiterates. For a description of such systems see Peill and E. J., "The Scriptures in Phonetic," 329–37. For the details of Bible translations in Chinese dialects, see You, "Shengjing fangyan yiben shumu kaolu" (A Study and Catalogue of Chinese Vernacular Versions of the Bible), 80–131. According to the compiler, the first

translations were distributed and used only among the language group that spoke the dialect. A Bible version accessible to more people, and especially northerners, was needed.

Meanwhile, missionaries were increasingly impressed with the extensive use of Mandarin, or *guanhua* 官话 meaning "official language," used in large parts of the empire by literati.[11] Clearly, Mandarin had no rival in all the other vernaculars as the *lingua franca* in China. Gradually, Mandarin versions of biblical books began to appear, NT books in the 1850s and OT books in 1860s. A major breakthrough toward complete vernacular use was the effort of the members of the Peking Committee, especially Blodget and Schereschewsky, to choose and use *guanhua* to translate the entire Bible.[12]

Finally, the first complete Mandarin OT, which was translated by Schereschewsky, was published by the American Bible Society in 1874.[13] This Mandarin version was widely used in the northern parts of China and Manchuria. Alexander Williamson suggested that Mandarin be supported "until it ultimately supplants all southern dialects and takes its place as the spoken and written speech of the Chinese." In the meantime, though not totally denying the value of *wenli*, he anticipated the final replacement of it by Mandarin in "two or three generations."[14]

Accordingly, *wenli* versions were suffering more and more attacks from those in support of Mandarin,[15] though it does not mean that high *wenli* versions in use would soon disappear and be replaced by vernacular

---

NT book in spoken dialect was the Gospel of John published in Shanghai in 1847 by Medhurst, while the first OT book appeared in 1854 by William J. Boone and C. Keith. Ibid., 83–84. A widely used Western catalogue for Bible translations in Chinese is Spillett's *A Catalogue of Scriptures*.

11. After the 1911 revolution, Mandarin was standardized and was called *guoyu* 国语, meaning "the national language."

12. For a detailed description of their efforts, see Eber, *Jewish Bishop*, 111–12.

13. For details of Bible translations in Mandarin colloquial, see Wylie, *Catalogue of Publications*, 28–30. As Lihi Yariv-Laor increasingly finds, the *Union Version* of 1919 relies greatly on Schereschewsky's translation. To what extent requires further research. See Yariv-Laor, "Linguistic Aspects," 101–21.

14. Williamson, "A Uniform Version," 231–32. Four decades later in 1919, the final replacement was realized just as Williamson predicted with the standardization of Mandarin as the national literary language.

15. For examples, see Juvenis, "One Bible for China," 224; and Sydenstricker, "Review of Schereschewsky's Plain *wenli* Rendering of the NT of 1898," 317–18, to name just two.

ones.[16] High *wenli* was gradually losing ground, and the distribution of high *wenli* versions declined year by year, whereas easy *wenli* and vernacular versions' distribution grew rapidly. Finally, even those missionaries who preferred the *Delegates' Version* had to acknowledge the inferiority of *wenli* to vernacular.[17] By the mid-1890s, the circulation of the Mandarin Bible was already much larger than that of high *wenli* and easy *wenli* combined, while considerable progress had been made in other vernaculars.[18] In the process, easy *wenli*, which was a simplified *wenli* style identical to Mandarin in terms and sentence structures, facilitated the transition from high *wenli* to Mandarin, just as Liang Qichao's "new style" facilitated the transition from *guwen* 古文 (ancient style) to *baihua* 白话 (plain speech) at the same time.

The contribution of missionaries to the vernacular movement also lies in their discussions about the relevance of the vernacular Bible to vernacular literature. While Chinese reformers were promoting an easy and plain language style for literature, the missionaries in favor of Mandarin declared simultaneously, if not earlier, that "The reign of high *wenli* in the literature of China was nearing its close" and that "The time is rapidly drawing nigh, if it has not already come, when the wise man who wishes to reach the largest number of Chinese and influence them for good will write, not in *wenli*, but in Mandarin . . ."[19]

The Mandarin Bible's connection to literature was natural to a Western Protestant missionary. Since Mandarin at last brought the sacred Scriptures into the speech, thought, and life of the common people, the Mandarin Bible would inevitably contribute to the literature of the nation.[20] J. A. Silsby wrote: "The progress of vernacular literature in China, as in Europe, will, in all probability, be closely connected with the circulation

---

16. In fact, the *Delegates' Version* continued to be the dominant Chinese Bible in the south. Even in northern places where Mandarin was spoken, the *Delegates' Version* was still preferred by the better educated and distributed, though in smaller numbers, alongside the Mandarin version. The *Delegates' Version* was used into the twentieth century and the love of its beautiful literary style among the missionaries was great.

17. For examples, see Baldwin, "Union Standard Version," 466; Moule, "On Certain Characteristics," 411n2; and Walker, Note in "Correspondence," 235.

18. For details, see Silsby, "Spread of Vernacular Literature," read at the monthly meeting of the Shanghai Missionary Association, 508–9; "Notes" (*CR* 32), 625; "Notes" (*CR* 34), 301; and "Vernacular Translations of the Bible," 563.

19. Silsby, "Spread of Vernacular Literature," 508–9.

20. Porter, "Missionary Invasion of China," 297–99.

of the Scriptures. The Bible in China will, no doubt, in time become as great a power in literature, morals and religion as it has already become in England, America and Germany."[21]

Certainly, the great power of the Bible in literature can be achieved, as Arthur Cornaby emphasized, only when the Bible is put into a colloquial language similar to how the vernacular *Authorized Version* contributed to British literature.[22]

Missionaries also argued for the unity of writing and speaking. With the Bible rendered in many different styles, including high *wenli*, easy *wenli*, southern dialects, Mandarin, and even transliteration, the wide divergence between versions and the urgent demand for a standard version was felt.[23] Increasingly, a standard version meant one Bible version in one speech for one nation. That standard should not be *wenli*, but rather a universal and pure vernacular. For that purpose, William Muirhead attacked the writers who wrote impure Mandarin with *wenli* expressions. A pure Mandarin free of both pedantry of book style and localisms of particular dialects should "gave rise to the desire and the effort to speak in accordance with the requirements of writing" and "forward this result by its pure and simple colloquial style."[24]

The General Missionary Conference of 1890 in Shanghai set in motion the significant enterprise of translating the Bible into not a local but a universal Mandarin.[25] From 1891 to 1919, the lasting and painstaking efforts to make a Mandarin *Union Version* were particularly meaningful to the vernacular movement, especially the final standardization of *guoyu*, in two aspects: making a pure universal Mandarin, and facilitating a gradual transmission to the Mandarin *Union Version*.

The Mandarin Executive Committee of translators established at the Conference in 1891 was chosen from widely distant localities, to principally eliminate local differences.[26] It was highlighted by Chauncey Goodrich, one of the translators, that translators would always attempt to find terms

21. Silsby, "Spread of Vernacular Literature," 508–9.
22. Cornaby, "Four Subjects for the Revisers," 274.
23. See Moule, "Correspondence to Editorial," 67; "Common Version of the Scripture," 151; Juvenis, "One Bible for China," 224; Baldwin, "Union Standard Version," 465–66.
24. Muirhead, "Style of the Mandarin Bible," 332. As to principles for such a pure Mandarin, see ibid., 332–35.
25. Goodrich, "Union Mandarin Bible," 552.
26. Goodrich, "Translation of the Bible," 589.

in universal use. It is worth noticing that, in the long process of elimination and evolution, the missionary translators or revisers had exceptional Chinese scholars as their associates and gladly deferred to these colleagues in matters of style.[27]

For the sake of purity, the style, being truly colloquial, must also be chaste, emphasized Goodrich.[28] This was also held as a principle by the Bible societies. The American Bible Society even brought the unifying of the easy *wenli* and the Mandarin Version as the practical question of the evangelical mission in China. According to these societies, in the use of terms and in the construction of sentences, the easy *wenli* and the Mandarin should be made identical so that these two would be one and then, throughout China, the colloquial versions would be brought into accord with the standard—and the churches could rejoice in one Bible in China.[29]

In the process of preparing the Mandarin *Union Version*, the Bible societies had been publishing and distributing individual books of it before it finally appeared in its entirety in February 1919. In the complete 1919 Bible, it is obvious that the parts previously published had undergone further careful revisions. This final review brought the earlier work up to the standard of the more finished translation of the latest period of their labors.[30] Obviously, such an updating process rendered the transition from an older version to a new one less prompt but also less painful by being gradual. That gradual transition finally made possible a speedy and wide acceptance of the *Union Version*. In a short period of time, the *Union Version* was so widely and abundantly distributed that it soon became the dominant version throughout the country. The success of the Mandarin *Union Version* demonstrated at the height of the vernacular movement that "The Mandarin colloquial, unlike the dialects in the south-east section of China, is a *written language*, and under the hands of a master, both for prose and poetry, is equal to nearly all the demands that may be made upon it."[31]

---

27. Goodrich, "Union Mandarin Bible," 553.
28. Ibid., 552.
29. DuBose, "Letter from Soochow," 351–52.
30. "*Union Version* Bible," 134.
31. Goodrich, "Union Mandarin Bible," 553.

Educational Reforms and Old Testament Education

Early in the twentieth century, a new system of national education was inaugurated by a number of provinces and the official literary examination system was abolished in 1905 by the Manchu government. The new educational system was composed of vernacular schools of various levels from primary school to university, where mixed curricula, which covered both modern Western subjects and traditional Chinese classics, were adopted. One aim of those new schools was to promote greater social literacy and the vernacular predominated in instruction.

These educational reforms led the missionaries to realize the great demand, the prominent part, and the promising future of public schools in China's development and in producing educated men. The Christian missions were determined to lead and control this movement by making schools not only centers of learning but also evangelical centers through proper arrangement of the curriculum.[32] Soon after the 1911 Revolution, provincial governments turned their attention to popular education as well.

As a result, Christian educational work in China developed fast and constituted an enterprise of considerable size. Until 1921, around 7,000 Christian schools from primary schools to universities were located in most of the provinces, especially the coastal ones. Christian societies and missions of diverse denominations, especially the Methodist and Presbyterian ones from America, were engaged in education. Christian schools, which were much imitated by government schools, were a great help to the government in the development of its educational system. Finally, the Christian educational system was bearing a generous share of the burden of education for the non-Christian community.[33] Many modern intellectuals attended the new schools.

To Protestant missionaries, the establishment of the Church was totally dependent on the Bible's use, and a sound knowledge of the Bible was of the utmost importance, either in intelligently beginning or faithfully living the Christian life.[34] Moreover, "Bible study is perhaps the most satisfactory way of getting a real grip on young men's minds and consciences."[35] However, due to the growth of secular subjects even in Christian schools,

---

32. Pitcher, "Vernacular Schools and Vernacular Education," 681–84.
33. Stauffer, *Christian Occupation of China*, 403–4.
34. Seymour, "Sunday School Work," 127.
35. Taylor, "Some Points," 341.

the Bible was in many cases relegated to the background or left out of the curricula entirely. That made it all the more convincing to the missionaries that Bible classes and Sunday Schools should be made a strong part of their educational system. To secure that, Christian missions in China launched the so-called "Sunday School Movement." The fundamental principle of the movement was that the Sunday School be the Bible study service of the church, having as its object the instruction of all ranks and ages in knowledge of the Scriptures.[36]

Responses to the missionary call for Bible study were positive among Christians. Sun Yat-sen 孙逸仙 (1866–1925) stated, "Our greatest hope is to make the Bible and education ... the means of conveying to our unhappy fellow-countrymen what blessings may lie in the way of just laws and what relief from their sufferings may be found through civilization."[37] Bible study classes were generally regarded as the best approach for influencing government students to become Christians.[38] The Peking Apologetic Group (北京证道团), which published the widely distributed Christian journal *Zhenli yu shengming* (Truth and life), proposed to prepare Bible study courses that would show how the teachings of the Bible were related to the needs of society and thereby proving that the Christian faith was practical in nature.[39] But how should the Bible be taught to Chinese youth? Among the missionaries around the country, a heated discussion concerning the methods of OT education was initiated by diverse institutions. As a result, the following principles for OT education were settled.[40]

36. White, "Sunday School Movement," 130–31.

37. See Sun's statement quoted at the opening of D. J., "Review of the 1911 Report of the China Agency of British and Foreign Bible Society," 495.

38. "Christianity and Government Students," 537–46.

39. "Christian Renaissance in China," 638.

40. From November 5 to 7, 1909, a Bible Institute was held in the Y.M.C.A. Shanghai. The subjects dealt with were: "Bible Study and Sunday School Work," "The Importance of Bible Study," "How to Study the Bible," "How to Lead a Bible Class," and the like. "Missionary News," 727. A series of Bible institutes for the promotion of Bible study, which were held in July and August the next year at such summer resorts as Beidaihe, Jigongshan, Lushan, and Moganshan, included many courses on the OT: "Some of the Greatest Paragraphs of the Bible," "Selected Studies in Isaiah," "Selected Studies in Jeremiah," "Israel and Neighbors," "Recent Oriental Research and the Old Testament," "Studies in the Minor Prophets," "The Wisdom Literature of the Old Testament," "Studies in the Biblical Philosophy of Religion," "The Method and Application of Biblical Apologetics," "Fundamental Doctrines in their Biblical Setting," "The Inter-Testament Period," and "The Social Teachings of the Old Testament." The audience comprised "English-speaking Chinese young men" as well as the Westerners. "Summer Schools in China," 432–33. At

Firstly, OT education should be systematic and graded. Curricula should be created with consideration of the development and capacity of the pupil, as suggested in the following account:

> Bible stories, especially those selected from . . . Genesis, Exodus, and 1 Samuel, can be most readily grasped by a little child under ten years old and fill his mind with the fundamental truths that are so wonderfully suggested, rather than stated. . . . The Bible work should change from the topical to the biographical, in accordance with the pupil's change of interest. . . . It is obviously best from a pedagogical standpoint, then, to use the historical narrative in teaching pupils (from ten to fifteen years old), laying special stress on the persons and their achievements. . . . From fifteen or sixteen years on, the pupils can make a more deeply historical study of the Bible, and a deeper study of its application to daily life.[41]

Generally, the course of study used in the schools demonstrates a high proportion of OT content. According to *Chuxiao shengjing ke yaomu* 初小圣经科要目 (Outline of a Course in Bible Study for Primary School) and *Gaoxiao shengjing ke yaomu* 高小圣经科要目 (Outline of a Course in Bible Study for Middle School), issued by the West China Christian Educational Union (1916), OT studies were required through most of the years for each grade. In lower primary grades, the focus was on the fatherhood of God, revealed in the stories from the OT. In the higher primary grades, the history of the chosen people progressed from Moses to Christ. In the first year of middle school, first, the history of Israel to the death of Solomon was briefly reviewed; and then the history of Israel to the Exile, which included the pre-exilic prophets and their message. Emphasized were political relations, social conditions, and religious and moral progress. In the second year, the history of Israel from the exile to the Roman conquest was covered, with special attention to Nehemiah, Ezra, and the prophets of the exile. Selections from the poetical and wisdom literature were also read.[42]

Zhejiang Christian Workers' Institute in Hangzhou in July 1912, Dr. Garritt taught Isaiah and Amos, whereas Mr. Chiang Tsong Hai and Dr. Yang Vi En taught how to preach the Bible and methods of Bible study. Bakeman, "Chekiang Summer Preachers' Institute," 581–82.

41. Lovell, "Some Suggestions," 289–93.

42. Wallace, "Bible Study in West China," 296–99. See similar cases with the East China Educational Union Bible Study Curriculum (1916), the Central China Christian Educational Union Bible Study Curriculum Revised (1916), the Uniform Bible Study Curriculum secured by Educational Association of Fukien Province (1915) in "Bible Study Curricula," 308–12. Those organizations were four of the ten affiliated associations

Secondly, OT education was made as literary and attractive as possible, with special attention to OT characters and their lives. Missionaries in China had preached the Bible to their Chinese audiences by emphasizing acts of human beings. Human beings are not to be converted to God by wonders but by human sympathy—the appeal of a kindred spirit. The sins of the patriarchs, the unfilial conduct of princes, the crime of Judas, and the imperfections of good human beings were considered essential parts of a complete revelation. The Bible, like man, was considered a microcosm.[43] William Ashmore said that one should study the OT:

> ... because its types and symbols ... have not yet exhausted their significance. Deeper meaning and wider sweep of application disclose themselves as the ages wear on.... Because in the Old Testament we have such minute and powerful delineations of human nature acting itself out under every conceivable variety of moral condition, all presented unerringly without flaw and without partiality. The number of these delineations and touches of character run up into the thousand, so that if one were to be only a student of human nature, the Old Testament would be worth to him more than a hundred Shakespeares; no man who wishes to understand human nature can afford to be a superficial student of the Old Testament.... Because in it we are brought into companionship and kinsmanship with all the holy men of the past—Abel, Seth, Noah, Abraham, Moses and Aaron, and Samuel among the prophets.... [It is] a portrait gallery of heroes whom we are to imitate.[44]

Educators resorted not only to OT readings but also to study aids prepared for students. For example, *Ridui guren* 日对古人 ("Daily Readings in the Lives of the Great Men of Israel"—according to *CR*) aims to make such human beings of old as Abraham, Moses, and Saul real human beings to the reader so that the lessons learned from a study of their lives may be positive factors in day-to-day life.[45] Similarly, OT narratives were to be translated into the daily language of the people so that they might truly understand

---

of China Christian Educational Association established in 1890 at the second National Missionary Conference in Shanghai.

43. See Butcher, "Bible in Its Missionary Aspect," 295 and Wheeler, "Bible in China," 543.

44. Ashmore, "Why We Should Study the Old Testament," 352–54.

45. Espey, "Review of *Ridui guren*," 620–21.

that those OT men and women were similar to themselves and that the God of Abraham, Isaac, Jacob, and David, was their God as well.[46]

As did Ashmore nearly thirty years earlier, the missionaries in the teens at the time of the Literary Revolution repeated the importance of the OT to literature.[47] P. F. Price wrote: "And think of the limitless materials there are to draw from—the stories of Scripture (so rich in suggestiveness that the playwrights of England are looking enviously upon the Bible as a yet unexplored field for reproduction on the stage), the words of the Scripture which may be so profitably laid up in the memory, and the Bible characters.[48] In *Short Stories for Chinese Students*, the author of the story of Joseph was considered as great as Nathaniel Hawthorne, Allen Poe, Honoré de Balzac, Guy de Maupassant, Bjornstjerne Bjornson, and Rudyard Kipling.[49]

Thirdly, the OT was taught not only as religion but also as science. Due to the importance ascribed to the New Learning, the need to make Bible study as thoroughly intellectual as any other study was apparent. The missionaries believed that the core of their faith, namely its history, geography, and even theology, was science.[50] The close study of the "science" of the Bible was to the missionaries useful in teaching Biblical theology.[51]

Finally, OT education emphasized history and its relation to the present. Christian missions and Bible societies paid close attention to political movements, hoping to make the best of new opportunities. The Bible "is preeminently the Book for the times," and the Word of God "is the Word above all others that China's awakening millions need."[52] The *CR* devoted the entire issue of May 1916 to Bible study. It was "essential," according to the editorial, that Bible classes be "historical" and "practical." On the one hand, Bible personages and events must be related to the ancient historical and geographical context and "the modern method of studying history in periods and grouping the facts around central figures can be applied with great benefit to the Bible." On the other hand, studies of any ancient, abstract, or general motifs in the Bible must be related to the concrete and particular context of modern

---

46. Neave, "West China Evangelism," 107.

47. The missionaries also noticed that Hu Shi emphasized the necessity of producing a literature in the spoken language. "Editorial" (*CR* 47), 288.

48. Price, "Place of Bible Study," 294–95.

49. E. J. A., "Review of *Short Stories for Chinese Students*," 569–70.

50. "Notes and Items," 36–37.

51. Evans, "Standard of Theological Education," 374.

52. "Editorial Comment," 279.

history.⁵³ Also, OT education should be related to the present because of the developing nationalism in China. Books like Frank K. Sanders and Henry A. Sherman's *How to Study the Old Testament*, the lessons of which carry through the Maccabean period to the destruction of Jerusalem, were recommended to Chinese students for the emphasis they place on the relationship between religious faith and national well-being.⁵⁴

Many Bible-study aids—such as dictionaries, commentaries, biblical studies, and even literary rewritings of Bible stories—were either translated or paraphrased or written by both foreign missionaries and native Christians. Mission presses played a crucial role in editing, publishing, printing, advertising, and distributing those study aids. That such literature be indigenous goes without saying.⁵⁵ For the composition of Bible commentaries, the works of Zhu Xi were recognized as the model for commentaries because their form was considered both logical and effective, while their style "in unimpeachable *wenli*" was delightful, easy to understand, and only a little harder than Mandarin. Early efforts at providing the Chinese with scriptural commentaries tried to follow that model. As a result, commentaries by J. L. Nevius, Ernst Faber, and J. C. Hoare were appreciated by the Chinese "not only on account of method, but also on account of matter, and style."⁵⁶

Similarly, many study aids were prepared on the basis of field experience in OT education. For example, *Chuangshiji shiyi* 创世记释义 (Commentary on Genesis) was the product of Bible teaching at Trinity College in Ningbo and consequently was well tested prior to publication.⁵⁷ *Shengjing gushi jiaokeshu* 圣经故事教科书 (A Textbook of Graded Bible Stories) won wide acceptance and popularity among teachers of the lower and higher primary schools, especially in Shantung. It was translated into Mandarin from William J. Mutch by Wang Yuande 王元德, who was long associated with Calvin W. Mateer (1836–1908) in Mandarin Bible revisions.⁵⁸ Such

53. "Editorial" (*CR* 50), 287.
54. J. L. S., "Review of *How to Study the Old Testament*," 417–18.
55. "Christian Literature in Chinese," 452. Wang Wandai from Changzhou predicted that Biblical history rearranged "in the form of history after the style of Chinese histories and biographies" would be enjoyed by the educated classes. Also see Lew, "Making the Christian Church," 305.
56. Garritt, "Bible Commentaries in Chinese," 673 and 675.
57. D. H. D., "Review of *Chuangshiji shiyi*," 245.
58. "Our Book Table," 125. Wang Yuande the translator was a professor at Shantung Christian University, Weihsien. Rev. W. J. Mutch of the Howard Avenue Congregational

works on the Bible suitable for use in modern schools, in the words of Cai Lianfu, Editor of *Xinmin bao* 新民报 (New Citizen Newspaper), Shanghai, were of great importance.[59]

However, despite the active use of Bible study aids, OT educators always considered the biblical text and its reading a first priority. The effort to produce and use study aids adhered to that principle.[60] As already mentioned, the OT in Mandarin was read the most. In fact, since the 1870s, Mandarin OT reading had been scheduled in Christian schools whose pupils spoke Mandarin.[61] The 1907 Missionary Conference called attention to the importance of teaching Mandarin in the hope that the ability to read and write in that vernacular might become general.[62]

When the *Union Version* appeared, the Phonetic Promotion Committee of the National Christian Council coined the motto: "Every Christian a Bible reader and every Christian a teacher of illiterates."[63] Meanwhile, the China Continuation Committee (中华续行委员会), in cooperation with the Chinese government, promoted the use of a national phonetic system. According to the plan of its special phonetic committee, literature, especially the Bible, should be put into the hands of China's illiterate millions.[64] No wonder the Popular Education Movement (平民教育运动) to teach the population to read was said to have its birth in a Protestant organization![65] Without exaggeration, Mandarin Bible reading enforced by the missionaries had an impact on the growth of the vernacular reading capability of large numbers of people.[66]

Church, New Haven, prepared a number of graded courses and introduced them in his school: "The Patriarchs," "Men of the Bible," "Christian Teachings," and "History of the Bible." These courses were published and used in a number of other schools. Keedy, "Movement toward Graded Sunday Schools," 42–43. Wang's translation was probably based on those courses.

59. "Christian Literature in Chinese," 450.

60. Luce, "Some Characteristics," 307. Even in making and using a study aid, writers and readers were encouraged to use the biblical text for reference and testimony.

61. "Common Version of the Scripture," 151.

62. "Introduction," 519–21; and Latourette, *History of Christian Missions*, 666.

63. Ch'eng, in *China Today through Chinese Eyes*, 131; and Latourette, *History of Christian Missions*, 781.

64. "Editorial" (*CR* 47), 289.

65. "Introduction," 519–21.

66. The Christian intellectuals emphasized that impact in particular. For example, see Xie, "Jidujiao yu shehui jinbu" (Christianity and social progress), 17–23. In this article, Xie wrote about the wide distribution of the Bible in the vernacular movement and the

Last, but not least, some Chinese intellectuals received their OT education abroad. Since the second half of the nineteenth century, increasing numbers of Chinese students went to European and Japanese universities. American university education became especially important to Chinese intellectuals after part of the Boxer Indemnity was turned over to China for scholarships. Almost all of overseas Chinese students were exposed in one way or another to Christianity and its evangelical preaching, and not a few were attracted by the Bible. Guo Moruo 郭沫若 (1892-1978), for example, read the OT intensively in Japan; Chen Yinke 陈寅恪 (1890-1969) studied biblical Hebrew in Germany; Hu Shi 胡适 (1891-1962) enjoyed the stories of Moses and the prophets in Professor N. Schmidt's class; and Li Rongfang 李荣芳 (1887-1965) even obtained a doctor's degree in OT studies and biblical Hebrew in America. Those Chinese students who were exposed to an OT education either at home or abroad were a constantly moving stream of young people emerging from schools and mingling with millions of others. Their influence was not noted in any statistics, but both knowledge of the Bible and new methods of interpreting the OT resulted from their education.

Christian Intellectuals, the Old Testament, and the New Literature

Chinese Christian intellectuals considered the OT a literary as well as a religious document. The new interest in the literary aspects of the OT shows the impact of vernacular OT versions and OT education on converts in the twentieth century, which made them different from converts of earlier times. Chinese Protestant intellectuals, especially in their role of contributing an indigenous theology, have merited considerable attention. The Chinese Bible of that time, especially the Mandarin *Union Version*, has also been the subject of some research.[67] Yet, research concerning Chinese Protestant intellectuals and the Chinese Bible are developing independently of one another. Moreover, major attention is being paid to the NT. Here, therefore, the Chinese OT will be discussed in reference to Chinese Protestant readers in order to understand more clearly the effects of OT reading. The literary issues, insufficiently noted by scholars, will be emphasized.[68]

---

function of the Bible to reduce illiteracy.

67. A major work is Zetzsche's *Bible in China*.
68. Irene Eber, Marian Gálik, Lewis Robinson, and some Chinese scholars like

The year 1919 is taken as the starting point, and the period ends with 1937 due to the undeclared war launched by Japan. The war disrupted and ended for all practical purposes the healthy intellectual development set in motion years earlier. The time of war is, therefore, a different period.

Between 1919 and 1937, converts were profoundly influenced by new concerns. First, in the anti-Christian movement in the 1920s, a Protestant Christian apologetics emerged in the Chinese church.[69] An existential as well as a hermeneutical question was how to interpret the Christian faith and its texts as compatible with new values and relevant to new concerns. Secondly, Christian intellectuals split into at least two camps: fundamentalists and liberals. In terms of theology and biblical interpretation, they disagreed among themselves.[70] Thirdly, Western literary classics and theories were translated and introduced, and writers experimented with new literary methods and vernacular as the language of literature. At the same time, the *Union Version* was widely distributed and used throughout the country.[71] Finally, Christian newspapers and magazines proliferated during this period, which shows most clearly the true face of the Chinese Church.[72] All

---

Wang Benchao and Yang Jianlong are exceptions, but they have paid more attention to non-Christian intellectuals.

69. Lam, "Emergence of a Protestant Christian Apologetics," 1978.

70. As Dong Jiangyang saw it, for the fundamentalists, the Word of God had the absolute authority and was the core of Christianity; everything said in the Bible was correct and true. The biblical text was accurate without mistakes. They resisted the liberal theology, the Theory of Evolution, the "higher criticism" in biblical studies, rationalism, and secularism. The keynote of the fundamentalist view was that the world was getting worse. For the liberals, the Bible was no longer the holy revelation from God but the historical expression of religious experience of human beings. There was no fundamental difference between Christianity and other religions. Nor was Christ super-human and Jesus was the perfect model for humankind. There will be salvation if one follows this model. Accordingly, the liberals were optimistic about the future. In the contest with the fundamentalists, the liberals gained the upper hand. There were also followers of a middle way. Dong, "Jidujiao jiyaopai de xingcheng yu fenlie" (The formation and split of Christian fundamentalism), 70–78.

71. This does not mean that other Chinese Bibles were not used. A Protestant intellectual might keep using, at least occasionally, an older version, especially when he was already accustomed to it or fond of it for various reasons, including style and literary significance. Therefore, it should not be surprising to find quotations from versions other than the *Union Version* in their writings. But by 1922, in Mandarin, the *Union Version* had no rival; in *wenli*, the *Delegates' Version* was still very popular; the only easy *wenli* version on sale was the one translated by Schereschewsky. Stauffer, *Christian Occupation of China*, 452.

72. Ibid., 454.

those made the so-called issue of Chinese Christian literature (中国基督教文字事业的问题), in which the OT occupied a crucial position, a main concern of the Chinese Church.[73]

Chinese Christian intellectuals regarded the language and literary excellence as an important criterion in evaluating an OT translation. Cheng Zhiyi 诚质怡 (1890-1977), president of the Nanking Theological Academy, referring to the *King James Version* (*KJV*), argued that it was crucial to preserve the literary excellence of the OT in Bible translating so that it could be appreciated by readers. Since preservation and appreciation of literary excellence are crucial to biblical exegesis, translating the OT into Chinese demands a good knowledge of both biblical and Chinese literary conventions.[74]

New translations by Protestant intellectuals, though limited in scope to a short book, a chapter, a few verses, and even a few words from the OT, demonstrated the dissatisfaction with existing renderings and the attempt to produce more appealing ones. Xu Dishan 许地山 (1893-1941) translated Song of Songs anew on the basis of R. G. Moulton's *The Modern Reader's Bible*. Xu divided the eight chapters of the OT text into seven independent parts. They are "Wedding day" (1:1-2:7), "Bride recalling the proposal" (2:8-3:5), "Day of engagement" (3:6-5:1), "Nightmare of the bride" (5:2-6:3), "King pondering over the bride" (6:4-7:10), "Bride missing her home in Lebanon" (7:11-8:4), and "Making an engagement again with the lover at a vineyard in Lebanon" (8:5-8:14).[75] As Xu explained in the preface to the translation, the reason for such a division is that Song of Songs should be read as a lyric pastoral (抒情的牧歌), which portrays love, family, and religious affairs of the nomadic Israelites.[76]

---

73. For evidence, see Peng, "'Zhongguo jidujiao wenzi shiye de wenti' gailun" (Introduction of the "Issue of Chinese Christian Literature"), 1-11; Liu, "'Jiaohui wenzi shiye de wenti' xulun" (Preface to the "Issue of Christian Literature of the Church"), 1-6; Zeng, "Zhongguo jidujiao wenzi shiye de wenti" (The Issue of Chinese Christian Literature), 9-29; and Jiang, "Yu youren lun jidujiao wenzi shiye shu" (A Letter to a Friend on the Issue of Christian Literature), 36-40.

74. Cheng, "Yanjing yizhu" (An Aid to Bible Study) and "Yanjiu shenjing de fangfa" (The Method of Studying the Bible), 25-27 and 50-59.

75. Xu, "Yage xinyi" (A New Translation of the "Song of Songs"), 1-18.

76. Xu, "Yage xinyi, xuyan" (Preface to the New Translation of the "Song of Songs"), 1-8. According to Xu, unlike the OT, the *Book of Songs* contains few eclogues because China finished the nomadic life very early. But Xu still found slight traces of pastoral in the songs of "Jingnü" (Silent Girl), "Baiju" (White Colt), and "Wuyang" (No Goat). For different interpretations of the "Song of Songs," see Taijian (Jian Youwen), "Shengjing

Poetic parts of the OT were frequently quoted and translated anew. The quotations often appeared in the form of traditional Chinese poetry, which reveals not only the translators' interest in biblical poetry but also their love for traditional Chinese poetry. For example, Li Rongfang translated "Lamentations" from biblical Hebrew into Chinese, using the *sao* style (骚体) from "Lisao 离骚" (Encountering Sorrow) by Qu Yuan 屈原 (ca. 340–278 BCE). Li justified using the *sao* style by arguing that the form of parallelism in the verses of "Lamentations" is similar to the *sao* style; a typical couplet in "Lamentations" is characterized by a longer verse followed by a shorter one. That characteristic helps arouse sorrow in the audience. Likewise, a couplet in the form of *sao* style consists of a longer verse with seven syllables ending with *xi* 兮 and followed by a shorter verse with six syllables.[77] Obviously, Li was drawing a forced analogy because the *sao* style is characterized by the use of six-syllable couplets, the two lines of each couplet being connected by a syllable *xi*, which represents a meaningless sound used presumably to carry the singing voice through parts of the melody for which there are no corresponding words.[78]

However, Li's translation earned immediate praise. The poet Zhao Zichen 赵紫宸 (1888–1979) supported Li and helped polish the translated text.[79] Professor Liu Tingfang 刘廷芳 (1891–1947) also appreciated the adoption of the *sao* style. In Liu's view, despite the differences in cultural heritage, living environment, and concerns, the authors of both "Lamentations" and the *Songs of the South* (楚辞) had very strong feelings of distress and poured out their broken hearts. Besides, both "Lamentations" and the *Songs of the South*—especially "Jiuge" 九歌 (Nine odes), "Tianwen" 天问 (Heavenly questions), and "Yuanyou" 远游 (A distant journey)—are rich in religious thoughts. The authors appealed to the transcendental being when in deep sorrow, thus unconsciously revealing their religious thoughts. Liu also praised Li Rongfang's translation as done completely by a Chinese as well as the first effort of a Chinese to translate an OT text from Hebrew.

---

lide qingju" (A drama of love in the Bible), 265–69 and Jia, "Yage" (The "Song of Songs"), no pagination.

77. Li, Preface I to "Aige," Li Rongfang's Chinese translation of Lamentations. For Li's serialized translation, see *ZLYSM* 4.12 (May 1930) 44–5; *ZLYSM* 5.1 (November 1930) 68–70; *ZLYSM* 5.2 (December 1930) 48–50; and *ZLYSM* 5.3 (January 1931) 67–69.

78. Wei, *Hanying cidian* (Chinese-English Dictionary), 1056 and 1318.

79. Zhao, "Xu er" (Preface II to "Aige," Li Rongfang's Chinese Translation of Lamentations), 49–50.

According to Liu, it was a contribution to both the religious life and the literature of the Chinese people.[80]

Whereas some Protestant intellectuals translated just a few verses or words as needed in their writings, others did not translate the OT text, but talked about the principles of Bible translating or passed judgment on other translators. Yu Muren 余牧人, for example, commented that Chinese Bible versions in his day were stylistically good enough but could be improved by making them more identical to the original meaning of the biblical text, on the one hand, and more "contaminated" with the charm of Chinese popular literature, on the other. Although the literary beauty of a Bible translation is secondary to its faithfulness to the original meaning, it enables the sacred Scripture to reach the masses as effectively as popular songs, dramas, and stories do.[81]

Also testifying to their interest in the literary essence of the OT, Chinese Christian intellectuals began to pay attention to Western literary criticism of the OT. Despite the Christian bias, the introduction of Western literary criticism helped Chinese readers appreciate literary aspect of the OT. Sometimes, they translated works of pure literary criticism. At other times, their works might be on non-literary topics but with literary criticism involved, as did the essays about *A Man of Property* by Rev. Dr. Harris Elliot Kirk (1872–1953).[82] Unlike mechanical and superficial Chinese folk tales, the OT has "real" stories that do not follow the simplistic law of retribution; therefore, enlightenment cannot be achieved until the reader reaches the end of an OT story.

Bible stories expose human experience, it was argued, because they reveal the "element of tragedy" throughout everyone's life. The story of Jacob, a long and interesting story, has characters similar to present day people in many ways. The key element of tragedy running through that story comes from the unresolved contradiction between material and spiritual desires in every human being. That contradiction makes man vacillate

80. Liu, "Xu san" (Preface III to "Aige," Li Rongfang's Chinese Translation of Lamentations), 50–52.

81. Yu, "Wenyi zai chuandao shigong shang de diwei yu gongyong" (The Status and Function of Art in the Missionary Work), 38–39.

82. Kirk, *Man of Property*. For the serialized adaptation, see Liu, "'Sage' de kaichang" (How the "Saga" of Jacob Began), 222–32; Liu, "You le chanye" (Having Property), 81–95; Liu and Yang, "Shen jinlai le" (Where God Breaks Through), 254–68; Liu, "Meng yu shengya" (The Dream and Business), 70–85; and Liu, "Buxing zhi nian" (The Pedestrian Years), 40–55.

now to rationality, now to impulse, and leads him astray from the righteous path, thus damaging whatever is perfect in human nature. That damage explains the spiritual pain in life, even when the desire for wealth and fame are satisfied. That is where the faith in God to resolve the controversy becomes meaningful.[83]

Kirk's ideas about human desire and the element of tragedy are comparable to Wang Guowei's 王国维 (1877–1927) idea about eternal pain in human life, which will be discussed in the next chapter. But whereas Wang was pessimistic, the author here is optimistic because of his final resort to God for redemption and because of his recognition of the "element of tragedy" as a necessary aid for man to know God. Kirk's ideas about God's redemption show the impact of Immanuel Kant (1724–1804), especially Kant's ideas about God and the acme of perfection, which will also be discussed in the next chapter. But different from Kant, Kirk was more interested in the function of OT literature in exposing the idea of God.

Significantly, Chinese Christian intellectuals developed their own literary criticism on the OT. Their discussions were of three kinds. The first was about the literary value of the OT. That value partially consists of the OT's place in world literature and its impact on the literature of many nations. This was highlighted by Li Rongfang in a lecture on Hebrew literature and by the well-known writer Zhou Zuoren 周作人 (1885–1967) in a speech on the topic of "The Bible and Chinese Literature."[84] According to Cheng Zhiyi, the Bible made the most important contribution to British literature, and the OT authors' contribution is even greater than that of Shakespeare. British literature cannot be understood if the impact of the Bible is ignored. A good example is the influence of the *KJV* on John Milton (1608–1674).[85]

The literary value of the OT also can be seen in the importance of the OT's literary excellence to its religious nature. Yu Muren wrote about the relationship between religion and literary art. Like the Chinese classics of the *Book of Songs* and the *Songs of the South*, the Bible has an inspiring power that never diminishes because it is both religious and literary. The two significant features together enable the Bible to reach the depth of the human mind. Like the authors of the Psalms, Song of Songs, and the Proverbs, real religious writers are often genuine literary masters and vice versa.

83. Liu, "'Sage' de kaichang," 222–32 and Liu, "You le chanye," 81–95.
84. Xie, et al., "Yanjing daxue (xu)" (Yenching University, continued), 1–8.
85. Cheng, "Yanjing yizhu," 25–26.

In Yu's words, religion is like the soul, while literary art is like the body. Neither the notion of God nor the ideal of religion can be fully revealed without literary devices and a literary work, if lacking religious spirit, is like a skeleton without life. Therefore, they are dependent on each other, though literary art is secondary to religion and must serve religious values. For that reason, Yu was opposed to Cai Yuanpei 蔡元培 (1868–1940), who advocated that religion be replaced by art or aesthetics. In Yu's view, secular literary works like *Water Margin* (水浒传) and *Detective Stories of Shi* (施公案), no matter how popular, are not lofty because they are likely to suggest to the reader crime or erotic desires. Since the love for literary art, like the love for beautiful scenery in nature, is an essential need of a human being, obscene secular literature is dangerous to society if not replaced by lofty religious literature. For the same reason, Yu was also against the so-called literary art for art's sake (以文艺为文艺) doctrine, proletarian literature (无产阶级文学), and national literature (民族主义文学), all of which denied the function of religion.[86]

The second kind of discussions was about the literary aspects of the OT. These were often undertaken in comparison with Chinese literary traditions. Zhang Yongxun 张永训, an associate professor of theology in the Nanking Bible Training Schools and Affiliated Schools of Theology, studied the figurative speeches in the OT text. When he discussed imitation and exclamations of sorrow, he observed their uses in both the OT and Chinese literature. He wrote that Jacob's lament for Joseph (Gen 37:33–35), David's lament for Absalom (2 Sam 18:33 and 19:4), and Isa 14:9–20 are comparable to the best eulogies and mourning orations in Chinese classical literature. He cited those of the Tang 唐 (618–907) and Song 宋 (960–1279) dynasties by such literary giants as Li Hua 李华 (715–766), Han Yu 韩愈 (768–824), Liu Tui 刘蜕 (ca. ninth century), and Ouyang Xiu 欧阳修 (1007–1072).[87] Lifelike uses of imitation and

---

86. Yu, "Wenyi zai chuandao shigong shang de diwei yu gongyong," 35–43. *Warter Margin* is one of the four great classical novels of Chinese literature. Attributed to Shi Naian (1296–1372), who some believe was Luo Guanzhong (1330–1400), it details the trials and tribulations of 108 outlaws during the Song Dynasty. The novel began as a series of folktales told from the Song to Ming dynasties, which were complied and published during the sixteenth century. *Detective Stories of Shi* is one of the three most famous detective fictions in Chinese literature. The book began as a script for storytelling and was published in the eighteenth century.

87. They are "Diao gu zhanchang wen" (Mourning the Ancient Battlefield) by Li Hua, "Ji eyu wen" (Lamenting Crocodiles), "Ji shierlang wen" (Lamenting the Twelfth Nephew), "Liuzihou muzhiming" (Epitaph of Liu Zihou) by Han Yu, and "Ji Shi Manqing

exclamation grant shape to the shapeless, feeling and emotion to the lifeless. Imitation and exclamation of sorrow also make these mourning writings so touching that readers feel as if they were on the scene or reunited with the deceased. At the end, Zhang remarked that passionate OT prophets liked to use exclamations of sorrow and concluded that Oriental peoples like the Israelites and the Chinese make habitual use of them.[88]

But it is worth emphasizing that Zhang, not knowing Hebrew, relied on the Chinese OT for study and comparison. The Hebrew original of Gen 37:33–35, 2 Sam 18:33 and19:4, and Isa 14:9–20 in the Masoretic Text does not show any use of the so-called exclamations of sorrow. Instead, the Hebrew expressed Jacob's and David's sorrow through repetitions (2 Sam 18:33 and 19:4) or the linguistic device of emphasis (Gen 37:33). Therefore, Zhang's conclusion about exclamations of sorrow in OT texts is not convincing. However, what matters here is that the Chinese OT, which follows the example of the *KJV* and keeps the uses of exclamations of sorrow, inspired Zhang to subject the OT and Chinese literature to comparison. Here is an example showing the literary impact of the Chinese OT on a Chinese intellectual, even if use of the Chinese OT might be misleading and the impact was the result of misinterpretation.

In distinction, Zhang, however, correctly implied in the same article that the OT prose style was similar to that of essays written in the Tang and Song dynasties. The essay writing movement (散文运动) inspired by Han Yu promoted a simple style characteristic of the Confucian classics emphasizing true and natural human feelings and straightforward but innovative language. The voluminous production of eulogies written by excellent essayists like Han Yu, Liu Tui, Ouyang Xiu was one of the immediate results of this movement.[89]

Zhang Yongxun also considered OT poetry and poetic prose as expressions of natural feelings with emphasis on personal freedom and creativity. In the essay "Shengjing shifu kao 圣经诗赋考" (On Biblical Poetry and Poetic Prose), Zhang described the uniqueness of Hebrew poetry as having no fixed tonal patterns and rhyme schemes,[90] thus enjoying more

---

wen" (Lamenting Shi Manqing) by Ouyang Xiu. Zhang, "Shijing jingyi" (Interpreting the True Meaning of the Canon), 17.

88. Ibid.

89. Wu, "On Chinese Sacrificial Orations *chi wen*," 25–26.

90. However, Zhang did not neglect the exceptions with tonal pattern and rhyme schemes such as are in Pss 72:10, 25, 34, and 145, Isa 1:9 and 10:6, and Judg 14:8.

freedom of expression, natural wording, harmonious sound effects, and rich parallelisms. In addition, Hebrew verse is compact but emotionally touching and deeply meaningful. Therefore, Hebrew poetry, even in Chinese eyes, is poetic because it expresses a poetic spirit. He also analyzed the talk of Laban to Jacob in Gen 31:26–32 and 31:36–53 as an example of poetic prose. As he understood them, the sentences are strongly emotional, modulating in tone, but terse in grammar, which resembles typical Chinese poetic prose. He concluded from this example that the Israelites were a sensitive people whose poetic mood was easily stimulated.[91]

Zhang's work with OT poetry and poetic prose is richly suggestive by its comparisons with Chinese counterparts. He discussed parallelisms in OT poetry with many examples from the *Book of Songs*. For example, he considered "Zhongsi 螽斯" (Locusts) and "Lin zhi zhi 麟之趾" (Unicorn's paw)[92] as having the same type of parallelism as Psalm 27:1 and 35:26–27. That is, the two parallel parts, though not having the same wording, match in sense and parts of speech, with the latter part continuing the meaning of the preceding one.[93] Zhang also saw the poetic form of Jacob's blessing Judah in Gen 49:8–12 comparable with the form of *fu* 賦 (poetic prose) in "Lisao" from the *Songs of the South*. Both have verses of differing lengths and are interspersed with frequent pauses. These freer forms are due to the authors' deep and rich feelings or thoughts, which demand less restriction in rhymes and rhythms.[94] Here too, Zhang did not resort to the Hebrew original but to the Chinese translation of the OT for comparisons and conclusions.

The third type of discussion involved OT motifs like events, characters, and objects. Such discussions tended to involve concerns with society, human life, Christian theology, and evangelical work. The pastor Cao Xinming 曹新銘 (1896–1984) discussed humble but virtuous women of

---

91. Zhang, "Shengjing shifu kao" (On Biblical Poetry and Poetic Prose), 19–33.

92. These are the fifth and the tenth poems from the collection entitled "Zhounan" (Southern Zhou) among the *Guofeng* (Folk Songs of the States) in the *Book of Songs*.

93. Zhang, "Shengjing shifu kao," 25–26.

94. Ibid., 28–29. The *fu* form developed during the Han dynasty (206 BCE–220) from its origins in the long poem "Lisao" by Qu Yuan. The *fu* was particularly suitable for description and exposition, in contrast to the more subjective, lyrical *sao*. Its prosody was freer than that of *sao*, the rhyme pattern being less restrictive. The elements of the *fu* form include a long line, caesura, and the use of balanced parallel phrases. The use of rhyme places it somewhere between poetry and prose. For a standard history of *fu*, see Connery, "Sao, Fu, Parallel Prose, and Related Genres," 223–47.

low status, such as the maid servant Bilhah, the concubine Zilpah, and the prostitute Rahab. To Cao, society should pay attention to and take care of the millions of low-status Chinese women like Bilhah and Zilpah.[95] The silence of the OT about Bilhah's and Zilpah's background allowed Cao to imagine how they had become maid servants and concubines. But Cao was actually telling sad stories about Chinese maid servants and concubines under the disguise of OT characters. When Cao discussed Rahab, he frequently quoted her,[96] implying that characterization of OT personalities was achieved through their conversations.

Some writers even adopted and retold OT motifs. It was commonly held among them that good Christian journals could stimulate the literary interest of Christians and attract non-Christian readers as well.[97] One way to do that was to encourage and publish qualified creative literary writings.[98] The journal *Zhenguang* (True light, henceforth *ZG*) even arranged a special column for poetic literature in every issue with the hope of inspiring the readers' religious passions, influence their personalities, and build their faith.[99] In fact, creative literature adopting OT motifs, especially poetry and drama, appeared in many Protestant journals.

Poems appeared in popular or traditional forms. For example, Yan Jiqing 严霁青 contributed to the special column for poetic literature in *ZG* a poem of forty lines, retelling the Joseph story from his dream (Gen 37) to his reunion with Jacob in Egypt (Gen 46), in the form of *tanci* 弹词 (folk ballad).[100] A *tanci* composition can have an unlimited number of verses. Each line has seven words ending with a rhyme and the language is easy to understand. The *tanci* form is particularly suitable for storytelling. Typical of the *tanci*, Yan's lesson from the Joseph story is in the ending stanza: man should cultivate his moral character to become united with the just way of God as Joseph did in Egypt.

Yan's work indeed inspired some readers as expected. In the following issue, Li Qianli 李千里 paid high tribute to Yan's work and responded with a set of poems in the form of *qiyan jueju* 七言绝句 (a heptasyllabic

95. Cao, "Pila he Xipa" (Bilhah and Zilpah), 40–41.

96. Cao, "Jinü-Lahe" (A Prostitute–Rahab), 44–46.

97. Tang, "Xianzai xuyao gaoshuizhun de jidujiao zazhi ma" (Is there a need for Christian Journals of High Quality?), 521–27.

98. Yu, "Wenyi zai chuandao shigong shang de diwei yu gongyong," 38–39.

99. See the notice inviting contributions to the column in *ZG* 27.8 (1928) 76.

100. Yan, "Eryue renwu shi—yuese" (Poems about Biblical Characters—Joseph), 76.

quatrain), retelling the stories of the first ten human generations from Adam to Noah. Li selected eight OT personalities for retelling, namely Adam, Eve, Cain, Abel, Enosh, Enoch, Lamech, and Noah, and composed a poem for each.[101] In the form of *qiyan jueju*, every poem has only four lines, each line having seven characters, with both tonal pattern and rhyme scheme. To summarize an OT personality in such a short poem, Li chose to compose the poem in compact style with allusions. For example, in the poem about Cain, Li used in the first line the allusion "*huoqi xiangqiang* 祸起萧墙" (trouble arises behind the walls of the home) from the *Analects*. Then Li used in the second line the allusion of "*zhudou ranqi* 煮豆燃萁" (burning beanstalks to cook beans—fratricidal strife) and reminded the reader of the well-known story about the Cao Pi 曹丕 (187–226) and Cao Zhi 曹植 (192–232) brothers at the time of the Three Kingdoms 三国时期 (220–280). In the last two lines, Li related Cain's murder of Abel to the ongoing civil wars in China.

But not all authors adhered to the OT narration when retelling stories. Chen Xuming 陈旭明 wrote a poem adopting an OT story with many imaginary details. When retelling the story of the serpent in the Garden of Eden, Chen described the natural environment of the Garden, personality of Eve, and added conversations between the serpent and Eve. Not surprisingly, many additional details appeared according to the taste of a Chinese audience. For example, Chen supplied a view of the Garden of Eden embellished with jade, red peach flowers, green willows, darting swallows, and singing orioles, suggesting happiness and good fortune to a Chinese.[102]

Aside from poetry, stories were also retold as dramatic plays, some of which, if not all, were successfully performed.[103] Traditionally, Chinese dramatists considered portraying individual characters more important than keeping the story as it is. Huang Ciyuan 黄次元's drama about Joseph (Gen 37–46) divided the story into thirteen acts, which are based on the most important events in Joseph's life.[104] The script followed the conventions of

101. Li, "Eryue renwu shi (you xu)" (Poems about Biblical Persons, with a Preface), 74–75.

102. Chen, "She" (The Serpent), 62. But, not all authors adhered to traditional poetic forms. For modern poems in free style using OT motifs, see Xie, "Chenji" (Quietude), 2; Guo, "Qingchen" (Early Morning), 24–25; and Zhao, "Yiye de yu" (A Night of Rain), 185–90, to name only three.

103. For evidence, see Liu, "Liangpian xiaoju—xuyan" (Preface to Two Short Dramas), 35.

104. Huang, "Juben xuyan" (A Preface for the Drama), 16.

kunju 昆剧,¹⁰⁵ a popular dramatic form. Since a typical *kunju* opera has an old man in it, Huang has an old Ishmaelite who bargains with the brothers when buying Joseph. He, moreover, added lively touches by modifying or expanding the biblical text. For example, Huang portrayed the brothers' sale of Joseph and their bargaining with the Ishmaelites through conversations, thus highlighting the brothers' greed and cruelty and inviting sympathy for the innocent and helpless boy. He made the drama acceptable to a Chinese audience by selling Joseph to a childless old Ishmaelite who gained an adopted son, a common practice in Chinese society.¹⁰⁶

There are also OT stories retold in the form of modern Western drama. Liu Guangzhi 刘广志 rewrote the stories of Rebecca (Gen 24) and Jacob in two three-act modern plays. In the preface to the drama about Rebecca, Liu confessed that he had come to know many interesting stories in the OT when instructed by Dr. Li Rongfang and that he had taught children these stories.¹⁰⁷ The drama about Rebecca was staged in a church at Christmas for the children and was reported to have enjoyed immediate success. To Liu, both Rebecca and Jacob were perfect models for his audience. Rebecca is a good daughter, sister, wife and a strong-willed pleasant girl, while Jacob is a good son, brother, husband, father, and righteous wise man who follows God. Similar to Huang Ciyuan's work, many details and conversations are added to the biblical stories to enliven the dramas. The ways in which Rebecca's parents treated their guest, namely the servant sent by Abraham, accord perfectly with Chinese manners.¹⁰⁸

Three principal reasons account for the Christian intellectuals' interest in the literary aspects of the OT: first, the appealing literary beauty; second, their importance to NT and Christian theology;¹⁰⁹ and third, their

---

105. Developed under Ming dynasty, *kunju* is one of the oldest forms of Chinese opera still performed today. It combines song and recital as well as a complex system of choreographic techniques, acrobatics, and symbolic gestures. The opera features a young male lead, a female lead, an old man and various comic roles, all dressed in traditional costumes.

106. "Diyi mu: xiaohai shuomeng" (Act One: The Child Telling His Dream) and "Dier mu: muyang beimai" (Act Two: Being Sold While Shepherding), in Huang, "Huo zhong fu—yuese gushi" (Fortune Out of Misfortune—the Story of Joseph), 17-20.

107. Liu, "Liangpian xiaoju—xuyan," 35-36.

108. Liu, "Libaijia" (Rebecca), 36-41 and "Yage" (Jacob), 46-57.

109. A non-Christian intellectual might see it rather differently. For example, Qian Xuantong (1887-1939) viewed the OT as a historical and literary document of the ancient Israelites that has not much to do with Christ just as the Six Classics in China do not have much to do with Confucius. See Qian et al., "Xinwenhua zhong jiwei xuezhe

relevance to the reality of modern China. These three dimensions were seldom separated from one another but closely inter-related. Like Confucian writers of the past, notably Han Yu, who advocated that literature convey the dao (文以載道), Christian intellectuals highly evaluated the literary art of biblical and Christian literature. However, while Confucian scholars valued the dao as much as literary power, for Christians Christian doctrines were a priority.[110]

Finally, after the pioneering and preparatory work of both Protestant missionaries and Chinese intellectuals in vernacular translations, modern education, and literary reading of the OT, the OT began to have a significant place in the New Culture Movement. The immediate impact of the pioneering and preparatory work can be observed in the discussions and appropriation of OT motifs, among both Christian and non-Christian intellectuals, during those years. However, crucial to the development of the Chinese OT commentary tradition is to understand the extent to which non-Christian intellectuals interpreted one of the most important OT ideas, the monotheist understanding of God.

---

duiyu jidujiao de taidu" (The Attitude of Some Scholars to Christianity), 1–4. According to Raoul Findeisen, the literary assessment of the OT in China was originally developed for apologetic purposes and was a way to defend part of the canon. That is because some OT readers moved in an intellectual environment not very favorable to Christianity in general and the OT in particular. Verbal Conversation with Raoul Findeisen on October 11, 2005.

110. According to reader-response theory of literary criticism, the meaning of a biblical text was derived from the reader through his reading process. In his experience of the text as a piece of literary work, namely in his role in creating the meaning of the literary work, he imposed preconceived notions about the way to react to it. For a detailed account of reader-response theory, see Tyson, *Critical Theory Today*. While the reader put his own ideas and experiences into a literary work, he was at the same time gaining new understanding through the text. This is likely to be overlooked in reader-response criticism.

4

Monotheism and Chinese Intellectuals in the New Culture Movement

MODERN CHINA FROM THE mid-teens till the 1940s was a period of intellectual ferment. The worship of science was prevalent and the interest in Western philosophy was strong. It was also a period of new moral standards. Freedom, equality, and universal love were highly valued. Diverse ideologies like individualism, humanism, nationalism, and universalism, to name only a few, were widely championed. At the same time, some intellectuals turned to Chinese traditional culture while many attempted to reconcile Chinese and Western ideas. It was a time of intense intellectual activity. Accordingly, the most serious problem for the modern reader of the OT was to know how to relate its ideas to current knowledge, moral standards, ideologies, and concerns.

Monotheism is not only the crucial idea of the OT and the greatest contribution the OT made to Western culture but also the most stimulating and interesting biblical idea as far as modern Chinese intellectuals were concerned. In this chapter, three major topics will be taken up. First, how the OT and its idea of God were generally interpreted by Chinese intellectuals in light of modern scientism, Western philosophy, and Chinese traditional culture. Second, how the idea of one God was utilized by Chinese intellectuals in their efforts to explain human nature and to promote individual morality. Finally, an attempt will be made to show how universal love, which was of special importance in the context of monotheism, was interpreted by Chinese intellectuals. Two major groups of intellectuals will be considered: Christian converts, primarily Protestant, and non-Christian intellectuals.

The Old Testament and the Idea of God in Light of Scientism

Scientism challenged the traditional authority of the OT and led to a controversy among Chinese intellectuals. To those with absolute faith in rationalism, like the philosopher and educator Cai Yuanpei, faith in God does not help one find the truth of the world, and God is not the final reason for everything. Inductive scientific theories of astronomy and Darwinism showed that God did not create the world, while deductive scientific theories of ethics and sociology repudiated the OT idea that God supervised human activities. Like polytheism, monotheism was esteemed by the semi-enlightened. Though more advanced than polytheism, monotheism is inferior to the philosophy of pantheism.[1] In other words, the OT demonstrates an early stage of human civilization when science and philosophy were intertwined with myth and religion. In Genesis, for example, philosophy was supported first by the myth of God the Creator. But with myths as the basis, the OT idea of God is inevitably an incomplete system. When philosophy develops independently as a result of the growth of science, there is no more need for religion.[2]

Nor did Cai believe that Judaism could really help a person develop his morality. He criticized the Jews for their lack of morality despite their "blind" piety and reluctance to give up the "old" religion of the OT.[3] In Cai's view, it is not religious doctrines like the Ten Commandments, but "human conscience" (良心) or the will to be moral, that is the only true criterion of human values. As a psychological phenomenon, human conscience is powerful because everyone recognizes an idea in conscience and follows it voluntarily.[4] This was to Cai a physiological process, and his psychological analysis of human conscience denied God as the reason for human conscience.

At the same time, however, wider distribution and reading of the OT showed its lasting power and splendor even within a hostile context.

---

1. Cai, "Zai xinjiaoziyou hui zhi yanshuo" (Speech at the Religious Freedom Conference), 723–24.

2. Cai, "Jianming zhexue gangyao" (A Concise Outline of Philosophy), 392–93 and 460–62; see also Cai, "Zhexue yu kexue" (Philosophy and Science), 249.

3. Cai, "Fu wujingheng han" (A Reply to Wu Jingheng's Correspondence), 110–11. Cai also related this lack of morality to the Jewish diaspora and warned his compatriots of the danger of repeating the fate of the Jews if they were not enlightened by education.

4. Cai, "Zhexue dagang" (Outline of Philosophy), 133–34.

What on earth is its authority, asked some Chinese intellectuals.[5] To Christian intellectuals, that authority consists first and foremost in the higher criticism of OT studies. It was believed that the application of scientific methods helped expose the true meaning and spirit of the OT to the people.[6] The reason, as Zhao Zichen indicated, is that textual research by means of historical criticism helps reveal the historical evolution of an OT idea.[7] In addition, this historical evolution is also the process of revelation facilitated by God's will.[8]

Secondly, the authority of the OT is indicated by the fact that the OT contains eternal values because it records religious experiences, problems of the human mind, and the needs of spiritual life, all of which remain the same throughout history.[9] Many Chinese intellectuals believed that science alone is not enough because it does not provide moral education, as proven by World War I. In contrast, OT teachings are full of life and excel in moral messages.[10] Xu Baoqian 徐宝谦 (1892–1944) highlighted in a translated article the OT's emphasis on benevolence (良善) as the highest moral value. That emphasis is demonstrated in the establishment of the moral idea of God, namely the development from the evil God of revenge of antiquity to the God of justice and benevolence of the prophetic period.[11] Li Rongfang related this moral value to human survival and evolution. The family of Noah survived not because of their superior intelligence or physical prowess, but because of their superior morality.[12]

---

5. Zhao, "Shengjing zai jinshi wenhua zhongde diwei" (The Place of the Bible in Modern Civilization), 2 and 11–13.

6. Ibid., 10; and Barton, "Yiselie de zongjiao-shenmingji" (The Religion of Israel), 24. The book was translated from George Barton, *The Religion of Israel*, New York: MacMillan, 1918, and published in the 1920s in the journal *ZLYSM*.

7. Shi Qide, "Kexue yu zongjiao de chongtu" (The Conflict of Science and Religion), 17. It is impossible to identify the author.

8. Yuan, *Jidujiao gailun* (Introduction to Christianity), 1–4 and 33n11. Similarly, Li Rongfang and Liu Tingfang claimed that a good example showing the development or evolution of the religious mind of human beings is the evolution of the idea or image of God in the OT. See Li, "Shengjing gaiwei xuanke hou" (What is the Position of the Bible?), 62–63; and Liu, "Shende xingxiang" (The Image of God), 176–78.

9. Cheng, "Yanjiu shengjing de fangfa" (The Method of Studying the Bible), 58–59.

10. Smith, "Zongjiaode quezheng zhi lunlide jichu" (Ethical Basis of Religious Assurance) 52. Smith also stated that the motives for freedom of scientific research are the sources of moral disintegration. Ibid., 48–49.

11. Montague, "Xinyang de jiefang" (Liberation of Faith), 28.

12. Li, "Xibolai zaonian gushi zhong de shehuixun" (Social Ethics in Some Early

To non-Christian intellectuals who had a keen interest in cultural problems and sympathy with religion, the authority of the OT was first in its importance to Hebrew culture. Regarding the religion of Israel as the core of Hebrew culture, they often used the terms "Hebrew religion" and "Hebrew culture" interchangeably. However, while Christian intellectuals always believed that in medieval times, Hebrew culture was as important as Greek culture and the two combined,[13] non-Christian intellectuals differed among themselves. In Cai Yuanpei's view, religion, Hebrew culture especially, should be blamed for the scholasticism of the medieval period. The weak point of scholasticism was its focus on deduction because it blindly used simplistic OT ideas to explain the origin of the world without inductive investigations.[14] Zhang Dongsun 张东荪 (1886–1973) had a more favorable view of Hebrew culture, when he wrote that Westerners fortunately absorbed Hebrew culture and, as a result, had Christianity for internal cultivation.[15]

Because of their concern with traditional Chinese classics, non-Christian intellectuals were inspired by the achievements of higher criticism in OT studies. Zhou Zuoren declared that the main reason no satisfactory progress has been made in research regarding Chinese classics is a stubborn obedience to ancient doctrines and the lack of independent study based on evidence like historical criticism applied to OT studies.[16] Stimulated by historical and literary studies regarding Song of Songs, Hu Shi claimed that, if the ancient Chinese classics like the *Book of Songs* were not considered

---

Hebrew Stories), 38–39.

13. Peng, "Ping Lishicen rensheng zhexue zhi yiduan" (A Review of Li Shicen's *Life Philosophy*), 303. It is impossible to identify the author's name. To Xie, the reason why Hebrew and Greek cultures could combine is that both call for the worth of individual character. Xie, "Wode zongjiao jingyan zhi sanjieduan" (Three Stages of My Religious Experience), 7.

14. Cai, "Zhongguo de wenyi zhongxin" (Chinese Renaissance), 809; see also Cai, "Zai jiujinshan" (Speech at the Reception), 60–62.

15. Zhang, *Sixiang yu shehui* (Thought and Society), 188. Zhang made this point as an addition to Liang Shuming (1893–1988), who proclaimed that Western culture seeks external material profits. For Liang's ideas, see Liang, *Dongxi wenhua jiqi zhexue* (Eastern and Western Cultures and Their Philosophies), 1922. Zhang also spoke highly of Hebrew culture as one of the two sources for Western culture. See Zhang, *Lixing yu minzhu* (Rationality and Democracy), 1968.

16. Zhou, "Shengshu yu zhongguo wenxue" (The Bible and Chinese Literature), 9.

sacred, they could be similarly approached with new and scientific methods as research material for social, political, and cultural studies.[17]

The Idea of God in Light of Western Philosophy

During the New Culture Movement, Western philosophy was widely translated and introduced to China as a leading branch of scientific learning to reveal the truth of the world. Some Christian intellectuals found inspiration in atheistic philosophers because of their faith in God. Zhu Weizhi 朱维之 (1905–1999), scholar of biblical literature, tried to reconcile the modern understanding of Song of Songs as a lyric of sexual love and the traditional interpretation of it as a religious book about God's love for man. On the one hand, Zhu agreed with biblical scholar E. J. Goodspeed, saying that, as far as the content is concerned, Song of Songs is not about religion. They are songs of love between men and women with details about the secular life of the people. On the other hand, love songs were collected in the Holy Scriptures and used by the Church for preaching even in medieval times with its dominant asceticism, because religious psychology is related to the love between man and woman.[18]

To strengthen his argument, Zhu turned to Sigmund Freud (1856–1939) and Kuruyagawa Hakuson 厨川白村 (1880–1923) for theoretical support. According to Freud's theory of psychoanalysis, all works of literary art originate in consciousness, namely, in sexual desire. Or as Kuruyagawa has it, all works of literary art are "symbols of depression" (苦闷的象征), the result of suppressed desires. Depression, in turn, cannot be expressed openly. Instead, it is released unconsciously or semi-consciously by means of so-called inspiration. Since literary works of religion also are the product of inspiration, they are naturally connected with the desire for sexual love. Zhu further argued that human faith in God as an eternal lover is supported by the instinct of sexual desire, and religious piety is a transformation of sexual desire.[19]

Other Christian intellectuals considered philosophy and the faith in God as one and the same. The evangelist Yuan Ding'an 袁定安 argued for a "philosophy of theism" and proposed verifying God through the

---

17. Hu, "Tantan shijing" (Speaking of the *Book of Songs*), 557–58.

18. Zhu, "Yage yu jiuge" (The "Song of Songs" and The "Nine Songs"), 107–08. For Goodspeed's points, see Goodspeed, *Shengjing de yanjiu* (Biblical Studies), 139.

19. Zhu, "Yage yu jiuge," 108.

philosophical method. Since it is human intuition to probe the question of deity as did Moses (Exod 33:8-13) and Gideon (Judg 6:36-40),[20] the faith in God is meaningful to human life. Therefore, the existence of God can be verified through the "pragmatist method" (实验法) advocated by such pragmatist philosophers as William James and Hu Shi. Unlike Lao Zi's "inconceivable" dao, a "dominant, sympathetic, and anthropomorphic" God whose ultimate purpose is man can be ascertained in religious life through conscious communication with him.[21]

Yuan defended monotheism against all other theistic ideas. Dualism stresses equally the god of the good and the god of evil, thus maintaining that two gods exist side by side. This is wrong because evil is not an attribute of the deity but that of the devil. Therefore, saying that there are two gods is a false statement. In polytheism, nature and human figures are worshiped together with the deity, thus failing to distinguish the deity from human beings and ghosts. Besides, philosophers have believed in a monotheistic God since antiquity. Socrates already recognized a monotheistic deity. The transcendentalists Plato, Aristotle, and Descartes also believed in a transcendental God who created and sustained myriad things (万物) in the cosmos. In the modern era, both Emmanuel Kant and Georg Hegel believed in a mystical God. In Kant's theory of nebula, the power of nature actually referred to God because it was taken as the reason for the cosmos. Later, even Jean-Jacques Rousseau, Thomas Huxley, and Charles Darwin were amazed by the idea of God. Those scientists and philosophers who supported atheism did not confess their belief in God only because they tried to create some novel ideas. Like Herbert Spencer, they tended to realize their error and accept God when they became older and more experienced.[22]

Regarding the concept of evolution, Yuan believed that the OT authors had identical views with Darwin. Originally no competition for survival and evolution existed in the world. However, after the Fall of Adam and Eve, God intended to show the effect of sin and evil through the cruelty of

---

20. According to reliable OT commentaries, Moses' plea has nothing to do with "human intuition." The plea is for a sign or guarantee of Yahweh's presence and guidance (Exod 33:12). The "ways of God" in Exod 33:13 are certainly meant in a wider sense of God. It is supposed that Sinai is the real place of the divine presence, and that with the departure from Sinai the further presence of God becomes questionable for Moses and Israel and needs to be mediated. See Noth, *Exodus*, 256-57.

21. Yuan, *Shende zhexue* (Philosophy of Theism), 77-79, 103, 139-40, and 148.

22. Ibid., 10, 54, 62 -65, 125, 134, 136, 143, 149, 159, and 163-64.

competition for survival and evolution. God did that for man's sake. Yuan did not think that the Darwinian theory of natural selection contradicts God's work of creation. They are two different ideas. Creation took place first and natural selection came next. Besides, the process of natural selection or evolution is facilitated by God. Spencer's social evolution theory is wrong in denying God's role.[23] When confronting Hu Shi, who denied God as the ultimate reason, Yuan claimed that only God could be considered as the reason and, as Plato argued, the starting point of the world, while everything else was an effect of that reason. On the basis of *The World of Life* by Alfred Wallace, Yuan indicated that the evolutionists limited the law of causality to the cellular world of biology and excluded the role of the transcendental dominating will of God.[24]

Zhao Zichen too advocated compatibility of the faith of God with philosophy. In his view, the OT does not lack philosophical content; it is apparent in such books as Ecclesiastes, Second Isaiah, Job, and Gen 1. More importantly, philosophy and monotheism are identical. For philosophy, the "first principle" (第一原理) or prerequisite is a hypothesis. The myriad beings (万有), heart-mind (心), substance (物), principle (理), and spontaneity (天然) are all observed in the framework of that hypothesis so that they can be well explained and united rationally. Similarly, it is also a "first hypothesis" or prerequisite to believe that the OT came from God. Since God is the reason for the myriad beings, heart-mind, substance, principle, and spontaneity, every kind of existence finds its origin and end in God. For that reason, Zhao considered Gen 1 as "pure" philosophy.[25]

However, Zhao also believed that, among peoples who made great contributions to humanity, the Israelites paid the least attention to philosophical thinking and were the least talented in that respect. Their unique contribution to Western civilization was felt only at the time of the Reformation. The Reformation transformed the interest of Europeans, especially those in Protestant countries, from rational Scholastic theology to religion as expressed in the Bible, especially the OT.[26] Zhao attributed the

23. Ibid., 46–49, 54, 57–61, and 101–4.

24. Ibid., 49–50 and 57–61. Wallace, *World of Life*, 1910. For Hu Shi's atheistic ideas, see Hu, *Zhongguo zhexue shi* (History of Chinese Philosophy), 1919.

25. Zhao, "Shengjing zai jinshi wenhua zhongde diwei," 7 and 12–13.

26. Shi Qide, "Fazhan yu fenhua," (Development and Breakup), 7. The original author cannot be identified. Yuan Ding'an in the 1930s also believed that the Israelites lacked philosophical thinking. According to Yuan, Judaism is the most pragmatic religion in the world. As a result, it has produced few poetic and philosophical giants. They saw God

lack of philosophical thinking to the prophets, who attacked the religious practices of their times, counting not on reason but on direct orders and instructions from God.[27]

Wang Guowei argued that all world religions have dualistic elements. It is significant that he analyzed these elements from a philosophical viewpoint. The opposition between good and evil is a universal phenomenon in human experience, which leads to endless disputes in the world, as well as such differences as between politics and morality, religion and philosophy. In the biblical tradition, the diametrically opposed characters of Yahweh and Satan are due to the impact of Zoroastrianism, in which Ormuzd was the good god of light and peace and Ahriman was the evil one of darkness. The motif of Adam and Eve's fall shows the struggle between good and evil.[28] Wang's interpretation contradicted Western OT commentary. Indeed, Persian religion dealt in opposites of light and darkness. However, as in Isa 45:7, Yahweh claims not to be those conditions, but to *create* both, and thus to overcome the inherent dualism in his sovereign rule over them.[29]

Feng Youlan 冯友兰 (1895-1990), like Yuan Ding'an and Zhao Zichen, also denied any principle difference between religion and philosophy. Religion is inherently philosophical. However, the philosophy of Christianity is different from "the philosophy of others," with which Feng actually implied Confucianism. In the philosophy of Christianity, God is the creator, while man and the world are the created. There is no internal link between the two except the covenantal relationship. God and man are opposites (Gen 2:7 and Isa 45:67). In Confucianism, the "thing-itself" (本体) of human spirit has comic implications. Secondly, in the philosophy of Christianity, the ideal world, in which human beings once lived and should return to, was concrete (Gen 2-3). In Confucianism, it is abstract. Thirdly, in the philosophy of Christianity, the lost paradise cannot be restored

---

through concrete substances. Yuan, *Youtaijiao gailun* (Introduction to Judaism), 1935, 20-21.

27. Shi Qide, "Fazhan yu fenhua," (Development and Breakup), 8.

28. Wang, "Shubenhua zhexue jiqi jiaoyu xueshuo" (The Philosophical and Educational Thoughts of Schopenhauer), 190-91. According to Wang, *shen* (god) and *mogui* (devil) can be contrasted. Evidence of dualism can be also noted between *xing* (nature) and *qi* (matter), *liangzhi* (innate knowledge) and *wuyu* (material desires), advocated by Lu Xiangshan (1139-1193) and Wang Yangming. Therefore, Lu Xiangshan and Wang Yangming, despite their faith in man's *xingshan* (natural goodness), were dualists, whereas Mencius was self-contradictory.

29. Watts, *Isaiah 34-66*, 157.

without absolution of men's sin. Who will be redeemed and who will not be redeemed depends not on men's achievements and virtues but totally on the will of God. In Confucianism, human beings can restore the ideal world they had lost with their own will power.

In Feng's view, those unique OT ideas in Christian philosophy explain why modern science and progressivism (进步主义) developed nowhere else except in Europe. The cardinal ideas of progressivism are that man and nature are opposed to one another, and man can control nature with human intelligence. As Feng understood it, that man and nature are not in harmony but in opposition reflects the relationship of man and God in the OT. The confidence in human knowledge about nature and power over nature is inspired by the idea of an anthropomorphic God as the world's creator and governor with unlimited wisdom and power. As to the concrete vision of paradise, it explains why modern Europeans hoped and worked so hard for a better world. Finally, under an autocratic God, people obviously can protest and hope to establish a human kingdom with their own power.[30]

The Old-Testament Idea of God and Traditional Chinese Culture

With the revived interest and confidence in traditional Chinese culture among many Chinese intellectuals after World War I, discussions of OT ideas were frequently undertaken in parallel with ideas from Chinese traditions. Like educated Christians discussed earlier, some New Culture Christian intellectuals also related OT ideas to Confucianism. Wu Zhenchun吴震春 (1869–1941) emphasized that in an age of evolutionary religion and changing academic thought, it is even more meaningful to mediate between the classics of Christianity and Confucianism.[31] On the subject of man's origin for example, Wu believed that Gen 2:7, the opening sentence of the *Book of the Mean*, and Zhu Xi's commentary to it all expressed the same idea.[32] In fact, in Zhu's commentary, "nature" is not

30. Feng, "Jinbupai" (Progressivists), chapter 7 in *Rensheng zhexue* (The Philosophy of Life). Feng was a person who generally argued that philosophy should replace religion, and so this claim from an earlier work of his would show a position which he later rejected.

31. Wu, "Jidujiao jing yu rujiao jing" (Christian and Confucian Classics), 5. By "Jidujiao jing" (Christian Classics), Wu meant the Bible.

32. Ibid., 1–2. The opening sentence is "What Heaven has ordained is called nature . . ." For Zhu Xi's commentary of it, see Zhu, *Sishu zhangju jizhu* (Collected Commentaries

limited to man; it embraces that of animals also. But by Christian intellectuals, "nature" was understood as the nature of man only, a difference that Wu Zhenchun neglected.

Yuan Ding'an explored the subject of God as the Creator in greater detail. According to Chinese etymology, he wrote, the authoritative dictionary *Shuowen jiezi* 说文解字 by Xu Shen 许慎 (ca. 58–ca. 147) states that "the heavenly god draws forth all things on the earth" (天神引出万物于地), whereas the *Shuowen jiezi xizhuan* 说文解字系传 (Notes on the *Shuowen jiezi*) by Xu Kai 徐锴 (920–974) states that "the heavenly lord lowers energy of life to inspire all things on the earth" (天主降气以感万物). According to the OT, God created the embryonic world at the very beginning and then simply commanded the production of things from the land. Command means that God spoke, and speech has the energy of life. Therefore, that all things were produced by God's command is the same as Xu Kai's idea. God's work at the second stage, stating and drawing forth things, confirmed God as the Creator at the first stage. Scientists describe the second stage of God's work, while religious leaders reveal the first.[33] Xu Shen's *shen* 神 (god or gods) can be understood in a monotheist sense. In Chinese, *shen* is a generic term for gods/spirits and can be either single or plural in number.[34] The use of *tianshen* 天神 (the heavenly god) does not exclude the existence of other gods. Although Xu Kai stated *zhu* 主 (lord) instead, *tianzhu* 天主 (the heavenly lord) in his day did not have monotheist implications either. Nonetheless, Yuan equated *shen* and *zhu* to God, as did, of course, many missionaries.

Yuan Ding'an believed that genuine Confucianism had a monotheist faith. Both *Tian* and *Shangdi* refer to a monotheist deity like God. But later, Confucianism became a polytheist religion due to the lack of a clear monotheist theory as well as the impact of Buddhism, Daoism, and superstitions. Originally Buddhism did not hold polytheistic ideas either, and only Buddha was worshipped until Bodhisattvas became gods. As to Daoism, Lao zi named God with an abstract word "dao" and, according to

---

to the Four Books), 17. For the English translation of the sentence and Zhu's commentary, see de Bary and Bloom, *Sources of Chinese Tradition*, 735.

33. Yuan, *Shende zhexue*, 4–5, 10, 71, and 121.

34. For a detailed discussion of the meaning of *shen*, see Eber et al., "Interminable Term Question," 136–47.

his description, advocated monotheistic ideas. Later, Daoism also became a polytheistic religion.³⁵

Zhu Weizhi also believed that the worship of *tian, di* 帝 (God), *tiandi* 天帝 (heavenly God) or *shangdi* in the religious thought of ancient China was identical with that of Yahweh:

> For the Yin [殷] people who practiced divination, *tiandi* as the highest consultant was anthropomorphic, dominating everything, and the same as Yahweh of the Israelite people.³⁶ . . . The Zhou inherited the worship of *tiandi* of the Yin. . . . The skeptical and complaining attitude of the Zhou about *tiandi* . . . reflects the diminished faith in *tiandi*. . . . Later the worship of ancestral gods developed and came into conflict with that of *tiandi*. In the Spring and Autumn Period [770–476 BCE], the traditional faith in *tiandi* became divided [into separate strands]. . . . Lao zi neglected the supreme authority of the anthropomorphic *tian* and replaced *tian* with the philosophical dao, which already existed before *shangdi*. Confucius also denied the anthropomorphic god. The so-called mandate of heaven [天命] is nothing but the operation of the Nature. Mo zi was more conservative concerning the traditional faith in *tiandi*. He believed in the anthropomorphic *tian* and the will of heaven [天志].³⁷

Among non-Christian intellectuals, a major person who interpreted OT ideas in accordance with those from Chinese culture was Liang Qichao. His comparison of Jewish and Chinese cultures was best exemplified by his understanding of God in the OT and *tian* in Confucian classics. First, he observed that God in the OT was identical with *tian* in an earlier phase of Chinese culture and that a similar religious passion to that of Jews was evident among China's ancients. In pre-history, before they established kingdoms, both Jews and Chinese were clan societies and tribes with a unity of religion and politics. Neither had a notion of politics but the worship of the divine will. It was the time of polytheism, and gods were anthropomorphic.

Monotheism appeared in historic times; the Divine was called Yahweh in reference to God by the Jews and *tian* or *shangdi* in reference to heaven

---

35. Yuan, *Shende zhexue*, 54n6, 154–55 and 160–62.

36. Zhu noted that Guo Moruo (1892–1978) had argued the same in his *Xianqin tiandaoguan zhi jinzhan* (The Evolution of the Notion of *tian* and dao in the Pre-Qin Era), 1982.

37. Zhu, "Zhongguo wenxue de zongjiao beijing" (The Religious Background of Chinese Literature), 42–47.

by the Chinese. Like God in the OT, *tian* referred to an anthropomorphic deity with sensations, sentiments, and will, who often directly watched and interfered in political activities, as related in the *Book of Songs* and the *Book of History*. As a result, worship of the divine will was replaced with the politics of God's and the will of *tian*. Liang named this type of politics "heavenly governmentism" (天治主义), which was still unified with religion. Up to this point, Jewish and Chinese thought were similarly underdeveloped.

Later, such primitive ideas were difficult to sustain. Therefore the notion of *tian* was gradually refined and became abstract.[38] By the time of Tangyu 唐虞 (2070–1046 BCE), like the God of Christianity, *tian* was less anthropomorphic but was still regarded as dominant and capable of seeing, hearing, speaking, and moving. By Confucius' time, *tian* was no longer anthropomorphic. Unlike the God of Christianity, *tian* was not omnipotent and transcendent. According to the *Book of Changes*, *tian* meant simply the motion and function of nature. Man is able to dominate nature, not *vice versa*. The mandate of *tian* was not anthropomorphic and became natural law.[39]

Liang rejected Mo zi's idea of the will of heaven.[40] In the Han dynasty, under Mo zi's impact, Dong Zhongshu 董仲舒 (179–104 BC) believed that man was created in the image and spirit of *tian*. Liang regarded Dong and the Han Confucians' view as a departure from original Confucianism that was not restored until Song and Ming dynasties.[41] Apparently, Liang regarded the philosophical idea of *tian* in the Confucian tradition as more advanced than the religious idea of God in the OT.

According to Liang, sometimes *tian* less directly supervised human politics and was then related to man through fundamental principles and cosmic natural laws assigned by *tian*. Those principles and laws were revealed to man when *tian* gave Yu 禹 (the twenty-first century BCE) the Great Plan with its Nine Divisions (洪范九畴), which is analogous to God giving Moses the Ten Commandments. This myth had much bearing on the thought of China's ancients. Since then, the anthropomorphic deity

---

38. Liang, "Xianqin zhengzhi sixiang shi" (A History of the Political Thought in the Pre-Qin Period), 18–22. "heavenly governmentism" of the Jews was also named "shenquan zhuyi" (ruling by divine right); see the term in Liang, "Guojia sixiang bianqian yitong lun" (On Changes in Thoughts about State), 20.

39. Liang, "Rujia zhexue" (Confucian Philosophy), 88–96.

40. Ibid. Liang criticized Mo zi's faith in the "truth of *tian*'s will," noting that it is is not convincing because it is impossible to have the "confession of *tian*'s will" and the "third judge." See Liang, "Zhongguo falixue fadashi lun," 41–94.

41. Liang, " Rujia zhexue," 88–96.

was identical with natural law in the eyes of Confucians. The religious *tian* was changed to the philosophical natural law; and thus the Chinese and Jews began to differ from one another.[42] Liang considered that change crucial. Chinese culture began to have its own direction of development and became specific, deserving a place in world civilization with a focus on observing "principles and laws" (理法) of human life.[43]

But Liang also believed that even the anthropomorphic *tian* was already different from God in the OT. Like comparative mythologists in the West, Liang suggested that the origin and uniqueness of a people's thinking should be investigated and understood through their myths. In doing so, comparisons with other peoples in the world should be encouraged. Therefore Liang compared Jewish and Chinese flood myths. In his view, the various tales of floods were independent of the biblical story and were about different floods.[44] According to the OT, human beings degenerated and enraged God, who penalized mankind with the flood. The Jewish people saw an irresistible power behind such a disaster, in the face of which mankind was powerless. Although China's ancients also dreaded penalties from *tian*, they did not believe that *tian*'s might was unlimited and could not conceive of a *tian* that destroyed all living creatures in a fit of rage. Therefore, when telling the myth of the flood, they did not say that the flood was caused by an enraged *tian* but emphasized that the flood receded because of *tian*'s blessing. Chinese myths, like that of Yu, who was best remembered for teaching the people flood control to tame the raging waters by using manpower, expressed the belief that man should withstand natural calamities and put nature in control instead of yielding to its pressure.[45]

---

42. Liang, "Xianqin zhengzhi sixiang shi," 18–22. See the motif of the Great Plan with Its Nine Divisions in "The Great Plan," *Zhoushu* (Book of Zhou), Book 4, 3. In a talk with Irene Eber, she asserted that the Ten Commandments and the Great Plan with Its Nine Divisions are not really analogous because the former concerns human society, while the latter does not.

43. Liang, "Xianqin zhengzhi sixiang shi," 1.

44. As to the reason for the Deluge, the unenlightened people did not have enough scientific knowledge to find it, thus attributing the catastrophe to some mystical cause. To explain why Jewish culture was rich in mystical flavor while Chinese culture not, Liang resorted to geographical determinism for help. For details, see Liang, "Dili yu niandai" (Geography and the Age), 2.

45. Liang, "Hongshui kao" (About the Flood), 19–20. With a nationalist agenda, Yuan Ding'an in 1930s interpreted the motif of Jacob overcoming God in the wrestling as evidence to show that man can triumph over nature and that Judaism is not an inert religion subject completely to fate. See Yuan, *Youtaijiao gailun*, 12–13.

Why did Liang compare the idea of God in the OT with that of *tian*? Through the comparison, a place for Chinese culture in world civilization was justified, because the idea of God in the OT was less developed and less comprehensive than the idea of *tian* in the Confucian classics. If the Jews had a place in world civilization, why not the Chinese? Moreover, to Liang, the inferiority of Jewish culture had been verified in history. Due to their strong religious consciousness, the Jews lacked a national personality (民族的人格),[46] unity in a political sense (政治的结合),[47] and a keen sense of nation-state (整个的国民)[48] in the Diaspora.

That Liang paid tribute to Moses, discussed in chapter 2, demonstrated his utilitarian and unsentimental adoption of any measure which may effect a positive change for the better; however, when he turned to his own cultural tradition after World War I, it revealed his proud faith in the existence of a national essence. By doing so, Liang found a solution to the conflict between shame and pride. Here was a new syncretism: the Mosaic or Western style in searching for material power and strength was inadequate. But by combining it with the spirit of Chinese culture, an efficient instrument could be created.

The Idea of God and Perfect Personality: Discussions on Human Conscience, Desire, Free Will, and Suffering

Chinese intellectuals did not limit themselves to attacking or defending the OT idea of God in the light of scientism, Western philosophy, and traditional Chinese culture. They also applied the OT idea of God to their search for both individual and social redemption. Among them, Christian intellectuals in particular, had an interest in the relevance of the idea of God to human personality (人格) and suffering. They generally held that individual redemption lies in moral perfection. To show that the faith in God is important to the moral integrity of an individual, many Christian intellectuals emphasized the perfection of God. The term God was even translated as the highest good (至善).[49]

---

46. Liang Qichao, "Zhongguo lishi yanjiufa" (Method for Research of Chinese History), 121.

47. Liang Qichao, "Zhongguo qiantu zhi xiwang," 8–9.

48. Liang Qichao, "Xinhaigeming zhi yiyi," 1–3.

49. Liu, "Cong shehui kexue shang guancha" (A Look at Christianity), 14–22.

This understanding of God reveals the impact of Immanuel Kant. According to Kant, the highest good meant being transcendental and being perfect. Being transcendental meant transcending everything and being free from limitations of the environment. Although nearly impossible in the mundane world, human beings can get increasingly closer to that goal through endless effort. Being perfect means a perfect combination of morality and pleasure. Since the motive of morality goes beyond the bounds of nature and cannot be the motive of nature, the combination of morality and pleasure is impossible unless there is a transcendental reason, namely God, which not only provides grounds for nature but also has morality.[50]

Needless to say, the human world is wicked. In Chinese culture, Xun zi 荀子 (ca. 313–ca. 238 BCE) advocated that human beings are bad by nature and must be reformed by education and cultivation. However, many Christian intellectuals believed, since man was created in the image of God, he is naturally good. Some suggested that even Adam and Eve's fall implies that human beings are good by nature. Natural goodness is human conscience (良心) and is put by God in the heart of every man including Cain.[51] Natural goodness is the deity in the heart as expressed by the Buddhist saying, "The heart is Buddha and Buddha is the heart." That is why conscience can be called heavenly conscience (天良). For the same reason, conscience is natural principle (性理) and no one can deny it or cast it aside.[52] Others explained that natural goodness referred to the heart of right and wrong (是非之心) as advocated by Mencius. Plato had said, the heart of right and wrong equips a person with innate knowledge and ability (良知良能).[53]

Although human beings are naturally good, they are inclined to be spoiled and bad because God granted them desires and free will to choose

---

50. Guo, "Kangde" (Kant), 26–32.

51. Li, "Zuide laiyuan" (The Origin and Effect of Sin), 11–12 and "Xiongfan gaiyin" (The Murderer Cain), 80.

52. Yuan, *Shende zhexue* (The Philosophy of Theism), 31–34 and 80–87. Yuan quoted from the *Book of History*, saying, "wei huang shangdi jiang zhong yu xia min" (The great Supreme God has conferred natural goodness even on inferior people). See the Chinese in Ruan, *Shisanjing zhushu* (Notes and Commentaries to the Thirteen Classics), 162.

53. Zhao, "Shengjing zai jinshi wenhua zhongde diwei," 11 and 18. See Mencius' words in *Mencius* 2A:6 and the English translation in Mencius, *Mencius*, 73. Yuan Ding'an noticed that Cheng Yi (1033–1107) highlighted the origin of innate knowledge and ability in *tian*. Yuan, *Shende zhexue*, 80–87.

good or evil. Desire can lead to immorality,⁵⁴ and desire was inherited from Adam and Eve. A person is good when due to his conscience he overcomes desire.⁵⁵ Desires are of three kinds: sensuality (肉欲), selfishness (我欲), and willfulness (意欲). Each kind can be beneficial or harmful. Religion aims to develop their helpfulness and check their harmfulness.⁵⁶

The interpretation of free will reveals once more the impact of Kant. Kant had stated, God allows for the existence of evil and gives human beings the freedom to choose good or evil so that they can exercise their moral responsibility.⁵⁷ Christian intellectuals regarded men's free will as evidence of human freedom. Adam and Eve had the freedom to decide what to accept and reject. God set rules yet respected their human freedom to decide what kind of persons they want to be.⁵⁸ Similarly, the covenant between man and God meant freedom of faith as was preserved by the Israelites. Therefore, the OT emphasizes self-determination according to one's conscience, using neither coercion nor cajolery.⁵⁹ Moreover, without men's free will, there would be no evolution to perfection of human beings and they would not renew themselves "ever newer from day to day" (日日新). The function of the Bible and Holy Spirit is not to compel but to help human beings to evolve until they become as perfect as God. Human beings should follow their conscience (良心) to understand this will of God so that they can obey it out of their own free will. Therefore, men's free will and God's will are not mutually exclusive.⁶⁰

The ideas of desire and free will led to discussions about the secondary good (次善) and the highest good (至善). The highest good refers to absolute faithfulness and obedience to God, whereas the secondary good means

---

54. Some non-Christian intellectuals also discussed the subject of human desire, but usually denied its relation to religion. For examples, see the discussions by Liang Qichao above and by Wang Guowei below in this chapter.

55. Yuan, *Shende zhexue*, 80–87.

56. Xu, "Women yao shenmeyang de zongjiao" (What Kind of Religion Do We Want?), 1.

57. Guo, "Kangde," 28.

58. Tashan, "Jiuyue xiyi" (OT Commentary), 2–4. For a similar argument, see Yan, "Dujing xinde" (Inspirations from Reading the Scriptures), 50.

59. Yuan, *Youtaijiao gailun*, 25–26.

60. Wang, "Kaocha shengjing de xinde" (What I Have Learned in Bible Reading), 9. See the Chinese quotation in chapter 42, *Liji* (The Book of Rites), and its English translation in Confucius, *Ta Hsüeh and Chung Yung* (The Highest Order of Cultivation and On the Practice of the Mean), 7.

to follow desire. Human beings are sinful when they chose the secondary good rather than the highest. Li Rongfang resorted to Chinese tradition for support. According to the *Great Learning* (大学), the ultimate goal is to "rest in the highest good" (止于至善). Mencius said, "Life is what I want; dutifulness is also what I want. If I cannot have both, I would choose dutifulness rather than life." (生亦我所欲也义亦我所欲也二者不可得兼舍身而取义者也)[61] He who chooses the highest good is a *daren* 大人 (great man) and he who choose the secondary good is a *xiaoren*小人 (small man). The gist of Li's argument is that when a person must choose, the choice is related to morality.[62] More than that, the morality of a sage like Moses must be attributed to God and "sageliness" is identical to holiness. Yuan Ding'an believed that Chinese tradition confirmed his view, arguing that the perfect moral integrity of a Confucian sage is a result of modeling after *tian* or God. Zhou Dunyi 周敦颐 (1017–1073), for example, also advocated that a sage is one who learns from *tian* (圣希天).[63]

Unlike their Christian contemporaries, non-Christian intellectuals did not necessarily concur that God endowed man with free will and that this free will is related to morality. Like Feng Youlan, the poet Xu Zhimo 徐志摩 (1897–1931) portrayed God as one who tried to restrain men's free will. God regretted having created man in His image and planned to recreate man without blowing a soul into his nostrils.[64] In another poem, Xu admired the knowledge and light as represented by the serpent. Adam was a "fool" who obeyed God blindly and lived without free will to open his eyes to see "heaven and earth," "the light," and "the marvelous world."[65]

---

61. Li, "Zuide laiyuan," 11–14. See the Chinese of the quotation in *Mencius* 6A:10 and its translation in Mencius, *Mencius*, 253. Note the change in the meaning of "the highest good" when it is used to describe God, an OT man of God like Abraham, and a Confucian sage.

62. Li, "Zuide laiyuan," 11–14. Li must have consulted *Lunyu* 4:16, which says that "junzi yuyu yi xiaoren yuyu li" (The gentleman is versed in what is moral. The small man is versed in what is profitable). See the English translation in Confucius, *The Analects*, 33.

63. Yuan, *Shende zhexue*, 8–9 and 138–39. See the quotation in Zhou, *Tongshu* (Explanatory Text), in *Zhouzi quanshu* (Complete Works of Zhou Dunyi), 1978. In *Tongshu*, Zhou defines sagehood in terms of *cheng* (sincerity). To be sincere is to be true to the innate goodness of one's nature bestowed by heaven and to actualize one's moral potential. With the modeling of a sage from *tian*, "tian ren heyi" (the unity of heaven and man) comes true. Adler, "Zhou Dunyi," 676.

64. Xu, "Youyici shiyan" (Another Experiment), 162–63. First published in the supplement *Shijuan* (Poems) of *Chenbao* (The Morning Post), No. 6, (May 6, 1926).

65. Xu, "Renzhong de youlai" (The Origin of Humankind), 351–54. First written in

Turning now to the idea of suffering, Christian intellectuals explained it as God's will that man evolve a perfect personality. The Bible explains human suffering most comprehensively because it was written by a people who had undergone centuries of suffering and oppression. Moreover, whereas suffering may be viewed as a fact rather than a problem by atheists and a commonplace phenomenon due to conflicts between gods by polytheists, the Israelites who believed in a monotheist and merciful God required an explanation for the problem of suffering.

Zhao Zichen introduced the evolution of the idea of suffering. In the early stages when a tribe or a clan was considered the unit of moral responsibility and a disaster was seen as God's punishment for the offence, the suffering of an individual, whether innocent or not, was considered part of God's punishment for the wrongdoing of a king like Saul (2 Sam 21:1–14) or an ancestor like Achan (Josh 7). But with the development of civilization, the individual became the unit of moral responsibility. Prophets like Jeremiah and Ezekiel introduced a new ethical idea of individual retribution, while the Book of Job rejected the idea that suffering was God's punishment. In some later books of the OT as in Prov 3:11–13, suffering was interpreted as God's means of training and educating man for moral improvement. Because of the Babylonian exile, suffering of a righteous person or nation began also to be interpreted as a universal and cardinal principle of the human world.[66]

Suffering as God's punishment for sins is compulsory in the process of human evolution because only through punishment can human beings recognize their sins as did Jacob and Joseph.[67] Support was also found in Exodus. God did not destroy the Egyptian troops earlier but let the Israelites live in anxiety because only then would the Israelites have the courage to risk crossing the Red Sea and benefit their future. The idea of suffering is certainly not alien to Chinese tradition. According to Mencius, to confer a

---

1922 and published June 21, 1923 in the supplement *Xuedeng* (Learning Lamp) of *Shishi xinbao* (News express) in Shanghai. "And God said, Let there be light; and there was light" (Gen 1:3, KJV) was quoted by Xu Zhimo at the beginning of his opening remark "Xinyue de taidu" (The Stand of *Xinyue*) in the first issue of *Xinyue* (Cresent Moon) on March 10, 1928. See Zhao, "Preface," 20.

66. "Zhansheng tongku" (Victory over Suffering), 27–33. Li Rongfang also believed that in his time, it was God's plan that righteous men sacrificed their lives for a better society. Li, "Hongshui de shexun" (The Social Ethics of the Flood), 282–83.

67. Li, "Xibolai zaonian gushi zhong de shehuixun," 37–38 and 41–42.

great office on a person, heaven also exercises the person's mind and body with sufferings, which is similar to the biblical sense of suffering.[68]

Although non-Christian intellectuals resorted to the OT in their search for a possible solution to the problem of suffering, they were more interested in the end of suffering than taking it for granted and they related suffering less to human perfection. Wang Guowei, for example, traced the reason for human suffering to the mistake made by the first ancestors of humankind, described in both the Book of Genesis and the first chapter of the *Dream of the Red Chamber* (红楼梦). However, he denied the possibility of happiness of the majority, as expressed in the biblical idea of redemption. One must rely on free will for release from suffering and a natural release can be achieved only temporarily in art.[69] Obviously, Wang's ideas of free will and release are not concerned with religious issues.

The Idea of God and the Ideal of a Perfect World

To Chinese intellectuals, it was not enough to search for the perfect personality. It was more important to educate or integrate moral doctrines into the heart of mankind to achieve a perfect society. Does the OT and faith in God contribute to the rebuilding of the nation and the making of a perfect world? Below I will discuss how that question was approached by both Christian and non-Christian intellectuals, and how the OT with its idea of God was relevant to their views about education and universalism.

Early in 1917, Cai Yuanpei wrote an article calling for replacing religion with aesthetic education. Cai's article led to controversies among his contemporaries in subsequent years. Many non-Christian intellectuals supported Cai's idea, but some also disagreed with him. The writer Shen Congwen 沈从文 (1902–1988) admitted that Cai Yuanpei made a great contribution to national rebuilding with his call for aesthetic education, but Shen did not believe that replacing religion with aesthetic education was useful. To make his point, he distinguished *shen* from *shangdi*. *Shangdi* refers to the OT God of Creator,[70] whereas *shen* is an abstract and panthe-

---

68. Yuan, *Shende zhexue* (The Philosophy of Theism), 91–94 and 98. See Mencius' argument in *Mencius* 6B:15.

69. Wang, "Hongloumeng pinglun" (A Study of the *Dream of the Red Chamber*), 92–93, 102–3, and 106.

70. Shen Congwen knew OT motifs well. For example, he used motifs from the Book of Genesis and the "Song of Songs" in his diaries. For details, see Shen, "Huangjun riji"

istic idea of deity. Nonetheless both *shen* and *shangdi* are relevant to his admiration of "beauty" (美).

On the one hand, everything in nature is created by God and has its own life. On the other hand, "beauty" is omnipresent in everything that has life. The pantheistic idea of *shen* is a symbol for and synonymous with "beauty." Although one cannot reach God, one can reach that which God has created, namely beauty or *shen*. In other words, if a person approaches a creature from a pantheistic perspective, he will find beauty in it. Therefore, the highest meaning of life is to know that *shen* is in life. Shen Congwen's view implied that the pantheistic idea of *shen* is superior to but dependent on the monotheistic idea of *shangdi*.

Shen Congwen's interpretation of beauty also suggested the impact of Chinese tradition, especially Daoism. He wrote that beauty found in a creature represents the highest "virtue" (德), which leads to human wisdom. This implies the daoist idea that "virtue" is the reflection of dao in the phenonmenal world. Therefore, the "disintegration of shen" (神的解体) leads to all kinds of disorder, evil, and immorality. If people were to "recreate," that is follow, *shen* and establish a new religion of beauty and love, it can stimulate the desire to be an upright person. Like the daoist dao, the abstract *shen*, or "beauty," or "love," will stop human degeneration, promote spiritual life, and arouse the sincere desire for a better future. National restoration would then become possible.[71]

Therefore, though both Shen Congwen and Cai Yuanpei advocated the dominant role of beauty or art in national rebuilding, Shen tried to reconcile his ideas with religion, whereas Cai emphasized the opposition between aesthetic education and religion. However, the OT's inspiration on aesthetics was generally recognized by Chinese intellectuals. Indeed, even Cai admitted that in medieval Europe, many works of art were inspired by the OT.[72] The reason for combining art and OT motifs, especially God, is that with the help of art, religion diverts a believer's attention and leads him to the noumenal world so that he can forget for a moment the phenomenal world of sufferings.[73]

(Diaries of Huang jun), 211 and 248–49.

71. Shen, "Mei yu ai" (Beauty and Love), 376–79.

72. Cai, "Yi meiyu dai zongjiao shuo" (About Replacing Religion with Aesthetic Education), first published in 1917, 45. Cai, "Yi meiyu dai zongjiao" (Replacing Religion with Aesthetic Education), first published in 1930, 206.

73. Cai, "Meiyu dai zongjiao" (Aesthetic Education to Replace Religion), first published in 1932, 276. Like Kant, Cai stressed the universal nature of the appreciation of

Christian intellectuals disliked Cai's idea of replacing religion with aesthetic education. On the one hand, they highlighted the importance of religion and the Bible to aesthetics. Although Hebrew thought (希伯来主义) as ethics neglects aesthetics and cannot appeal to the majority of people, there is nonetheless some kind of uncultivated and unsophisticated beauty in the occupations and trifles of the OT prophets. That beauty may inspire masters of fine arts.[74] Art is part of human life and the Bible is a document about human life, therefore art must also be a part of the Bible.[75] The OT stories, moreover, reveal eternal truths as do fine arts (美术的真理) because both OT myths like those in Genesis and works of fine art portray the nature of human life with simple and practical symbols.[76]

On the other hand, Christian intellectuals denied the universal value of art, declaring that improper and excessive use of art endangers religious faith. To Liu Tingfang, the second of the Ten Commandments—"Thou shalt not make unto thee a graven image, nor any manner of likeness, of anything that is in heaven above, or that is in the water under the earth" (Exod 20:4)—forbids art to negate theology so that human beings will not sully their outlook of God with material expressions. He explained that, although most people have to resort to art when they hope to express a spiritual idea (灵的观念) like that of God, there is a decline in the worship of God when fine arts become popular. Fine arts are likely to become coarse and crude forms of humanization (人化主义) and make people forget the original intention of religion.[77]

To Christian intellectuals the OT and the idea of God were also helpful to national affairs. They did not find a conflict between serving people or country and serving God.[78] Indeed, the OT was sometimes considered as a literature of nationalism. All the OT historical books hold the same national as well as philosophical idea that Israel had the heavenly mandate

---

beauty and its capacity to provide a feeling of emotional detachment. Duiker, *Ts'ai Yüan-p'ei: Educator of Modern China*, 28.

74. Lu, "Jidujiao yu meishu" (Christianity and Fine Arts), 177–78.

75. Zhao, "Shengjing zai jinshi wenhua zhongde diwei" (The Place of the Bible in Modern Civilization), 14.

76. Li, "Rende laiyuan" (The Origin of Man), 474–78.

77. Liu, "Shende xingxiang" (The Image of God), 176–81 and 187. See the Hebrew and English of Exod 20:4 in Cohen, *Soncino Chumash*, 458–59.

78. Liu, "Yige daxue de zongjiao xueyuan" (The Mission and Standard for the College of Religion), 332.

to represent God before the nations.[79] This kind of "religious nationalism" was considered the focus of all the OT books: whereas the historical literature describes the rise and fall of the Israelites, the prophetic literature is concerned with national restoration. Even the Psalms, which seem to be works of religious philosophy, do not lack a nationalistic flavor for example in Psalm 122.[80]

Well educated in Confucian classics and proud of his own traditional culture, Yuan Ding'an was concerned with the fate of Chinese culture. He found the national doom in 586 BC particularly meaningful, since it brought Judaism to a new developmental stage. First, during the Babylonian exile, Judaism was liberated from the control of the priests and became a religion of the common people. Second, it became a revolutionary religion as the result of the zeal to restore the kingdom. Yuan thought that the reason why the life of the Israelite people never perished, even in the Diaspora, is that their culture has not disappeared and Judaism as the life of the nation and the principal part of national culture has been preserved. He concluded that there can be no national restoration for a country if the intrinsic culture of the nation cannot be preserved and its superiority cannot be assured. He warned his compatriots that the perishing of culture is even more horrible and lamentable than the captivity of their country.[81]

However, the ideal of many Chinese intellectuals was not only nationalism but also universalism. Non-Christian intellectuals generally traced the origin of universalism to Chinese tradition as did Kang Youwei. But the OT attracted their attention as another source during the New Culture Movement. As Chen Duxiu 陈独秀 (1979–1942) wrote, the problem of Christianity in modern Chinese society is a major issue worthy of study. The Chinese have not yet benefited from the religious spirit of Christianity; that spirit is the spirit of universal love and can be traced back to the OT. He declared that the basic teachings of Christianity are faith and love, as stated in Gen 9:5–6.[82] In light of OT theology, however, the divine sovereign right over human life is absolutely inviolable—not for man's sake because of some law of humanity or reverence for life, but because man is God's possession and was created in God's image.[83]

79. Li, "Jiuyue daoyan" (Introduction to the OT), 2.
80. Yuan, *Youtaijiao gailun*, 94–96.
81. Yuan, *Youtaijiao gailun*, 52–55.
82. Chen, "Jidujiao yu zhongguoren" (Christianity and the Chinese), 5.
83. Von Rad, *Genesis*, 132.

Christian intellectuals called for a heavenly kingdom on earth, namely a perfect society with universal love and world peace, and in that respect, the OT with its idea of God was particularly valuable and inspiring. Some tried to prove that the OT and Judaism restrained nationalism and upheld universalism. Since man must love God and other people to complete the law, the prophet Amos introduced to the Jews a God of universal love for all nations (9:7).[84] Some advocated that universalism was the destiny of human evolution. Universal love was the prerequisite for many other virtues necessary for a perfect society, such as equality and mutual aid.[85] Darwin was wrong to ignore universal love's role in the spiritual realm. "Survival of the fittest" meant not physical fitness like that of "the heroes of old, men of renown" (Gen 6:4, NIV) but moral fitness like that of Noah and his family.[86] The defeat of Germany and survival of Poland in World War I revealed the same.[87]

Of course, Christian intellectuals did not believe that universal love can be disseminated by Judaism. Instead, it was Christianity that makes universal love possible. Even those who believed that Judaism was originally universal resolved the contradiction by stating that Judaism was later spoiled. According to Yuan Ding'an, at a later time, by stressing the way of holiness, Judaism lacked learning and no longer practiced the way of love. Although Judaism spared no effort in attacking evil, it denounced aliens without respecting their value as human beings.[88]

Universalism was considered by some as closely related to humanism. The Bible is sacred because it upholds all humanity. If one takes a monistic and practical outlook on life, he will regard human relations as the supreme and genuine principle.[89] Zhao Zichen argued that the primary essence of modern

---

84. Li, "Xibolai zaonian gushi zhong de shehuixun," 34; and Li, "Minzu tongxibiao" (The Table of Nations), 434.

85. For an example, see Liang, "Rensheng yiyi" (The Meaning of Human Life), 6–7.

86. Li, "Hongshui de shexun," 287.

87. Wang, "Kaocha shengjing de xinde," 3–6.

88. Yuan, *Youtaijiao gailun*, 32–33. In Yuan's view, the Christian idea of God emphasizes God's universal love. The ancient Hebrews and the ancient Chinese had almost identical notions about deity and had the same limit: prejudice or discrimination against the aliens. Ibid., 3–10 and 13–22. Still, not all Christian intellectuals believed in the universal love of Christianity. Xu Baoqian thought that Judaism excludes outsiders as does Christianity. In contrast, Chinese culture incorporates things of a diverse nature. See Xu, "Jidujiao zai zhongguo de qiantu" (The Future of Christianity in China), 336.

89. Jian, "Shengjing lide qingju" (A Love Drama in the Bible), 265–67.

culture is humanism or the high regard for character. The main concern of the Bible is the human being (Gen 9:5–6). Man is the center because God, living in man, is the center of the whole world. Faith in God and universal love in the world are the main ideas of the Bible, and these created the foundation for culture and made genuine democracy possible.[90]

For the sake of universalism, therefore, there is the need to emphasize human relations based on peace, equality, mutual love and aid among human beings and nations, which only faith in God can help achieve. Given this assumption, it was claimed that both Mo zi's theory of universal love (兼爱) and Peter Kropotkin's theory of mutual help (互助论) were testimonies of God's revelation.[91] Due to a lack of faith in God, many atheists are not concerned about other people. Although some advocate mutual-aid, socialist ideals, or universal love, they are not as far reaching as those of the theists.[92] Li Rongfang emphasized the love between husband and wife as the foundation of family life and of society. Therefore, the motif of God creating women (Gen 2:18–24) is valuable because God considered it impossible for man to achieve happiness without a partner's cooperation, especially love from women.[93]

But how to justify nationalism and the diversity among nations within the context of the universalist ideal? The answer is that diversity was planned for the purpose of human evolution toward a perfect world. God stopped human beings from building the Tower of Babel and scattered them over the face of the earth. As a consequence, people began to speak different languages. God did that for humanity's sake because a people can develop only when separated from others and independent.[94] Such an interpretation differs from most of the classical Jewish commentaries. Regarding the latter, Rashi (1040–1105) for example, wrote that the dispersal of the nations in Gen 11:1–9 represents God's judgment on man's ungrateful and sinful attempts to make for himself a name. The tower of Babel puts man's deeds

---

90. Zhao, "Shengjing zai jinshi wenhua zhongde diwei," 15 and 17.

91. Yuan, *Shende zhexue*, 80–87. But Yuan did not think the two theories were equal. Since Kropotkin's argument is detailed and based on biological findings, it is more significant than Mo zi's theory and has made a great contribution to world peace.

92. Ibid., 115–20.

93. Li, "Xibolai zaonian gushi zhong de shehuixun," 35–37. Tashan and Zhou Weitong (?–1983) interpreted Eve's creation out of Adam's rib as representing equality, unity, and mutual aid of humankind. See Tashan, "Jiuyue xiyi," 2–3; and Zhou, "Shengshu renwu zhuan" (Biographical Notes about Biblical Characters), 19.

94. Li, "Kouyin bianluan" (God Confused the Languages), 491–95.

in question. He is not master of his fate. Indeed, when rebelling he will be humiliated and suffer. God will curtail his grandiose dreams.[95]

Because of their differences, the nations make different contributions to a perfect world. The same is true of individuals and families. Independent individuals are the prerequisite of happy families and independent families are the prerequisite of flourishing countries, whereas independent countries are the prerequisite of universalism.[96] Therefore, neither individualism nor nationalism hinder but promote the realization of universalism. Chinese nationalists who fought for national self-determination actually aim for universalism in the long run. Before the Chinese reach the goal of a harmonious world, they must strive for liberation and freedom of China. Of course, nationalism differs from imperialism. The former is a stage on the road toward universalism, whereas imperialism deviates from the universal spirit since imperialists do not recognize a universal brotherhood that demands universal love.[97]

The OT ideal of universalism is not foreign to Chinese traditions. The genealogy of Gen 10 reveals that all human beings can be traced to one ancestor; that one should be respectful toward others as a gentleman in society; and that "all within the Four Seas are brothers" (四海之内皆兄弟).[98] The traditional Chinese ideal of Great Harmony (大同理想) is also that of a perfect society. Confucius presumably declared that when the great dao prevails, the whole world will be harmonious (大道之行也天下 . . . 大同). The prerequisite of realizing the ideal of Great Harmony is that human beings should consider each other brothers.[99]

The attempt was made in this chapter to show how OT views and ideas were related to current concerns of May Fourth intellectuals. For most intellectuals, faith in God was a secondary concern to their interpretation of the problems of their times. OT views and ideas were, moreover, transposed into a new cultural context with different assumptions and readers. In the process, Chinese intellectuals resorted to different resources to legitimize their contextualized reading of the OT. Western ideas of science and

---

95. See Cohen, *Soncino Chumash*, 52–54 and Wenham, *Genesis 1–15*, 209.

96. Li, "Kouyin bianluan," 491–95.

97. Li, "Minzu tongxibiao," 433–35.

98. Li, "Xibolai zaonian gushi zhong de shehuixun, 39–40. See the quotation in *Lunyu* 12:5 and its English translation in Confucius, *The Analects*, 111.

99. Li, "Minzu tongxibiao," 433–35. See the Chinese quotation from *Liji* in Ruan, *Shisanjing zhushu*, 1414.

philosophy, especially the evolutionary theory, were considered; whereas the use of Chinese conventions was not limited to Confucianism and attention was also paid to Daoist ideas. As discussed by these men, OT views and ideas did not contradict scientific thinking. That is, there was to Chinese intellectuals no contradiction between the introduction of science, on the one hand, and the OT, on the other. Science and the OT only had different emphases. Chinese argumentation tends to be inclusive rather than exclusive on nearly every topic. The introduction of the OT took the same course. Therefore, this chapter suggests that during the May Fourth period the first tentative steps were taken for creating a genuine Chinese commentary tradition of the OT.

5

Moses, the Prophets, and Chinese Intellectuals

FROM THE 1920S AND for the next twenty and more years, a common and constant agenda for Chinese intellectuals was how to construct their nation with ideal human beings and an ideal society. To do this, they not only resorted to the OT idea of God for theoretical support, but also made use of important OT personages. That is, they found OT characters inspiring and interpreted them as perfect examples of ideal men. Biblical images of OT persons in their interpretations were in most cases receptor culture and reader oriented, and interpretations were adjusted to their own urgent concerns. In addition, modifications were also frequently made to accord with modern Western ideas of the period. Due to space limitations, my discussion relies to a large extent on several commentators only, but they are representative enough to demonstrate the growth and development of Chinese OT commentary at this era.

Moses as an Ideal Leader

The image of Moses underwent a number of changes between 1920s and 30s, and in the 30s he was regarded mainly as an ideal leader. Chinese intellectuals were also interested in the God of Moses in the 1930s and a discussion of this is included below with an explanation regarding Moses' role as a religious leader. Finally, Moses' relevance to nationalism in the 1930s and 40s must be addressed. One problem that preoccupied Chinese intellectuals was how to save their country from foreign aggression. For the majority, especially the youth, their credos covered a wide range, but nationalism was the common denominator. They were attracted to an intermediate array of Chinese and Western heroes who shared little of anything in common but their success in uniting their nation or defend it against foreign invasions.¹ The nationalist image of Moses was thus employed as common currency and appealed to a broad, emotionally volatile public.

After World War I, many intellectuals introduced Moses less favorably in comparison with Confucius. Liang Qichao, who had written admiringly about Moses before the war, now regarded him as merely a religious founder, considering his personal appeal only among his disciples and followers.² In contrast, the appeal of Confucius as a religious founder was felt "among all the Chinese." China is Confucius' China, while Judea was not Moses' Judea, Liang declared. In Liang's opinion, the important reason was that as a religious founder in a "remote" place like Judea, Moses lived in a world of "naïve humanity and decadent learning." Even if he could remain pure and noble, he "was like spring water in a mountain flowing beneath the fallen leaves and he could never see the scene of greatness."³ No wonder that Moses was intolerant of other religions.⁴

In the early 1920s, the literary giant Lu Xun 鲁迅 (1881–1936) expressed his sympathy for such an interpretation in the translated novelette "Zai shamo shang 在沙漠上" (In the Desert).⁵ It contains the gruesome vision of primeval violence raging among the Israelites on their journey from Egypt to the Promised Land.⁶ Although neither Lunz the author nor Lu Xun the translator intended to disparage the OT, the novelette suggests negative images of God, Moses, Aaron, and the Levites. According to Lu Xun's quotation of Yonekawa Masao 米川正夫 (1891–1962), Lunz wrote the tale in 1921, trying to interpret the revolution in Russia while rewriting the OT story.⁷

1. For examples, see Israel, *Student Nationalism in China*, 180.

2. Liang Qichao already regarded Moses as a religious founder in "Xin shixue," 13–17. For Liang's earlier and favourable interpretations of Moses, see chapter two.

3. Liang, "Kong zi" (Confucius), 65 and 68–69.

4. Liang, "Zhongguo lishi yanjiufa bupian" (Method for Research of Chinese History, continued), 139–42.

5. Lev Lunz, "Zai shamo shang," 39–49. The Chinese translation was made from Yonekawa Masao's Japanese version of the story in 1927 or 1928 and first published in January 1929. See Yonekawa's Japanese in Yonekawa Masao, *Laonong luxiya xiaoshuo ji* (Collection of Russian Novelettes), 1925. Like other members of *Serapionsbrüder*, a major literary group established in Russia in 1921, Lunz was not attached to any political party and denied all political ideologies, though he had sympathy with the toiling masses. See Lu Xun's preface to *Shuqin* (The Harp) written September 9, 1932, ibid., 7–11.

6. Gamsa, *Chinese Translation of Russian Literature*, 180n203.

7. See Lu Xun's postscript to *Shuqin* written September 10, 1932, ibid., 243–245.

In Lunz's tale, the march toward Canaan full of suffering and immorality symbolizes the revolutionary struggle for a utopian society. The golden sunshine, a symbol of the revolutionary ideal, made daytime even more terrifying than night because it killed the human soul. The so-called righteous God, who stood above the Israelites and indicates revolutionary dictatorship, was also the God of slaughter. Between God and the masses of Israel were the sky and Moses. The blue but terrifying sky reflects the society established by the Russian Revolution. Moses, on whom the Holy Spirit relied, instructed the masses and symbolizes the teacher of the revolution.

The frightened Israelites, guilty or innocent, all repented and pleaded for absolution. Whenever the suffering and desperate Israelites expressed their suspicion and reluctance to proceed, Moses pronounced a judgment. He would step onto a high altar and communicate with God in a foreign language, inexplicable, and terrifying, which the author considered as the preaching of revolutionary doctrines. Aaron, who stood nearby not as Moses' brother but as the Head Priest, would ask the Levites, who were his relatives, to kill whoever expressed dissent. Aaron and the Levites stand for the lackeys of revolutionary dictatorship, while the Levites' sword represents the state apparatus. After the bloody suppression of dissent, the Israelites were forced to continue on their endless course with their private property confiscated.

During the high tide of the Nationalist "revolution" in 1926 and 1927, as most biographers have pointed out, Lu Xun was shocked by Chiang Kai-shek's 蒋介石 (1887–1975) massacre of Communists in Canton on April 15, 1927, following his coup in Shanghai a few days later. The random arrest of the innocent shattered the hope Lu Xun might have entertained for the "revolutionary men" of the Guomindang 国民党. The very meanings of revolution were most confusing and the impression was negative: the reality of revolution itself was rather a world of total chaos and confusion.[8] In this

---

According to Western scholars like Patrick Hanan, Lu Xun was inclined toward symbolism or symbolic realism, especially in the early phase of his creative career. Lee, "Tradition and Modernity," 9; and Hanan, "Technique of Lu Xun's Fiction," 61. Douwe Fokkema has also argued that Lu Xun was interested in works of fantasy. Fokkema, "Lu Xun," 94.

8. Lu, "Xiao zagan" (Mini-thoughts), 532 and Lee, *Voices*, 138–39. For Lu Xun uncertainty about the revolutionary movement's outcome in his student days in Japan and utter despair with the 1911 revolution, see Lin, "The Morality of Mind," 108. Dismayed by warlord politics, Lu Xun observed cynically in 1925, "I feel that before the revolution, I was a slave, but shortly after the revolution, I have been cheated by slaves and become their slave." Lu, "Huran xiangdao" (Sudden Thoughts), 16.

period until 1929, Lu Xun's ideas were not fully crystallized and he had not committed himself to a proletarian or Marxist point of view.[9]

In 1932 when Lu Xun wrote the "preface" and "postscript" to the book, which contains "Zai shamo shang," he was already a Communist sympathizer and his view of Lunz's work should accordingly have been changed. The inclusion of the tale in the selected works proved, as Leo Ou-fan Lee pointed out, that the "Russianness" of Soviet literature continued to fascinate him, as he tried to keep pace with the collective suffering of a whole people and social transformation of a nation of the proletariat. The traits revealed in the tale such as terror and despair were in Lu Xun's eyes spiritual hallmarks of the Russian people.[10] The aim of Lu Xun was to establish a mirror for the Chinese people and for literature.

Although Sun Yat-sen, the pioneer and leader of democratic revolution in modern China, was often compared to China's Moses, Sun himself considered the contribution of Moses limited. Although he had led the Israelites in the exodus, he failed to make them a truly independent nation before they reached Canaan. The Chinese people were subjected to autocracy of the Manchus for hundreds of years and lived in abject misery as did the Israelites in Egypt. Now the Chinese cast off the yoke of the Manchus just as the Israelites were liberated by Moses. However, like the Israelites, they still needed a Joshua to end their state of disunity.[11]

Christian intellectuals too discussed the limitations of Moses from a non-theological perspective.[12] According to the OT scholar Li Rongfang's translation of George Barton, Moses was the leader of a group of barbarians, who damaged whomever they conquered. They were saboteurs of culture. Therefore, Moses' religion was naïve and underdeveloped. Even Moses' achievement in the exodus was called in question. Because not all the Israelites were in Egypt at Moses' time, Moses led only part of the Israelites out of Egypt.[13]

Despite the ambiguous image and limitations, Moses could still be inspiring. The following favorable comments about Moses anticipate the urgent

9. Lee, *Voices*, 110–29; Peters, "Die Ansichten," 149–57; and Huang, *Lu Hsün*, 120–22.

10. Lee, *Voices*, 168.

11. Sun, "Mian zhongguo jidujiao qingnian shu" (A Letter to Encourage), 1448–49.

12. For an example of theological discussion on Moses' limitation, see Porter, "Lishide yesu" (A Historical Jesus), 17–18. Such discussions were usually based on traditional ideas of Christian theology.

13. Barton, *Yiselie de zongjiao*, the preface by Li Rongfang, 3, 10, and 29–30.

need for a powerful leader in China after the chaotic years of the 1920s and the growing interest in Moses in the 1930s as a great leader of his people. Liang Qichao, who discussed the limitations of Moses but believed in the dominant role of heroes, highlighted the importance of a "distinguished figure" (首出的人格者) like Moses to his nation. Liang wrote that the personality of such a figure would penetrate the entire society and change its form and content so that the character of the public could take shape.[14]

As a response to the renewed interest in traditional Chinese culture, Moses was considered by some Christian intellectuals as a Confucian style sage. According to Zhao Zongfu 赵宗福, God sent Moses to enlighten the Israelites just as *tian* had sent Confucius to the Chinese. Chinese tradition values highly the learning of a sage. Since modern learning referred to Western Learning or New Learning, particularly the natural and social sciences, Zhao emphasized accordingly that, to prepare Moses, God made Moses spend forty years in Pharaoh's palace to be educated in such subjects as astronomy, mathematics, and politics.[15]

In addition to sound learning, perfection in behavior and morality is an equally important attribute of a sage, according to traditional Chinese thought. Since perfection cannot be achieved without suffering, a person charged with important tasks by *tian* must be tried and be physically tempered. For that reason, Zhao explained further, as an impatient and short-tempered person, Moses was not well accepted by his people when appointed by God as their leader. Therefore, Moses had to spend another forty years as a shepherd in the wilderness, where he led a hard life in tough circumstances. After those preparations, Zhao no longer mentioned Moses' shortcomings, implying that Moses had become a perfect man like a Confucian sage. Such a sage was surely a brilliant political as well as religious leader who would bring order out of chaos. For this reason, political and religious affairs were united without conflict in Moses' time.[16]

14. Liang, "Zhongguo lishi yanjiufa," 113–21.

15. Rowe, "Jiuyue de lijie" (Etiquette in the OT, continued), 24–27. For another example, Zhu Baohui, also a Christian, introduced Moses as a learned and erudite person with remarkable literary talents. See Zhu, "Yueboshu xiaoyin" (A Brief Introduction to the Book of Job), 20.

16. Zhao, "Jiuyue de lijie," 24–27. Yuan Ding'an in the 1930s argued the opposite. Moses was inspired by Jethro and established the Tent of Congregation, which was the beginning of theocracy. In the theocracy of Judaism, religion and politics were separated, which was seen in the role of the priests. Yuan, *Youtaijiao gailun*, 30–31.

Liu Tingfang admired Moses so much as to compare his hero to Sun Yat-sen. Sun had a strong faith in God and considered himself a messenger sent by God to fight against the devil similar to Moses on Mount Horeb. Sun established the Republic of China and liberated the Chinese from the shackles of the Manchus like Moses who led the Israelites out of Egypt. Sun devoted forty years to revolutionary work similar to Moses who spent forty years guiding the Israelites in the exodus. Sun did not achieve his goal of a better republic similar to Moses who failed to enter Canaan. Sun died with the vision of "a Canaan-like Republic of China flowing with milk and honey" in the future just as Moses saw Canaan in the distance and died. Even Sun's will on his deathbed is similar to Moses' last words on Mount Nebo.[17]

For such positive images of Moses, Christian intellectuals, especially those in the 1930s who encountered less hostility to Christianity, naturally resorted to Moses' idea of God. As shown in chapter four, interest in the OT idea of God in the 30s was considerable. The relationship between God and Moses was also recognized and discussed, especially by Christian intellectuals. Therefore, their interpretation of Moses' idea of God helps explain Moses' role as a religious and cultural leader in their eyes. What the interpreters cared about was Moses' God as a religious phenomenon but also as crucially instrumental to Moses' leadership.

According to Liu Tingfang, the history of a religion is an evolutionary process of replacing an old idea of God with a new one and the best example to show the struggle between an old idea of God and a new one is the motif of Mount Sinai. Moses ascended the mountain to obtain a new idea of God. Aaron, without a real teacher's insight, instructed the masses with the old idea. When Moses returned from the mountain, a conflict between the two ideas ensued. The old had the upper hand at first and the two tablets were destroyed. But the final victory, as usual, belonged to the new idea and the revised Ten Commandments were successfully transmitted through history.[18] Moses with his idea of God represented the new and the new idea was the progressive force in the evolution of history.

To Yuan Ding'an, it was most meaningful that Moses introduced God's name of "Yahweh," which means "I am that I am" (Exod 3:14, KJV), because

---

17. Liu, "Zhonghua jidutu yu sunzhongshan" (Chinese Christians and Sun Yat-sen), 90–93. To the article, Liu Tingfang attached two poems, one by him and the other by his wife Wu Zhuosheng, to lament Sun's death. Both poems compared Sun's life to that of Moses, 94.

18. Liu, "Shende xingxiang," 176–78.

that established God from the gods of others at the transition period from the Zoomorphic Age to Anthropomorphic Age.[19] Different from living beings and not subject to the law of nature, the God of Moses was transcendental. Therefore, Moses' idea of God was indeed innovative in contrast to the worship of natural objects or phenomena and was a great leap forward. Besides, the God of Moses was holy and pure. The impact of God's holiness and purity on the Israelites' ethical life is considerable, as well as on the making of laws, rites, and systems; otherwise the Israelites should acquire bad habits from heathens.[20] According to classical Jewish commentaries, nevertheless, the repetition of "I am," which should be translated literally from the Hebrew *ehyeh* as "I shall be," signified God's assurance to Moses at the time of suffering.[21]

Moses' idea of God was progressive as well as innovative also because Moses related the religious faith in God to the political responsibility for his people. The bush on fire was explained by Liu Tingfang and Yang Yinliu, who was a Christian musicologist, as Moses' imagination when he saw the senna in bloom. The sight reminded Moses not only of God's glory but also of his responsibility for his people in slavery and danger. God in His glory would not tolerate that the Israelites led such an inhumane life because the world created by God was originally perfect. To worship God is to fight against any damage to the world. Therefore, the lesson of the bush on fire is that seeing God is facing His challenges and engaging in service for the oppressed people. Inspired by Moses, Liu and Yang exclaimed, "how can we live in ease and comfort while our [Chinese] compatriots are still groaning bitterly?!"[22]

Li Rongfang regarded Moses as the most important figure in the history of Israel because of his idea of God, which made him the national leader of the Israelites and the "inspiring man" (启示人) of their faith in Yahweh. The problem that had always bothered Moses during his years in Midian

---

19. The English used by Yuan was "I am that I am" probably from the *KJV*, while the Chinese used by him was "woshi ziyou yongyou zhe" (I Am that I Was from Time Immemorial and that I Shall Be Eternally) from the *Union Version* since both versions were dominant at the time.

20. Yuan, *Youtaijiao gailun*, 21–22. Li Rongfang introduced a similar idea that the religion of the Israelites took shape when Yahweh revealed His name to Moses in Exod 3:14–15. James, *Jiuyue renwu zhi* (Personalities of the OT), 5 and 7.

21. See the commentaries by Rashi, Nachmanides, Sforno, and Rashbam in Cohen, *Soncino Chumash*, 332.

22. Liu and Yang, "Huoyan zhong de jingji" (The Bush on Fire), 239–56.

was that he loved his people and was eager to find a solution for their suffering, but he was neither powerful nor resourceful enough to achieve that. At last on Mount Horeb, Moses found the answer and realized that God was his comrade in the protest against the power of oppression. The core of Moses' religion was that Yahweh was the God of the Israelites and the Israelites were God's chosen people. Moses' God had mercy on his people and was ever-victorious over the enemies of the Israelites, His chosen people. The First Commandment (Exod 20:3) laid the foundation of the intimate relationship and the covenant between Yahweh and the Israelites.[23]

According to Li Rongfang's translation of Barton, the unique covenantal relationship between God and the Israelites was established at a crucial moment in the nation's destiny. Unlike the ties of kinship between Semitic deities and their worshippers, which were thought to be insoluble and from which it was difficult to develop ethics, the covenantal relationship, which could be readily undone, enabled the later Israel prophets to advocate an ethical and moral covenant with Yahweh, thus distinguishing their religion from others in the world.[24] Li introduced uncritically Barton's view and failed to point out the speculative nature of the hypothesis. The vital question about the growth of the ethical element was inconclusive and did not allow for such a positive conclusion.[25]

Aside from his God, Moses himself was viewed from different perspectives. For example, Moses' killing the Egyptian who beat an Israelite was a display of inexperience, patriotic passion, and soaring aspirations of the young Moses.[26] On the other hand, Moses was also regarded as a philosopher, educator, cultural founder, political leader, intermediary between God and the masses, sage, hero, prophet, preacher, priest, and even as a king of ancient Israel.

---

23. Li, "Moxi de zongjiao" (The Religion of Moses), 441–44. Li apparently based himself on George Barton. See similar points in Barton, "Chapter IV: Moses and the Covenant with Yahweh," in *Yiselie de zongjiao* (The Religion of Israel), 56–73. But Li did not always follow Barton. For example, Barton emphasized the covenantal relationship of God with the Israelites as a result of God's jealousy (Exod 34:14), whereas Li highlighted that God was chosen as the only god of the Israelites.

24. Barton, *Yiselie de zongjiao* (The Religion of Israel), 35–36.

25. "Book notices," 653.

26. See Zhao, "Moxi zhi mengzhao" (Moses' Being Called), 2; Liu and Yang, "Huoyan zhong de jingji," 241; and Li, "Zongjiao shenghuo de fazhan" (The Development of Religious Life), 171.

To Cai Yuanpei the philosopher and educator, Moses was also a philosopher and educator. Like the Chinese myth of Pangu, OT myths like that of Creation, which were attributed to Moses, aimed to explain man, nature, life, and death. Such myths offered sustenance to philosophy and set limits for man. Moses said he received the Ten Commandments on Mount Sinai just as China's ancients talked about *tian*'s mandate when Yu received the Great Plan with Its Nine Divisions. With the Ten Commandments, Moses initiated the establishment of Jewish religion, which eventually replaced the OT myths.[27] Since there was no science in primitive times, Moses with the help of religion answered systematically questions about the world and human beings. Therefore, Moses was also an educator.[28]

Like many others, Yuan Ding'an regarded Moses as the founder of Judaism and Hebrew culture. Moses brought the Israelites to Mount Sinai, made the covenant with them by the order of God, explained theology, issued holy laws, made ceremony and propriety, set up the Tabernacle, selected priests, and created order among his fellow believers. Moses thus took care of everything: religion, ethics, politics, education, and hygiene. Moreover, Moses represented cultural progress. He consulted the Code of Hammurabi and other ancient conventions, but he went beyond these and made a superior code. For example, his idea prohibiting all work on Sabbath caused people to abandon prevalent bad habits of exploitation acquired in Babylon and Egypt.[29]

Occasionally, Chinese intellectuals interpreted Moses as a prophet. However, their meaning of the term differed. To Zhu Weizhi, Moses was a prophet because he was a real and great preacher.[30] Li Rongfang introduced Moses as the first prophet God sent to bring to Israelite laws (Deut 18:15).[31] Moses as a prophet implied that he, unlike Adam and Eve, had perfect personal morality (人格) and did not sacrifice the highest good (至善) for the

---

27. Cai, "Jianming zhexue gangyao," 460–62. By the same token, from Moses' religious doctrines to Jesus' revolution is in fact a philosophical development, according to Cai. Liang Qichao also compared the myths of Moses and Yu but with a different focus.

28. Cai, "Meiyu dai zongjiao," 274–75.

29. Yuan, *Youtaijiao gailun*, 18 and 26. Liu Tingfang and Yang Yinliu considered Mosaic law as a national constitution. Liu and Yang, "Huoyan zhong de jingji," (The Bush on Fire), 239–56.

30. Zhu, *Jidujiao yu wenxue* (Christianity and Literature), 188–89. Zhu believed that Moses was the first preaching prophet in history and had remarkable literary talent. For a detailed discussion of Moses' literary talent, see 196–97.

31. James, *Jiuyue renwu zhi*, 118.

secondary good (次善).³² And, as mentioned earlier, the image of Moses as a cultural founder and a master-like prophet with concern for society and perfect morality made him comparable in the eyes of some to Chinese sages like Confucius.³³

However, Moses was portrayed most often as a brilliant leader of his people, whether in a religious, military, or political sense. As a religious leader, in addition to his idea of God already mentioned, Moses was considered unique because he was an intermediary between God and the people as portrayed in the Book of Numbers. Similar to priests and prophets, intermediaries worked between God and men. But whereas a priest worked on behalf of human beings and a prophet on behalf of God, an intermediary was responsible for both sides. God's laws were delivered to human beings through Moses, on the one hand; on the other, Moses prayed to God for men's sake so that God would desist from punishing them for their crimes.³⁴

Moses was a military leader with foresight, sagacity, and diplomatic talents. Seeing that most Israelites were still cowardly after he sent some human beings to explore Canaan, Moses decided to keep them in the wilderness longer so that they could be better trained for the conquest of Canaan. After another thirty-eight years of political training and military education, the younger generation was ready. When Pharaoh's army retreated from Canaan, Moses realized that the time had come for the Israelites to enter. He defeated the strong Amorites and conquered a large area east of the Jordan.³⁵ Western commentators, however, have claimed that Moses' role in the military encounters, in which Israelites were involved, is very limited.³⁶

Discussed by most was that Moses was a great political leader. Some intellectuals highlighted Moses' qualification. Li Rongfang paid special

32. Li, "Zuide laiyuan" (The Origin and Effect of Sin), 12–14.

33. For an example, see Porter, "Zhongguo de jiuyue" (China's OT), 241–43.

34. "Moxi wei zhongbao" (Moses as Intermediary), 3–4. Li Rongfang also introduced the image of Moses who prayed for his people. Even the story of the Golden Calf in Exod 32 showed not Moses' anger with Israelite but his praying for them. *James, Jiuyue renwu zhi*, 15–16.

35. Yuan, *Xibolai de minzu yingxiong moxi* (Moses: the National Hero), 21–23. Liu Tingfang, Yang Yinliu, and Zhu Weizhi also portrayed Moses as a militeary man, while Li Rongfang claimed that Moses initiated the era of military leaders. For details, see Liu and Yang, "Huoyan zhong de jingji" (The Bush on Fire), 239–56; Zhu, *JDJYWX*, 238; and James, *Jiuyue renwu zhi*, 74–75.

36. van Seters, "Moses," 10:117.

attention to Moses' cooperative and democratic leadership. The story at Mount Sinai showed Moses as a man ready to accept advice and be trusting. That made Moses a pre-eminently successful leader, trusted by his people; they were attached to him and did not protest against him. He managed to unite his people by giving them religious faith and ethics. At the very beginning he had learned to recruit human beings of worth and he entrusted them with authority. Numbers 11:14, 17, and 29 presented Moses as a man ready to share his responsibilities with others.[37]

The heroic morality of Moses as a political leader was also highly praised. Moses could have voluntarily surrendered to Pharaoh's mercy after he killed the Egyptian. But being a real man, Moses despised that and considered it betrayal of his self and people. Even in exile, Moses was always ready to defend the weak without considering personal interests, which was the true quality of a hero. His experience as a shepherd familiarized him with the life of nomads and conditions in the wilderness as formative. The forty years of wandering changed Moses from a reckless teenager to a mature leader who kept the general goal in sight while accomplishing daily tasks.[38]

The evangelist Zhao Liutang 赵柳塘 likewise emphasized the impact of suffering on a heroic leader. Only suffering can help a person cast off his old self. All those to whom God assigned important positions grew up in suffering. Moses was born into a world of difficulties and hardships.[39] Having gone through the test of suffering, Moses devoted himself to becoming a leader and could not be defeated even by the threat of death. When Moses knew that he would soon "be gathered to your people" (Num 27:13, NIV), he did not become despondent. Instead, he worked even harder until he finished all his tasks. Moses died neither of old age nor of any mistake (Num 27:14) but because he had finished his work. Even the motif that Moses saw Canaan with his eyes was interpreted as a special favor bestowed by God because Moses could then see the fruit of his hard work and feel satisfied.[40]

37. James, *Jiuyue renwu zhi*, 11, 13, 17, and 19–20.

38. Yuan, *Xibolai de minzu yingxiong moxi*, 9–10. Liu Tingfang and Yang Yinliu believed that because of his earlier education, Moses was able to learn wisdom and survival techniques in the desert. The many years he spent in the desert also transformed Moses into a man of courage, resourcefulness, and strong faith, which were necessary for a leader of a large group of urban slaves wandering about in the desert. Liu and Yang, "Huoyan zhong de jingji" (The Bush on Fire), 239–56.

39. Zhao, "Moxi zhi dansheng jiqi shaonian" (Moses' Birth and Early Years), 24.

40. Zhao, "Moxi zhi wannian" (The Last Years of Moses), 1–7. Unlike the Reubenites and the Gadites, who asked for the land on the eastern bank of Jordan, Moses requested

Jiang Yizheng, a Christian scholar and translator of scientific books, also valued Moses' patience and perseverance. When Moses saw the Israelites worship the Golden Calf, he angrily smashed the tablets. However, he did not give up, but rather climbed Mount Sinai for the second time and finally got the Ten Commandments carved on stones. In contrast to Moses, Chinese leaders vacillate now to the left, now to the right. They have no insight, are not confident and patient, and do not have fixed aims. As a result, they fail in most matters.[41]

Besides Moses' qualifications, his role of servant to his people and his leadership was particularly inspiring. Although Moses was a person, he was able to hear "God's voice." God's voice, which Moses heard on Mount Horeb, was a "human voice" (人声) because it was made for the sake of humankind. This is vastly different from the noise in the modern world made by those who treated other people like beasts, crushing their bones and chewing their flesh. A man like Moses who refused to be contaminated by evil influences and consented to serve the common people at God's call is surely able to hear the human voice of God. The problem at the present time is not that God keeps silent but that no one hears His voice.[42]

A leader like Moses who heard God's human voice was prepared to make sacrifices for his people. Moses was like Mount Tai that carries a heavy burden.[43] Moses was also as tolerant as an ocean with room for hundreds of rivers. He who wants to be a leader and servant of his people must follow Moses' example. He must willingly and gladly be subjected to every kind of maltreatment and never lose the love for his people. Otherwise, he is destined to abandon the task halfway. Although Moses could not save his own life and died in the wilderness, with his death he saved

---

to have a look at Canaan across the river. To Zhao, the Reubenites and the Gadites cared about only immediate personal interests, while Moses was concerned with long-term interests for his nation. Zhao criticized the many leaders of his time who scrambled for power and profit, while seeking ease and comfort. Zhao, "Moxi zhi wei lingxiu" (Moses as a Leader), 6–15.

41. Jiang, "Xiandai de lingxiu you ci jianxin ma" (Do Modern Chinese Leaders Have So Strong a Faith?), 10–17.

42. Jiang, "Rensheng" (Human Voice), 58–59.

43. Mount Tai was thought to carry a burden probably because of a quotation from Sima Qian (ca.145–90 BCE), "ren guyou yisi, huo zhongyu taishan, huo qingyu hongmao" (Though death befalls all men alike, it may be weightier than Mount Tai, or lighter than a feather). See Sima, "Bao Ren'an shu" (A Letter to Ren An) in Ban Gu, "Simaqian zhuan" (Sima Qian's Biography), *Hanshu* (A Historical Account of Han Dynasty).

the lives of thousands of his people. Moses was like a seed that must die for the new plant to sprout.

He was not a born leader and servant of his people. Before Moses determined to devote himself to deliver his people, he was a different person. Selfish, cowardly, and lazy, he hid like a hermit in the depth of a mountain for forty years. Even when God called him in the flaming bush, he was still reluctant and afraid to accept God's command that he go to save his people. Full of suspicion, Moses had no self-confidence and did not believe that his compatriots were worth saving. However, after he had realized his error and repented, he made a fresh start and was no longer his old self.[44]

Still, the image of Moses as a leader could be negative as in the short story "Xinai shan 西乃山" (Mount Sinai) by Liu Yu 刘宇, which portrayed Moses as a fraud. The short story was adapted from Exod 19–20, 24, 32, and 34. It deals with Moses and Joshua's actions at Mount Sinai but does not include the presence of God. As a political leader, Moses was fairly successful by using fraudulent tricks. He called upon the Israelites in the guise of God, invented the myth of Canaan to strengthen their resolve to leave Egypt, made laws in God's name to restrain them, and forbade them to go up to Mount Sinai so that nobody would expose his lies. However, Moses was a naïve idealist who lacked sober-mindedness, political experience, and iron-handedness.

In contrast, Joshua as Moses' right-hand man was imbued with the very qualities Moses lacked. By following Joshua's advice, Moses suppressed the traitors led by the ambitious Aaron and headed off the political crisis by destroying their idol, smashing the two imperfect tablets, and killing the traitors. Moses and Joshua added two new commandments and carved them as the first two on the new tablets: "You shall have no other gods before me. You shall not make for yourself an idol (偶像)." By using these high-handed measures, Moses made the Israelites believe in him.

In this short story, Liu Yu created a human and not a superhuman image of Moses. Moses received a lively characterization through details of conversation, behavior, and psychological traits. He felt relaxed, delighted, and proud when he was about to finish carving the first two tablets. He was puzzled and hesitated to believe Joshua who questioned the loyalty of the Israelites at the foot of Mount Sinai. He was upset when Joshua reminded him of the Israelites' servility. He first felt stunned, then angry, and finally sad and dejected when he was informed of Aaron's

---

44. Jiang, "Xiandai de lingxiu you ci jianxin ma," 10–17.

betrayal. He deeply worried when Joshua convinced him that the elders might have seen through the fraud about Mount Sinai. He could not bear to see the worshipers of the Golden Calf killed and questioned the validity of violent suppression. But his cheerfulness was boundless when he succeeded by violent means.[45]

In Liu Yu's rewriting, in spite of the image of a naïve idealist, lack of sober-mindedness and political experience, Moses was a firm patriotic leader. As Liu Tingfang and Yang Yinliu had argued, despite education and life in the Pharaoh's palace, Moses retained his Hebrew identity because of his patriotic passion. It was the same kind of patriotism that united Israelites in the Diaspora.[46] However, as many Chinese intellectuals understood, patriotic passion was not enough. China was in urgent need of a national hero or a revolutionary like Moses who would take action and bring his people to act.[47]

For many of these intellectuals, Moses exemplified nationalism. Well committed to nationalism in the 1930s, Yuan Ding'an, though a Christian, believed that it was neither God nor the people but Moses who moved history forward. Once out of Egypt, Moses could not find a destination for his people, hence the forty years of their wandering. During this time Moses managed to alleviate the people's suffering, dispel their complaints, tap their intellectual resources, and develop their talents so that they became increasingly civilized and finally reached Canaan. Because of those efforts, Moses was even greater than Confucius and Socrates. He was not only a cultural founder but also a national hero. Moses to Jewish liberation was similar to Cromwell to British democracy and Washington to American independence.

Yuan claimed that Moses led a movement of national liberation and did everything due to nationalist ambition. He received a nationalist education in childhood and was aware of the fate of his people. The Egyptian national revolution, which brought about the establishment of the Eighteenth Dynasty, aroused Moses' ambition to be a national hero. Seeing the misery of the Israelites with his own eyes, Moses considered it shameful to seek a good life while his compatriots were suffering. He carried out

---

45. Liu, "Xinai shan (Mount Sinai)," 632–38.

46. Liu and Yang, "Huoyan zhong de jingji," 239–56. For other interpretations of Moses as a patriot, see Adams, "Renshi shengjing de jizhong fangfa (Some Ways to Know the Bible)," 277–78; and Zhu, *JDJYWX*, 113, 171–72, and 196–97, to name only two.

47. Zhao, "Moxi zhi dansheng jiqi shaonian," 23. Zhu Weizhi called Moses the earliest national revolutionary in the world. Zhu, *JDJYWX*, 196–97.

careful investigations to prepare for future national liberation. With hopes to arouse his people and plot revolution, Moses tried to instill a nationalist spirit in his people. After he was betrayed, Moses fled into exile and waited for an opportunity to resume.

Following the Pharaoh's death, he, though becoming old and infirm, thought the time was ripe for action and returned to Egypt to lead the movement of national liberation. Moses engaged in peace talks with the new Pharaoh in order to win freedom and equality for his people to establish a country of their own with equal international rights. With unrelenting diplomatic efforts as well as the help of unprecedented natural disasters that occurred in Egypt, Moses conveyed to most Egyptians that it was useless and even dangerous to detain the Israelites. At last, Moses considered the time ripe for further action and plotted the exodus.

Aware of strong hostile tribes ahead and his people's low combat effectiveness, Moses made a detour in the wilderness with which he was familiar and during which he had time to train the Israelites. Since they were docile and accepted their fate, Moses' paramount concern was to build up their self-esteem and cultivate their national consciousness. To construct a culture for national education, Moses introduced the ideas of Canaan, Yahweh, and chosen people, thus distinguishing their religion from the polytheism of other nations.[48]

Religion was interrelated with national consciousness. Moses' keen religiosity together with the inspiration of Jethro's pantheistic religion prepared Moses for his return to Egypt to bring about national liberation through missionary work. He realized that the confidence of his people in him would not be strengthened unless they believed that he was entrusted with a mission by God. For that reason, Moses announced that God had seen and heard the suffering of the Israelites and would punish the Egyptians for their cruelty. He was sent by God to deliver and teach the Israelites. Both the Israelites and Pharaoh should obey his heavenly mission. As a result, Israel was granted the unparalleled status in the world of becoming the chosen people of God. Judaism in Yuan's view was a kind of nationalism.[49]

---

48. Yuan, *Xibolai de minzu yingxiong moxi*, 1, 8–10, 12–17, and 24–25.

49. Moses' ultimate goal of establishing Judaism, Yuan wrote, was to extend it to the whole world in the interest of all humankind. Unfortunately, that responsibility has been ignored by Jews and was undertaken by Christians instead. For that reason, Yuan claimed that Judaism pursued nationalism, while Christianity advocated universalism. Yuan Ding'an, *Youtaijiao gailun* (Introduction to Judaism), 18–20 and 26. In the light of a different agenda, Moses could also be interpreted as a statist with a narrow-minded idea

Compared with Jesus, Moses is a lively and more acceptable image to Chinese readers who lack the traditional faith in transcendental beings. Moses was born an ordinary human being, with both character weaknesses and physical defects. Moses, like many of us, was humble. He had a temperament similar to ours. He was not even a genius and he needed many years of education. He also learned lessons from his own failures and suffering before he became successful. Moses was at once impetuous, timid, shallow, unreliable, had no confidence in himself, arrogant, and impatient. He made mistakes and even tried to disobey God, which made God angry and sad. He was helped not only by God but also by his parents, brother and sister. It was such a man who became great, a hero, and a savior of his people.[50]

However, those who did not believe in national heroes might argue the opposite. Lu Xun who translated Lunz's novelette "Zai shamo shang" (In the Desert) avoided portraying an optimistic heroic protagonist. That avoidance reveals Lu Xun's as well as Lunz's uncertainty about the positive role of revolution and the revolutionary hero or leader in the history of human civilization. But no matter what kind of leader Moses was and what role he played in the eyes of Chinese intellectuals in the 1930s, Moses undoubtedly proved to be a most interesting and stimulating prototype in their arguments.

Although it is understandable that Moses was attractive to Chinese intellectuals, generally Western theology does not interpret Moses as an ideal leader or a great hero of crucial importance. In the OT, the theme of Israel's oppression is often mentioned elsewhere as the condition of the people from which God redeemed them, often without any reference to Moses. Moses' initial attempt at deliverance (Exod 2:11–15), whereby he kills an Egyptian for beating a Hebrew, is anti-heroic because it leads only to his flight. This prepares the way for the biblical author to present Moses as a most un-heroic leader, totally dependent on the divine word for each action he takes.[51]

---

of God as shown in Exod 9:15 whose religion originated in cruel wars. See James, *Jiuyue renwu zhi*, 9. A statist here is one who advocates complete sovereignty.

50. Zhao, "Moxi zhi mengzhao," 1–8.
51. van Seters, "Moses," 116–17.

Prophets and Modern Chinese Intellectuals

Moses was by no means the only OT character who was attractive to Chinese intellectuals. Many also turned to the OT prophets and created idealized images of them in their interpretive efforts to set ideal examples.[52] More than ever before, the period of the May Fourth and New Culture witnessed a remarkable interest in the OT prophets among Chinese intellectuals. To understand this interest, the meaning of "prophet" according to translators and the Chinese interpreters of the OT must be clarified. Secondly the modern outlook of OT prophets according to Chinese intellectuals, and finally the significance of OT prophets within current ideas of patriotism, nationalism, and universalism must be explored. Some prophets, such as Amos and Jeremiah, were more important than others among them.

Although the word "prophet" in the OT was usually rendered *xianzhi* 先知 (literally "he who foreknows"), most Chinese intellectuals were more interested in its more complex meaning in the OT. Prophets were responsible to both God and man.[53] As a result, the prophet was called a "person who demonstrates and recounts God's edict,"[54] "God's spokesman," "inspired preacher of foresight,"[55] or "tongue person." Li Rongfang complained that the term *xianzhi* for OT prophets already lost the two meanings, namely "a person who speaks in place of God" and "a person who speaks in front of the masses," whereas greater importance was attached to the sense of "a person who foretells." As a result the true idea was lost and the prophetic spirit did not develop in Chinese society.[56]

The remoteness of the prophetic spirit from Chinese society brought about the decline of morality and ethics. Ethics referred to the relationship between human beings and God similar to Confucian ethics that was explained as the unity of heaven and man (天人合一). The differences between OT prophets suggested that different prophets had different revelations

---

52. Almost all the interpretations of OT prophets were positive. Cai Yuanpei nevertheless noted that OT prophets were superstitious and irrational. See Guo, "Caiyuanpei de shidai" (Cai Yuanpei's Times), 1633.

53. Zhuo, "Shangdiguan de yanjin" (The Evolution of the Idea of God), 8.

54. Tang and Ye, "Shengjing zhi wenxue de yanjiu," translation of W. H. Hudson's "The Bible as Literature," 18–25.

55. Zhu, *JDJYWX*, 196–97. According to Zhu, Christianity developed the art of preaching to its climax by combining the spirit of the ancient Hebrew prophets and Greek and Latin rhetoric.

56. Li, *Amosi zhushi* (A Commentary on Amos), 1. See also Li, *Xiandai qingnian jiuyue bidu* (OT Selections for Present-Day Youth), 48 and 89–90.

from God; and that the closer relationship human beings have with God, the more human beings will know about God and God's will, the more human beings will become aware of their inadequacy, and consequently the more human beings will improve their personal morality. The more human beings improve their personal morality, the closer they will be to God until they finally are united with God.[57]

For intellectuals who respected both biblical and Chinese culture, the OT revealed that there was no significant difference between a prophet and a historian. Although prophets were more interested in the present and future, while historians paid more attention to the past, both attempted to exert an impact on human life. Therefore, the prophetic and the historical writings in the OT were the same kind of literature despite their different perspectives and should not be separated when being discussed.[58] Indeed, the masses do not understand the intention and meaning of history, which explain God's will and action. God enlightened the prophets so that they would interpret the meaning of history and introduce the truths to the unenlightened masses.[59]

Also because of the respect for both biblical and Chinese culture, some believed that the ideal man in the modern era should be a combination of OT prophet and Chinese sage. As a professor of Protestant theology at Yenching University, Zhao Zichen believed that the first objective of higher theological education was to train and develop prophets. But he criticized the old type of prophet in the OT for showing "only one side of the picture." He explained that, in antiquity, even a shepherd could be a prophet as long as he truly heard God's call; whereas in modern China, the new type of prophet must have perfect learning and be socially engaged.[60] Zhao's emphasis on perfect learning and social responsibility reveals the impact of the traditional idea of a sage.

---

57. Li, "Shengjing de xiaoyong" (The Usefulness of the Bible), 86. Zhang Xisan suggested that the writings of the prophets were different one from the other because they had different talents, personalities, and backgrounds; and because the prophets were human beings themselves, their writings would be better understood by men. Ai Silan, "Xinyue yu jiuyue" (The NT and the OT), 3–5. It is impossible to identify the author's original name.

58. Li, *Xiandai qingnian jiuyue bidu*, 48 and 89–90.

59. Ai Silan, "Xinyue yu jiuyue" (The NT and the OT), 3–5.

60. Zhao, "Wo dui zhongguo gaodeng shenxue jiaoyu de mengxiang" (My Dream about Higher Theological Education in China), 344–45.

Treating *tian* as equal to God and OT prophets equal to Chinese sages, Liu Songjun 刘松筠 quoted *Mencius* that "Heaven, in producing the people, has given to those who first attain understanding the duty of awakening those who are slow to understand" (天生斯民也以先知觉后知). The reason why merciful *tian* or God sent a *xianzhi* or prophet into the world and bestowed on him extraordinary spiritual enlightenment was to assist heaven in governing the world. The aim was to help the masses see what is right, warn them of future judgments, alert them, and save them from "the sea of retribution."[61] Some intellectuals even wrote that the OT prophets, like Chinese sages, were interested in this world and believed in rewards through one's own effort.[62]

Westerners too joined the discussion, arguing that OT prophets and Chinese sages emphasized the same ideas. According to Lucius C. Porter for example, both reveal the same outlook on historical philosophy, which can be easily seen by comparing the Book of Deuteronomy and *the Book of History*. Secondly, both highlight rites (礼), which originally came from *tian* and took care of national, family, and personal affairs. In this aspect, the Books of Leviticus and Numbers can be compared with *the Book of Rites*. Thirdly, both emphasized morality, private or public. Righteousness advocated by the prophets is identical with Mencius' ideas of benevolence and righteousness (仁义). The Hebrews stressed personal morality (人格), while Confucius advocated loyalty and consideration (忠恕). Finally, both longed for an ideal society in the future.[63]

As the Chinese sages were highly esteemed, the importance of the OT prophets to Judaism and Christianity was highlighted and even exaggerated. Yuan Ding'an declared that prophets and law are synonymous with Judaism, while Zhu Weizhi wrote that prophetic literature reflects the main features of Hebrew and biblical literature, that is, their intuitive recognition of God in trials and tribulations.[64] Christian intellectuals argued that the impact of OT prophets on Jesus and Christianity was all pervasive. Christian ethics

---

61. See the Chinese of the quotation in *Mencius* 5B:1 and its translation in Mencius, *Mencius*, 217. Liu, "Lun yisaiyashu shangban zhi dazhi" (The Main Idea of the First Isaiah), 21.

62. Yuan, *Youtaijiao gailun*, 20–21.

63. Porter, "Zhongguo de jiuyue," 241–43.

64. Yuan, *Youtaijiao gailun*, 72; and Zhu, *JDJY WX*, 52 and 55.

originated in the thoughts of the prophets. Not only Jesus' religious experience but also his wisdom and virtues were under their influence.[65]

Not only Christian intellectuals, others also, like Hu Shi, believed in an inherent relationship between OT prophecy and Christian messianism.[66] However, they did not consider the role of God because what excited them were the prophets themselves, whom they interpreted as ideal men. They usually showed more freedom to advocate their own ideas and went beyond the limits of apologetics. Two best examples for that phenomenon were Zhang Dongsun and Lu Xun.

Zhang Dongsun believed that Amos the religious leader, like Jesus, was actually an idealist in ancient times. Human society improves because the ideals of such men, like sunshine, light the way for the masses so that they can keep marching toward the sun. Since the masses can never reach the sun or realize those ideals, human beings like Amos are also called "enthusiasts with fantasy" (空想的热心家) just as socialists are called utopians. However, Zhang preferred "ideal" to "fantasy" as the word for the thoughts of those enthusiasts because an ideal is always realistic to some extent, thus having some force of changing and improving the uncertain situation of reality.

Amos and others like him are not necessarily political leaders similar to Moses. They are independent minded individuals of action with special insights. They criticize their times and tell people what it should be like ideally. That is why idealists like Amos are particularly praiseworthy. The Chinese only saw the superficial "principle" (理) and were satisfied with retaining the present order, thus lacking progress, because the superficial principle implied a non-challengeable authority. In contrast, Westerners see the profound and transcendental "rationality" (理性), or the so-called "natural law" (自然法). They realized that no system is really perfect, hence the constant demand for correcting mistakes. As a result, Westerners became wiser and had more achievements to their credit.

Zhang further compared idealists like Amos to the scientists of modern times. By scientists Zhang actually meant individuals who have the scientific spirit of emancipation or idealists who follow a scientific way. In Zhang's view, science itself contains ideals because science always wants to find a deeper level of rationality. Zhang highly praised the combination of

---

65. For examples of such arguments, see Yuan, *Jidujiao gailun*, 6–8 and 20–24; Montague, "Xinyang de jiefang" (Liberation of Faith), 36–37; Toyohiko, "Yesu de zhihui" (Wisdom of Jesus), 28–29; and Zhao, "Shengjing zai jinshi wenhua zhongde diwei," 19.

66. Hu, "Shuo ru" (About the Ru), 38.

science and idealism as was the case with Karl Marx (1818–1883) because this combination explains why Western culture has overwhelmed others and has become the world culture.⁶⁷

In Lu Xun's eyes, Jeremiah was most praiseworthy because he was an unyielding "spiritual fighter" for his people's interests. Jeremiah's voice was completely sincere and most powerful because he voiced the aspirations of people.⁶⁸ According to Kuriyagawa Hakuson who admired Jeremiah and whose thoughts were introduced by Lu Xun to Chinese readers, when the prophets were inspired by God, they in fact gained knowledge of the people's unconscious desire for life. This is so because the people's voice is God's voice (*Vox populi, vox Dei*).⁶⁹ Such an image of Jeremiah reflects how Lu Xun understood himself as a writer in the society. Like Jeremiah, the writer voices feelings of discontent which people in general are not yet aware of.

Lu Xun also translated an essay by Anatolij V. Lunačarskij, in which the author argued that, after the nomadic Israelites settled in Canaan, they were spoiled by their heathen agricultural neighbors, who believed in alien gods and encouraged class oppression and exploitation. As a result, Israelite aristocrats established monarchic politics and lived by exploiting the poor. It is the prophets who strongly opposed the new order of oppression and who advocated the only legitimate life—the life of truth, equality, universal love, and simplicity, which once was Israel's lifestyle and that God permitted.

Moreover, some modern thinkers like Thomas Carlyle, Lev Tolstoy, and Jean Jacques Rousseau were similar to the prophets because they also resorted to antiquity to protest the degenerate world of the modern era. In their view, directed against capitalism and the bourgeoisie, the past is better than the present because people then lived a God-like existence without malevolent competition and deviation from the original perfection of human nature. Human beings should restore a primeval organization of society and an organic existence of mutual love.⁷⁰

---

67. Zhang, *Lixing yu minzhu* (Rationality and Democracy), 110–12 and 114. Zhang did not necessarily agree with Marxists. He wrote, an ideal is often distorted in practice due to "social inertia" or "habituation in the intellectual process" or lack of "intellectual adaptation" that is neglected by Marxists; forces countering social mobility or reform remains even after the fundamental change of the economic system. Zhang, *Sixiang yu shehui* (Thought and Society), 187.

68. Lu, "Moluo shili shuo" (On the Power of Mara Poetry), 55–56 and 101.

69. Kuriyagawa, "Kumen de xiangzheng" (The Symbol of Depression), 96, 101, and 104.

70. Lunačarskij, "Tuoersitai yu makesi" (Tolstoy and Marx), 265 and 288–97. See

Since Lu Xun probably had followed the idea of the unity of heaven and man as Lin Yüsheng suggested, the idealized God-like human life in antiquity advocated by the OT prophets, Carlyle, Tolstoy, and Rousseau must have sounded most natural and acceptable to Lu Xun. According to Lin, the Confucian conception of the unity of heaven and man (or of the mind of the Way and the mind of man) entails that transcendental reality is immanent in the cosmos of which man is an integral part.[71] Also, if the novelette "Zai shamo shang" indicates Lu Xun's awareness of the destructive possibilities of a revolution and distrust of Communism in an earlier period, the translation of Lunačarskij reveals Lu Xun's ideological commitment, or sympathy at least, with Marxism in the post May Fourth era. The implication may be Lu Xun's rejection, or suspicion at least, of evolutionism and his development from a lover of the people to a class-conscious Marxist.[72]

Many admired the prophets because they considered them to be spokesmen for their people. Zhu Weizhi declared that the people's voice is God's voice. The great Book of Amos in the language of the people was written by the people, owned by the people, and read by the people. It should be read by the Chinese because their times are similar to those of Amos, the poet of complete sincerity.[73] Zhu compared great poets to OT prophets because great poets, he suggested, had prophetic consciousness.[74] Admiration for the prophets sometimes led to rather untenable comparisons. Zhu Weizhi freely compared Jeremiah to Moses, Confucius, Jesus, Zhu Xi, Martin Luther, and Sun Yat-sen. The strong sense of mission or responsibility made Jeremiah into a great preacher, a model teacher, a hero, a real ruler of society, and an eloquent literary giant of his time. Jeremiah even deserved the title of "Model Teacher of Myriad Ages" (至圣先师) as Confucius enjoyed.[75]

Finally it was patriotism, nationalism and universalism that were seen as the prophets' particularly attractive features. They were passionate patriots, as was most notably expressed in the Book of Lamentations, the author of which was widely believed to be Jeremiah. And even if he was not, the

---

the opposite views of Zhang Dongsun above regarding prophets and social ideals.

71. Lin, "The Morality of Mind," 114–15.

72. For Lu Xun's ideological development, see Eber et al., "Reception," 258–65.

73. Zhu, "Amosi" (Amos), 112–13. The article was first published in SXZ in September 1949. See Amos as a poet in Zhu, JDJYWX, 161.

74. Zhu, "Wen yiduo lun zongjiao" (Wenyiduo's Comments on Religion), 14.

75. Zhu, JDJYWX, 188–89 and 198–99.

author would have been a prophet living at the same time as Jeremiah and was influenced by the latter.[76] Moreover, the Book of Lamentations was often compared to "Lisao" by Qu Yuan because both mourned the national calamity.[77] Zhu Weizhi pointed out the patriotic passion in both texts, and he analyzed Jeremiah's impact on the patriotic poet George G. Byron.[78]

The patriotic passion of OT prophets was often interpreted differently. Proponents of nationalism did not always distinguish it from patriotism, and to them patriotic prophets were simply nationalists. The essential facts of life at the time were national suffering as well as moral decline. National suffering gave birth to a heroic spirit among the prophets. Whenever national suffering was looming, or imminent, or unbearable, the prophet played a crucial role in warning his compatriots, making them repent and mend their ways, and giving them hope of redemption.[79]

As a response to those who advocated the incompatibility between Christianity and nationalism, the Christian scholar Wu Leichuan 吴雷川 (1870–1944) claimed that the best way to implement nationalism in modern China is to arm the disorganized Chinese people, who lacked the capacity to unify, with the true spirit of Christianity, exemplified by the strong national unity of the Jewish people. Jewish prophets throughout the ages were patriots; therefore, the Jews always remained an independent people, attempting to restore their state despite the many setbacks in history.[80]

For others who aimed for universalism, the patriotic prophets were not nationalists but universalists. Tang Chengbo and Ye Qifang proposed that since the function of prophets broadly speaking is to promote the spirit

---

76. Li, Preface I to *Aige* (Lamentations), 1–5.

77. Zhou, "Shengshu yu zhongguo wenxue," 14–15.

78. Zhu, *JDJYWX*, 66 and 75. Zhu also saw similarities between the Book of Lamentations and "Lisao" in their literary styles and religious morality. Professor Raoul Findeisen kindly read this part of the chapter and pointed out that comparing Jeremiah to Qu Yuan was "a strategic perspective of early Chinese readers of the OT." Qu Yuan was "a stereotype of the twentieth-century literary history writing that merits critical assessment." Verbal Conversation with Raoul Findeisen on October 11, 2005.

79. Zhu, *JDJYWX*, 50–52, and 55. Jian Youwen introduced G. B. Smith's call for a "democratic" interpretation of biblical doctrines, which focuses on the "heroic" attitude to the "facts of life as well as sincerity of morality" of the Biblical authors, many of whom were believed to be OT prophets. Smith, "Shenxue lunli de gaizao" (Reform in Ethical Theology), 52. See the original in Smith, *Social Idealism and the Changing Theology*, 1913.

80. Wu, "Guojiazhuyi yu jidujiao shifou chongtu" (Is Christianity in Conflict with Nationalism?), 4–5.

of the bad world, prophets are not nationalistic.[81] It was the universalism expressed by such prophets as Amos, Isaiah, Micah, Jeremiah, and Jonah since the eighth century BCE that was important.[82] Amos, for example, believed in a God of all the nations.[83] Promotion of morality and spiritual faith of the people would help solve social and religious problems once and for all.[84] Li Rongfang praised Amos and Jeremiah among the prophets most highly. Amos advocated ethics and faith in a monotheistic God. He emphasized justice and warned of God's punishments. One who is morally degenerate and did evil would surely be punished by God. No ritual can help those who are without sincerity and morality. Amos regarded righteousness as the foundation of a good society. He called for a sense of responsibility and action in accordance with a person's conscience.[85]

Li Rongfang maintained that Jeremiah was the first to preach ethical monotheism. Not only did he pronounce the idols of the nations "worthless" (Jer 10:15 and 14:22, NIV), he also emphasized personal responsibilities and the internal experience of faith. Jeremiah was the prophet of all nations because he advocated that God was for all peoples. This commitment granted Jeremiah a keen sense of responsibility.[86]

Like Lu Xun, Li Rongfang also introduced Jeremiah as an unyielding fighter but for a different reason. Jeremiah was a fighter for perfection. He had a perfect personality because, unlike Adam and Eve, Jeremiah did not

---

81. Tang and Ye, "Shengshu zhi wenxue de yanjiu," 29.

82. Li, "Jiuyue li de guoji guannian" (International Ideas in the OT), 22.

83. Li, *Amosi zhushi*, 3–10, 18; and James, *Jiuyue renwu zhi*, 92–93. Nonetheless Li also wrote that such universalism without Jesus was no more than imperialism. Those prophets contributed indeed to the formation of the Messianic idea, but what they really longed for was a Jewish empire, whose monarch would be a descendent of David. Because the monarch should rule "nanbei" (from north to south) and govern "tianxia" (the land under heaven), it is an imperialist ideal that must be understood as political Messianism. Li, "Yesu yu jidu" (Jesus and Christ), 5. According to Li, a similar political idea is also found in some psalms. Ibid., 6–8.

84. Li, "Yiselie de xianzhi" (The Israel Prophet), 42.

85. Li, *Amosi zhushi*, 3–10, and 18. Zhao Zichen's translation similarly proposes that Amos was the first prophet to establish ethical monotheism as the religion of Israel though the prophets who followed him were not completely successful in educating their people until the birth of Jesus. See Shi Qide, "Fazhan yu fenhua" (Development and Breakup), 9.

86. Barton, "Yiselie de zongjiao" (The Religion of Israel), 4–5; and James, *Jiuyue renwu zhi*, 124 and 132. Li even considered Jeremiah similar to Jesus more so than any other OT prophet. Li, *Xiandai qingnian jiuyue bidu*, 143–52.

lose his personal morality by sacrificing the less perfect for the perfect.[87] For the same reason, Jeremiah opposed all his contemporaries. Moreover, he believed that destruction helps ultimately with construction and considered it his mission to destroy, thus becoming the public enemy of his people.[88]

The prophets, moreover, believed in national salvation by promoting personal virtue and morality. They eventually made not nationalism but universalism their ideal.[89] Even Yuan Ding'an with a strong commitment to nationalist ideas admitted that, if Judaism was a tribal religion from Abraham to the period of Judges and a national religion during the time of Kingdom, it had become a universal religion at the time of the prophets. The prophets at the end of the Kingdom period already transformed Judaism into an ethical religion. When the Judaism of the prophets will spread to the entire world, there will be perpetual peace.[90]

Interestingly, this idea of evolution from nationalism to universalism among the Hebrews was also held by others. After losing their state, Jews held a belief in a national hero or Messiah who would arise in the future and lead the conquered people to national rejuvenation. After years of failure to attain that hope, the dream of political revival was shattered and changed in content. Namely, the zeal for political rejuvenation decreased, while the desire for religious or cultural rejuvenation increased. The national hero of restoration was transformed into a great sage who would deliver humankind. Jewish Messianic expectation came true in Jesus. Although Jesus' death ended the Jews' dream of restoration, he became "a light unto the Gentiles" and brought salvation "to the ends of the earth."

Hu Shi pointed out that the Yin 殷 people of the Shang dynasty (ca.1600–ca.1046 BCE) in Chinese history also had a prophecy of a national hero for national and political rejuvenation: "Every five hundred years a true king should arise" (五百年必有王者興).[91] The Yin people's prophecy materialized partially in Confucius. Confucius, like Jesus, also died with the dream of national rejuvenation unfulfilled. But Confucius also revived after death because "It is Man who is capable of broadening

---

87. Li, "Zuide laiyuan," 12–14.

88. James, *Jiuyue renwu zhi*, 128–29 and 134. Jian Youwen also subscribed to the fighting image of Jeremiah. For his argument, see Smith, "Zongjiaode quezheng," 53–55.

89. Zhuo, "Shangdiguan de yanjin" (The Evolution of the Idea of God), 10.

90. Yuan, *Youtaijiao gailun*, 46–47.

91. See the Chinese quotation in *Mencius* 2B:13 and the translation in Mencius, *Mencius*, 98–99.

the Way" (人能弘道).⁹² He broke through the limits of local cultures and laid a universal foundation for Ruist culture. Confucius thus also became "a light unto the Gentiles."⁹³

Amos and Jeremiah especially inspired Chinese Christian intellectuals because they believed that the two upheld ethics and demonstrated a harmony between patriotic passion and the universalist ideal. These major concerns of Chinese Christian intellectuals at the time of social wickedness, national crisis, and imperialism clearly shows the changed perspectives of Chinese intellectuals regarding the OT prophets. Jeremiah, for example, spent much of his career prophesying doom. Yet the implication that a radical change of human nature was possible became a universal value. As a result, in the history of religion, the words of the prophet became a legacy of hope.⁹⁴ For the Chinese interpreters, the radical change of human nature did not mean repentance as Jeremiah had advocated but a message of universal moral perfection, hence the need to promote ethics.

However, the example of Jeremiah and Amos does not suggest that other OT prophets were irrelevant in the new context and not interesting to Chinese intellectuals. In fact, different prophets provided various interpreters with different inspiration. In many ways this would seem an evolving Chinese exegesis. More research is needed, to be sure, to substantiate such a bold suggestion. Nonetheless, whereas Jesuits and Protestant missionaries tried to give the Chinese their commentaries, here the Chinese are at last speaking. Still, it should be stressed that this evolving Chinese commentary tradition shows the impact of only the Christian exegesis. Intellectuals like Zhao Zichen, Jian Youwen, and Li Rongfang relied mainly on Christian commentaries that they translated and not on Jewish commentaries. These more often than not differ from the Christian ones, presenting vastly different perspectives about their past and its meaning. However, with the increasing involvement of non-Christian intellectuals like Liang Qichao, Cai Yuanpei, and Lu Xun, the Chinese commentary tradition was stepping on a path toward independence.

---

92. See the Chinese quotation in Verse 29, Book 15, *Lunyu* and its translation in Confucius, *The Analects*, 157.

93. Hu, "Shuo ru," 38–39 and 50–52. But Hu denied that Confucius is a Messiah like Jesus. For details, see ibid., 80–81.

94. Sperling, "Jeremiah," 8:6.

6

Concluding Reflections

Throughout the nineteenth century, as had happened previously, there was the remarkable receptivity of the periphery where Christian and Old Testament (OT) ideas spread. Protestant missionaries followed two basic strategies in introducing the OT to educated Chinese. Together with the introduction of Western learning, they emphasized that the OT was an important part of Western learning. But it was their repeated efforts in translating the OT into Chinese with the help of Chinese coworkers that demonstrated the beginning of the OT ideas and human beings being interpreted and transformed in the context of Chinese culture. Each translating effort was an accommodating effort, which involved different translators, coworkers, modes, styles, principles, and aids.

Protestant missionaries and the Chinese OT had a major shaping influence on the culture of the littoral, and many Chinese living there either became Christian or were conspicuously affected by OT teachings. At times, the OT text itself was less important than the booklets about the OT. Knowledge of the OT was also spread through secondary literature mainly prepared by Protestant missionaries. Since mid-nineteenth century, with the development of the publishing industry, and the appearance of journals like *JHXB* and *WGGB*, the missionaries sponsored and organized on a larger scale Chinese OT commentary activities among Chinese readers and contributors. In the process a Chinese OT commentary tradition slowly took shape and contributors interpreted the OT text often in conformity with Neo-Confucian concepts, with which they were familiar. OT commentaries in this first stage were largely the work of converts.

Missionary publications were fairly widely distributed and were also read by non-Christian literati at this time. The reformist thinkers' discussions about OT persons and ideas are particularly significant when we trace the development of the Chinese OT commentary tradition. For the first time, the OT and its motifs merited serious attention from non-Christian scholars. Although interpretations were undertaken by a small number of scholars and often occurred together with interpretations of Chinese traditional culture as was done by converted literati, the reformist thinkers' perspectives were different because of their absolute confidence in Confucianism and a strong commitment to it when confronting Western challenges.

After 1894, many Chinese literati related historic events in the OT to contemporary Jews in the Diaspora and saw in the condition of the Jews a lesson for the Chinese about what would happen to them if they did not change. However, no matter from what perspective they interpreted Jewish history in the OT, their focus was on the Chinese ruling class and social elite. Liang Qichao took a large step forward by introducing ideals of the new citizen and transitional heroes in his interpretation of Moses. Responding to discussions on the OT from the camp of conservative and orthodox Confucianism were meaningful because they demonstrated that OT ideas and human beings had exerted an impact on a wider area and a large segment of the gentry.

In this transitional period, the increasing number of Scriptures which were circulated spread a general knowledge and tended to correct false stories like the Hunan placards. The reconstruction of Chinese tradition was under the impact from OT as well as indigenous sources. After the pioneering and preparatory work of Protestant missionaries as well as Chinese intellectuals in vernacular translations, modern education, and literary-historical study of the OT, the OT began to have a significant place in the 1920s and the following decades. An immediate impact is best seen in the common interest among Chinese Christian intellectuals when they considered the literary significance of the OT. Their writings show the involvement of the OT in the development of modern Chinese literature and signify a unique place of the OT in the history of modern Chinese literature.

In the May Fourth and New Culture periods, a wider interest in OT persons and ideas among both Christian and non-Christian intellectuals was enhanced by current intellectual controversies, the anti-Christian movement, and developing nationalism. It is of special help to understand the extent to which they interpreted one of the most important OT ideas, the monotheist understanding of God. In the process, Chinese intellectuals resorted to different resources to legitimize their contextualized reading of the OT. Western ideas of science and philosophy, especially the evolutionary theory, were considered; whereas the use of Chinese conventions was not limited to Confucianism and attention was also paid to Daoist and other ideas. The major concerns of Chinese Christian intellectuals at this time when they considered social wickedness, national crisis, and imperialism also merited their changed perspectives regarding human beings like Moses and the prophets, Jeremiah and Amos.

This work paid special attention to the dynamic development of the OT as an important source of spiritual inspiration to educated Chinese in modern China. The development lies in the basic facts that the knowledge of the OT was increasingly popularized; that OT literature was increasingly recognized as religious, literary, and historical documents; that the appeal of the OT was increasingly felt by non-converts; and that a Chinese OT exegesis gradually took shape. The history of the OT in modern China is a history of re-interpretation and transformation of OT persons and ideas in a Chinese context, which were inseparable from Chinese tradition. The intellectual tradition a Chinese interpreter had inherited and had been educated in furnished a framework of meaning that enabled him to make sense of the OT text. Even radical intellectuals at the turn of the twentieth century and the May Fourth period were unable to jettison inherited modes of thinking. Therefore, when interpreting the OT, they felt they could not but engage the OT inter-scripturally with the Chinese classics.

However, despite the readability of the Chinese OT and art of the OT narrative, the gap between the OT and Chinese classics, especially Jewish monotheistic and Confucian non-theistic views, is obvious. The relationship between human nature in Confucian classics and the divine grace in the OT are at odds. Personal perfection in Confucianism can be obtained through man's own effort but can only be realized in absolute obedience to God in Jewish faith. According to the Chinese view, man and nature form a continuum and do not stand in a dichotomic relation as in the OT but in a relation of reciprocal complementarity. It is worth asking why Chinese literati were interested in the OT and why Christian converts resorted to the OT and its human beings rather than the NT and Jesus.

To orthodox Confucian gentry and anti-Christian intellectuals, the principle differences between the OT and Confucian teachings supported their opposition to the OT. But other intellectuals took these differences for granted. They tended to highlight the incompleteness of both Confucian and OT texts, while asserting that both were canonical and complementary. Christian intellectuals, for example, subsumed the Confucian self-cultivation ethic as grounded on *ren* and *li* but also based on the idea of God. To them, these two traditions together encourage a complete obedience of faith. A balanced worldview that is both theo-centric and anthropo-cosmic could be most beneficial; otherwise, religion would become divorced from ethics, alienating divine grace from human endeavor.

Some interpreters emphasized that OT teachings are basically the same as those of the ancient Chinese sages. Both the OT and Chinese classics embody normative and communal wisdom of two great civilizations. And the ideals and precepts of the two classics transcend the historical circumstances of their origin and shape the modern world. Christian intellectuals in particular believed that no culture system is beyond God's power and the OT is meaningless if not reconciled with Chinese culture, though by doing so, they may have endangered the uniqueness and authority of the OT.

To Chinese intellectuals, the OT and Confucian classics seek to overcome social conflicts, moral collapse, and spiritual chaos. Both Judaism and Confucianism emphasize human responsibility to make the world a better place through self-improvement. From this point of view, moral bankruptcy was the source of all problems. This was a typical Confucian diagnosis of social ills. The idea of God that can help reform Chinese society through moral teachings is not opposed to the Confucian belief in the basic goodness of human nature that can be transformed through effective moral education. Individual moral character can ultimately save a country by removing corruption, greed, and injustice in human hearts. Only by reconciling both views could Chinese Christian intellectuals identify themselves as Chinese as well as Christian. Whereas missionaries at first gave the Chinese their commentaries, here the Chinese are at last speaking and presenting rather different perspectives. With the increasing involvement of non-Christian intellectuals, the Chinese commentary tradition was embarking on an independent path.

Some common emphases can be identified among the Chinese interpreters: a keen awareness of the OT's authority in Western civilization and a claim on its readers; a clear aim to cultivate morality despite differences in understanding the term; and the final purpose to benefit the whole nation. Underlying these emphases is a Chinese pragmatic concern for life at the present time. It is in response to evil, suffering, and injustice that Chinese interpreters attempted to find meaning in the OT for their own day. The development of OT commentaries in modern China shows the conviction among Chinese interpreters in the continuous usefulness of the OT for China and the ongoing need to search for it in new situation. Such an approach to the OT may indeed have made them oblivious to historical and cultural gaps as well as led to misinterpretations of the OT at times. Yet this closer contact with the OT text enabled many Chinese intellectuals to find an inner logic in the OT and the book's existential claims on a reader's life. The process by means of which the contact was established is best described as accommodation.

In the process, Chinese readers demonstrate various modes in which the otherness of the OT manifested itself. Missionaries with Chinese coworkers translated the OT and often conveyed it in terms of Chinese culture. This mode of translation inevitably transformed the Chinese OT into a part of the spiritual and intellectual life of modern Chinese literati. Educated converts recognized OT culture as primordial and their call to responsibility and personal ethics frequently demanded a joint commitment. Encountering the OT also awakened awareness of plurality which resulted in an experience of difference. Although conservative and orthodox Confucian scholars rejected concern with the OT, the rejection in fact allowed for an exploration of difference that raised the question of why there were such disparities. Reformers and radicals after 1894 saw reflections of their own condition in the Jewish Diaspora, which entailed heightened self-awareness. In this transitional period, vernacular translations of the OT and the vernacular movement within missionary and Protestant Christian educational institutions, which were interwoven with the challenges of the time, played a pioneering and preparatory role in the mass educational movement of national enlightenment. In an effort to build Chinese church, Chinese Protestant theologians and evangelists incorporated the OT and aimed at assimilation. Non-Christian as well as Christian intellectuals in the New Culture period and its aftermath appropriated the OT and highlighted goals of utilization that were meant to remedy existing deficiencies.

Also, the liberal theology of Christianity became a dominant part of the picture because of its optimistic vision of human nature and a heavenly kingdom on earth. The compatibility and balance between these different viewpoints provided fertile ground for cross-cultural communication as did the transposition of the OT into the Chinese context by means of OT reading and interpretation in modern China. The introduction of the OT provides another example of the Chinese tendency to be inclusive rather than exclusive. More research is needed to substantiate this idea. It is especially relevant today to understand such work with a revived interest in the OT among the Chinese people. Not only is the reading of the OT becoming increasingly popular, the encounter between China and the world is unrivaled in history.

Bibliography

Adams, Marie. "Renshi shengjing de jizhong fangfa" (Some Ways to Know the Bible). Translated and edited by Pan Yumei. *Zijing* (The Amethyst) 7.2 (December 1934) 273–78. 党美瑞："认识圣经的几种方法"，潘玉梅译，《紫晶》

Adler, Joseph. "Zhou Dunyi: The Metaphysics and Practice of Sagehood." In William Theodore de Bary and Irene Bloom, eds. *Sources of Chinese Tradition*. Vol. 1. 2nd ed. New York: Columbia University Press, 1999.

Ai, Silan. "Xinyue yu jiuyue" (The NT and the OT). Translated by Zhang Xisan. *Shengming* (Life) 3.6 (March 1923) 1–11. 艾思兰："新约与旧约"，张锡三译，《生命》

Allen, Young John. "Wenxue xinguo ce xu" (A Preface to *Literature Helps China*). *Wanguo gongbao* 25 (Globe Magazine) (May 1896) 3b–6a. 林乐知："文学兴国策序"，《万国公报》

———. *Zhongxi guanxi luelun* (On Sino-Western Relationships). Shanghai: Gezhi Shuyuan, 1876. 林乐知：《中西关系略论》

Álvarez, Román, and M. Carmen-África Vidal, eds. *Translation, Power, Subversion*. Clevedon, UK: Multilingual Matters, 1996.

Ashmore, William. "Why We Should Study the Old Testament." *The Chinese Recorder* 23 (June 1892), edited by James Cha Shih-chieh, 249–55. Taipei: National Taiwan University Press, 2011.

Bakeman, P. R. "Chekiang Summer Preachers' Institute." *CR* 43 (October 1912) 581–83.

Baldwin, C. C. "Union Standard Version of the Bible in Chinese." *CR* 11 (November-December 1880) 465–74.

Ban, Gu. *Hanshu* (A Historical Account of the Han Dynasty). Beijing: Zhonghua Shuju, 1962. 班固：《汉书》

Bangu yongren. "Qing meiguo linmushi xudeng shenjing tiwen shu" (A Letter Requesting the American Pastor Allen to Publish the Other Prize Essays on the Bible). *Jiaohui xinbao* (Church News) 3 (November 12, 1870) 52a–b. 半瞽庸人："请美国林牧师续登圣经题文书"，《教会新报》

Barton, George A. *Yiselie de zongjiao* (The Religion of Israel). New York: Macmillan, 1918.

———. "Yiselie de zongjiao-shenmingji yu yelimi" (The Religion of Israel: The Books of Deuteronomy and Jeremiah). Translated by Li Rongfang. *SM* 2.3 (October 1921) 1–6. 巴尔腾："以色列的宗教-申命记与耶利米"，李荣芳译，《生命》

Bays, Daniel H. "Christian Tracts: The Two Friends." In *Christianity in China: Early Protestant Missionary Writings*, edited by Suzanne Wilson Barnett and John King Fairbank, 19–34. Cambridge: Department of History/Council on East Asian Studies, Harvard University, 1985.

———. *A New History of Christianity in China*. Blackwell Guides to Global Christianity. Malden, MA: Wiley-Blackwell, 2012.

B., C. C. (surname unknown) "Review of *The Beginnings of History According to the Bible and the Traditions of Oriental Peoples from the Creation of Man to the Deluge* by Francois Lenormant." *CR* 14 (March–April 1883) 152–62.

———. "Review of *Youtai dili zeyao*" (An Essential Geography of Judea). *CR* 14 (March–April 1883) 152–62. 评《犹太地理择要》

"The Bible: Its Adaptation to the Moral Condition of Man; with Remarks on the Qualifications of Translators and the Style Most Proper for a Version of the Scriptures in Chinese." *CRP* 4.7 (November 1835) 297–305.

"Bible Study Curricula in Primary School." *CR* 47 (May 1916) 308–12.

Bohr, P. Richard. "Liang Fa's Quest for Moral Power." In *Christianity in China: Early Protestant Missionary Writings*, edited by Suzanne Wilson Barnett and John King Fairbank, 35–46. Cambridge: Department of History/Council on East Asian Studies, Harvard University, 1985.

"Book Notices." *Harvard Theological Review* 53.6 (1919) 653.

Butcher, Dean. "The Bible in Its Missionary Aspect." *CR* 9 (July–August 1878) 295–99.

Buwang. "Kongyou xingyin wangru yisao" (See that No One Is Sexually Immoral or Absurd Like Esau). *WGGB* 7 (February 1878) 369b–70b. 补网："恐有行淫妄如以扫"，《万国公报》

Cai, Hongzhang. "Quandu shengjing wen" (Exhorting People to Read the Bible). *JHXB* 6 (July 18, 1874) 310b–11b. 蔡鸿璋："劝读圣经文"，《教会新报》

Cai, Yuanpei. "Fu wujingheng han" (A Reply to Wu Jingheng's Correspondence). First published in 1910. In *Caiyuanpei quanji* (Complete Collection of the Works by Cai Yuanpei), edited by Gao Pingshu, 110–11. Beijing: Zhonghua Shuju, 1984. 蔡元培："复吴敬恒函"，《蔡元培全集》

———. "Jianming zhexue gangyao" (A Concise Outline of Philosophy). In *CYPQJ*, edited by Gao Pingshu, 392–462. Beijing: Zhonghua Shuju, 1984. 蔡元培："简明哲学纲要"，《蔡元培全集》，高平叔编

———. "Meiyu dai zongjiao" (Aesthetic Education to Replace Religion). First published in 1932. In *CYPMYLJ*, edited by Gao Pingshu, 274–76. Changsha: Hunan Education, 1987. 蔡元培："美育代宗教"，《蔡元培美育论集》

———. "Yi meiyu dai zongjiao" (Replacing Religion with Aesthetic Education). First published in 1930. In *Caiyuanpei meiyu lunji* (Cai Yuanpei's Works on Aesthetic Education), edited by Gao Pingshu, 206–7. Changsha: Hunan Education, 1987. 蔡元培："以美育代宗教"，《蔡元培美育论集》

———. "Yi meiyu dai zongjiao shuo" (About Replacing Religion with Aesthetic Education). First published in 1917. In *CYPMYLJ*, edited by Gao Pingshu, 43–47. Changsha: Hunan Education, 1987. 蔡元培："以美育代宗教说"，《蔡元培美育论集》，高平叔编

———. "Zai jiujinshan zhongguo guomindang zhaodaihuishang de yanshuoci" (Speech at the Reception Held by the Guomindang in San Francisco). First published in 1921. In *CYPQJ*, edited by Gao Pingshu, 60–62. Beijing: Zhonghua Shuju, 1984. 蔡元培："在旧金山中国国民党招待会上的演说辞"，《蔡元培全集》

———. "Zai xinjiaoziyou hui zhi yanshuo" (Speech at the Religious Freedom Conference). First published in 1917. In *Caiyuanpei xiansheng quanji* (Complete Works by Mr. Cai Yuanpei), edited by Sun Changwei, 723–25. Taipei: Commercial, 1968. 蔡元培："在信教自由会之演说"，《蔡元培先生全集》孙常炜编

———. "Zhexue dagang" (Outline of Philosophy). First published in 1915. In *CYPXSQJ*, edited by Sun Changwei, 103-43. Taipei: Commercial, 1968. 蔡元培："哲学大纲",《蔡元培先生全集》

———. "Zhexue yu kexue" (Philosophy and Science). First published in 1919. In *CYPQJ*, edited by Gao Pingshu, 249-54. Beijing: Zhonghua Shuju, 1984. 蔡元培："哲学与科学",《蔡元培全集》

———. "Zhongguo de wenyi zhongxin" (Chinese Renaissance). First published in 1923. In *CYPXSQJ*, edited by Sun Changwei, 809-15. Taipei: Commercial, 1968. 蔡元培："中国的文艺中兴",《蔡元培先生全集》

Camps, Arnulf. "Father Gabriele M. Allegra, O. F. M. (1907-1976) and the *Studium Biblicum Franciscanum*: The First Complete Chinese Catholic Translation of the Bible." In *Bible in Modern China: The Literary and Intellectual Impact*, edited by Irene Eber et al., 55-76. Monumenta Serica Monograph Series 43. Sankt Augustin: Monumenta Serica Institute, 1999.

Cao, Jian. "The Chinese Mandarin Bible: Exegesis and Bible Translating." *The Bible Translator* 57 (July 2006) 122-38.

Cao, Xinming. "Jinü-lahe" (A Prostitute-Rahab). *Zhenguang* (True Light) 36.6 (June 1936) 44-46. 曹新铭,"妓女一喇合",《真光》

———. "Pila he Xipa" (Bilhah and Zilpah). *ZG* 36.4 (April 1936) 40-41. 曹新铭："辟拉和悉帕",《真光》

Cary-Elwes, Columba. *China and the Cross: A Survey of Missionary History*. New York: Kenneday, 1957.

Chen, Chi-yun. "Liang Ch'i-ch'ao's 'Missionary Education': A Case Study of Missionary Influence on the Reformers." *Papers on China* 16. Cambridge: Harvard University, 1962.

Chen, Duxiu. "Jidujiao yu zhongguoren" (Christianity and the Chinese). *Xin qingnian* (New Youth) 7.3 (February 1, 1920) 15-22. 陈独秀："基督教与中国人",《新青年》

Chen, Shenxiu. "Shangdi shijie shi" (A Poem of God's Ten Commandments). *JHXB* 2 (December 18, 1869) 79b-80a. 陈慎修："上帝十诫诗",《教会新报》

Chen, Xuming. "She" (The Serpent). *ZG* 36.7 (July 1936) 62. 陈旭明："蛇",《真光》

Cheng, Zhiyi. "Yanjing yizhu" (An Aid to Bible Study). *Zhenli yu shengming* (Truth and Life) 4.14 (March 1930) 24-27. 诚质怡："研经一助",《真理与生命》

———. "Yanjiu shengjing de fangfa" (The Method of Studying the Bible). *ZLYSM* 6.1 (October 1931) 50-59. 诚质怡："研究圣经的方法",《真理与生命》

Ch'eng, Ching-i, T. T. Lew, Hu Shih and Y. Y. Tau. *China Today through Chinese Eyes*. London: Student Christian Movement, 1922.

China Mission Year Book. Shanghai: Christian Literature Society for China, 1923.

"Chinese Version of the Holy Scriptures: Need Revision; List of Words Claiming Particular Attention; Proposed Meetings of Delegates." *CRP* 15.2 (February 1846) 108-10.

"Chinese Version of the Bible: the Manuscript in the British Museum; One Version Undertaken in Bengel, and Another in China; with Brief Notices of the Means and Measures Employed to Publish the Scriptures in Chinese Previous to A. D. 1830." *CRP* 4.6 (October 1835) 249-61.

Chiping sou. "Jinchang bian" (On Prohibition of Prostitutes). *Shen bao* 35 (Shanghai Daily) (March 29, 1872) 1-2. 持平叟："禁娼辩",《申报》

———. "Nü tanci xiaozhi" (A Brief Biographical Note of a Female Storyteller). *SB* 53 (April 19, 1872) 2-3. 持平叟："女弹词小志",《申报》

"Christian Literature in Chinese: A Symposium." *CR* 49 (July 1918) 450–55.

"Christian Renaissance in China: Statement of Aims of the Peking Apologetic Group." Translated by T. C. Chao (Zhao Zichen). *CR* 51 (September 1920) 636–39.

"Christianity and Government Students—A Symposium." *CR* 50 (August 1920) 537–46.

Cohen, A., ed. *The Soncino Chumash—The Five Books of Moses with Haphtaroth: Hebrew Text and English Translation with an Exposition Based on the Classical Jewish Commentaries.* London: Soncino, 1956.

Cohen, Paul A. *China and Christianity: The Missionary Movement and the Growth of Chinese Anti-foreignness, 1860–1870.* Cambridge: Harvard University Press, 1963.

———. "Littoral and Hinterland in Nineteenth Century China: The 'Christian' Reformers." In *The Missionary Enterprise in China and America*, edited by John K. Fairbank, 197–225. Cambridge: Harvard University Press, 1974.

Collins, W. H. "On Some Early Scriptural Traditions" *CR* 9 (March–April 1878) 100–108.

"A Common Version of the Scripture," in "Editor's Corner." *CR* 9 (March–April 1878) 151.

Confucius. *The Analects.* Translated by D. C. Lau. 2nd ed. Hong Kong: The Chinese University Press, 1992.

———. *Ta Hsüeh and Chung Yung* (The Highest Order of Cultivation and On the Practice of the Mean). Translated by Andrew Plaks. Chapter 42: "Liji" (The Book of Rites). London: Penguin, 2003.

Connery, Christopher Leigh. "*Sao, Fu,* Parallel Prose, and Related Genres." In *The Columbia History of Chinese Literature*, edited by Victor H. Mair, 223–47. New York: Columbia University Press, 2010.

Cornaby, Arthur. "Four Subjects for the Revisers." *CR* 30 (June 1899) 273–78.

Crawford, T. P. "The Ancient Dynasties of Berosus and China Compared with Those of Genesis." *CR* 11 (November–December 1880) 411–29.

Dampier, W. C. *A History of Science and Its Relations with Philosophy and Religion.* Cambridge: Cambridge University Press, 1971.

de Bary, William Theodore, and Irene Bloom, eds. *Sources of Chinese Tradition.* 2nd ed. New York: Columbia University Press, 1999.

D'Elia, Pasquale M. *The Catholic Missions in China: A Short Sketch of the Catholic Church in China from the Earliest Records to Our Own Days.* Shanghai: Commercial, 1941.

D., H. D. (surname unknown) "Review of *Chuangshiji shiyi*" (Commentary on Genesis) by W. S. Moule, *CR* 44 (April 1913) 245–46. 评《创世记释义》

D., J. (surname unknown) "Review of the 1911 Report of the China Agency of British and Foreign Bible Society." *CR* 43 (August 1912) 495.

Dong, Jiangyang. "Jidujiao jiyaopai de xingcheng yu fenlie" (The Formation and Split of Christian Fundamentalism). *Zongjiao* (Religion) (May 2002) 70–78. 董江阳："基督教基要派的形成与分裂",《宗教》

Drake, Fred W. *China Charts the World: Hsu Chi-yü and His Geography of 1848.* Cambridge: Harvard University Press, 1975.

———. "Protestant Geography in China: E.C. Bridgman's Portrayal of the West." In *Christianity in China: Early Protestant Missionary Writings*, edited by Suzanne Wilson Barnett and John King Fairbank, 89–106. Cambridge: Harvard University Press, 1985.

DuBose, Hampden C. "A Letter from Soochow on June 10, 1898, on the Subject 'One Bible or Three' to the *CR* editorial." *CR* 29 (July 1898) 351–52.

Duiker, William J. *Ts'ai Yüan-p'ei: Educator of Modern China.* University Park: Pennsylvania State University Press, 1977.

Eber, Irene. "The Interminable Term Question." In *Bible in Modern China: The Literary and Intellectual Impact*, edited by Irene Eber, et al., 136–47. Monumenta Serica Monograph Series 43. Sankt Augustin: Monumenta Serica Institute, 1999.

———. *The Jewish Bishop and the Chinese Bible: S. I. J. Schereschewsky (1831–1906)*. Studies in Christian Mission 22. Leiden: Brill, 1999.

———. "Introduction." In *Bible in Modern China: The Literary and Intellectual Impact*, edited by Irene Eber, et al., 13–26. Monumenta Serica Monograph Series 43. Sankt Augustin: Monumenta Serica Institute, 1999.

———. "Reception of Lu Xun in Europe and America." In *Lu Xun and His Legacy*, edited by Leo Ou-fan Lee, 258–65. Berkeley: University of California Press, 1985.

———. "Translation Literature in Modern China: The Yiddish Author and His Tale." *Journal of Asian and African Studies* 8.3 (1972) 291–314.

———. *Voices from Afar: Modern Chinese Writers on Oppressed Peoples and Their Literature*. Ann Arbor: Center for Chinese Studies, University of Michigan, 1980.

Eber, Irene, et al., eds. *Bible in Modern China: The Literary and Intellectual Impact*. Monumenta Serica Monograph Series 43. Sankt Augustin: Monumenta Serica Institute, 1999.

"Editorial." *CR* 47 (May 1916) 283–89.

"Editorial." *CR* 50 (May 1919) 288–90.

"Editorial Comment." *CR* 37 (May 1906) 278–79.

Eliade, Mircea, ed. *The Encyclopedia of Religion*. New York: Macmillan, 1987.

"Eren jiongqu youtairen" (Russians Expel Jews). *Zhixin bao* (The Reformer China) 91 (June 28, 1899) 10b–11a. "俄人窘驱犹太人", 《知新报》

Espey, J. M. "Review of *Ridui guren*" ("Daily Readings in the Lives of the Great Men of Israel"—according to *The Chinese Recorder*). *CR* 41 (September 1910) 620–21.

Evans, R. K. "The Standard of Theological Education." *CR* 45 (June 1914) 371–76.

Fairbank, John King. "Introduction: The Many Faces of Protestant Missions in China and the United States." In *The Missionary Enterprise in China and America*, edited by John King Fairbank, 1–19. Cambridge: Harvard University Press, 1974.

———. "Introduction: The Place of Protestant Writings in China's Cultural History." In *Christianity in China: Early Protestant Missionary Writings*, edited by Suzanne Wilson Barnett and John King Fairbank, 1–13. Cambridge: Harvard University Press, 1985.

Feng, Youlan. *Rensheng zhexue* (The Philosophy of Life). Chapter 7: "Jinbupai—dikaer, peigen, feixitui " (Progressivists—Decartes, Bacon, Fichte). Shanghai: Commercial, 1926. 冯友兰：《人生哲学》

Fokkema, Douwe. "Lu Xun: the Impact of Russian Literature." In *Modern Chinese Literature in the May Fourth Era*, edited by Merle Goldman, 89–101. Cambridge: Harvard University Press, 1977.

Gálik, Marián. *Influence, Translation and Parallels: Selected Studies on the Bible in China*. Collectanea serica. Sankt Augustin: Monumenta Serica Institute, 2004.

Gadamer, Hans-Georg. *Truth and Method*. New York: Continuum, 1997.

Gamsa, Mark. *The Chinese Translation of Russian Literature: Three Studies*. Leiden: Brill, 2008.

Garnier, Albert J. *Chinese Versions of the Bible*. Shanghai: Christian Literature Society, 1934.

Garritt, J. C. "Bible Commentaries in Chinese." *CR* 40 (December 1909) 673–75.

Goodrich, Chauncey. "A Translation of the Bible for Three Hundred Million: An Address before the Missionary Conference at Battle Creek, Mich., January 5th, 1912." *CR* 43 (October 1912) 587–91.

———. "The Union Mandarin Bible." *CR* 49 (August 1918) 552–54.

Goodspeed, E. J. *Shengjing de yanjiu* (Biblical Studies). Translated by Ma Honggang. Shanghai: Qingnian Xiehui Shuju, 1941. 古兹匹德：《圣经的研究》，马鸿纲译

Graves, Rosswell Hobart. *Youtai dili zeyao* (Essence of Jewish Geography). Translated and narrated by Chen Juemin. In *Xishi tongzhi*, edited by Yuan Zonglian and Yan Zhiqing. Shanghai: Wenshengtang, 1902.《犹太地理择要》，陈觉民译述；《西学通志》，袁宗濂和晏志清编

Graves, R. H. "Studies on Biblical Animals and Plants." *CR* 10 (March–April 1879) 124–28; *CR* 14 (November–December 1883) 479–85; *CR* 22 (April 1891) 157–61; *CR* 22 (June 1891) 253–55; and *CR* 23 (April 1892) 158–62.

Gulick, John. "The Theory of Evolution in Some of its Relations to Christian Theology." *CR* 16 (1885) 295–97.

Guo, Bendao. "Kangde zhi shangdi cunzai linghun bumie ji yizhi ziyou lun" (Kant's Ideas about the Reality of God, Conservation of Human Soul, and Free Will). *ZLYSM* 7.1 (October 1932) 26–32. 郭本道："康德之上帝存在灵魂不灭及意志自由论"，《真理与生命》

———. "Qingchen" (Early Morning). *ZLYSM* 4.3 (April 1929) 23–25. 郭本道："清晨"，《真理与生命》

Guo, Moruo. *Xianqin tiandaoguan zhi jinzhan* (The Evolution of the Notion of *tian* and *dao* in the Pre-Qin Era). Beijing: Renmin Chubanshe, 1982. 郭沫若：《先秦天道观之进展》

Guo, Xiaoxia. *Wusi nüxing zuojia he shengjing* (The Bible and Women Writers During the May Fourth Period). Beijing: Zhongguo Shehui Kexue Chubanshe, 2013. 郭晓霞：《五四女作家和圣经》

Guo, Zhanbo. "Caiyuanpei de shidai he tade sixiang" (Cai Yuanpei's Times and His Thoughts). First published in 1965. In *CYPXSQJ*, edited by Sun Changwei, 1604–50. Taipei: Commercial, 1968. 郭湛波："蔡元培的时代和他的思想"，《蔡元培先生全集》

Gützlaff, Karl Friedrich A. "Literary Notice." *Chinese Repository* 2.4 (August 1833) 186–87.

———. *Moxi yanxing quanzhuan* (Complete Biography of Moses' Words and Action). Singapore: Jianxia Shuyuan, 1836. 爱汉者：《摩西言行全传》

———. "Remarks on the History of China." *CRP* 2.3 (July 1833) 119–27.

———. *Shengshu liezu quanzhuan* (Complete Biographies of the Patriarchs in the Holy Bible). Singapore: Jianxia Shuyuan, 1838. 爱汉者：《圣书列祖全传》

Haishang shanren. "Wei er yan wo wei shui" (Who Do You Say that I Am?). *JHXB* 3 (November 12, 1870) 52b–53b. 海上山人："惟尔言我为谁"，《教会新报》

Hanan, Patrick. "The Technique of Lu Xun's Fiction." *Harvard Journal of Asiatic Studies* 34 (1974) 53–96.

He, Yuquan. "Shengshu lun qier" (On the Bible II). *WGGB* 10 (June 1879) 553a–54a. 何玉泉："圣书论其二"，《万国公报》

Hu, Shi. *Hushi koushu zizhuan* (Oral Autobiography of Hu Shi). Edited by Tang Degang. Beijing: Wenhua, 1989. 胡适：《胡适口述自传》，唐德刚编

———. "Shuo ru" (About the Ru). In *Hushi wencun* (Selected Works by Hu Shi), vol. 4, edited by Hu Shi, 1–83. Taipei: Yuandong Tushu Gongsi, 1953. 胡适："说儒"，《胡适文存》，胡适编

———. "Tantan shijing" (Speaking of the *Book of Songs*). First published in 1930. In *Hushi wencun* (Selected Works by Hu Shi), vol. 4, edited by Hu Shi, 556–66. Taipei: Yuandong Tushu Gongsi, 1953. 胡适:"谈谈诗经",《胡适文存》, 胡适编

———. *Zhongguo zhexue shi* (History of Chinese Philosophy). Beijing: Beijing University, 1919. 胡适:《中国哲学史》

Hu, Weiqing. "Jindai laihua chuanjiaoshi de kexueguan" (Attitudes Toward Science among the Missionaries in Modern China). In *Jidujiao yu zhongguo wenhua congkan* 3 (A Series on Christianity and Chinese Culture), edited by Zhang Kaiyuan and Ma Min, 217–58. Wuhan: Hubei Jiaoyu Chubanshe, 2000. 胡卫清:"近代来华传教士的科学观",《基督教与中国文化丛刊》3, 章开沅和马敏编

Huang, Ciyuan. "Juben xuyan" (A Preface to the Drama) and "Huo zhong fu—yuese gushi" (Fortune Out of Misfortune—the Story of Joseph). *Xiwang yuekan* (Christian Hope) 6.8 (August 1929) 16–20. 黄次元:"剧本绪言"和"祸中福——约瑟故事",《希望月刊》

Huang, Pinsan. "Daoying leibian xiaolu" (Brief Measuring by the Standards of the *Dao*). *WGGB* 8 (June 1878) 575b–78a. 黄品三:"道影类编小录",《万国公报》

Huang, Sungk'ang. *Lu Hsün and the New Culture Movement of Modern China*. Amsterdam: Djambatan, 1957.

Huang, Zunxian. *Ribenguo zhi* (Introduction to Japan). First published between 1890 and 1895. Tianjin: Tianjin Renmin Chubanshe, 2005. 黄遵宪:《日本国志》

Hudson, W. H. "The Bible as Literature." In *Peake's Commentary on the Bible*, edited by Arthur Samuel Peake, 18–25. London: T. C. & E. C. Jack, 1920.

———. "Shengjing zhi wenxue de yanjiu" (A Literary Study of the Bible). *Xiaoshuo yuebao congkan* (Selected Writings of *Short Story Monthly*) 25 (April 1925) 20–65, translated by Tang Chengbo and Ye Qifang from Hudson's "The Bible as Literature." Originally published in *Xiaoshuo yuebao* (*Short Story Monthly*) 13.10 (1922) 1–17. 汤澄波和叶启芳合译:"圣经之文学的研究",《小说月报丛刊》

Hutchison, William R. "Modernism and Missions: The Liberal Search for an Exportable Christianity, 1875–1935." In *The Missionary Enterprise in China and America*, edited by John K. Fairbank, 111–12. Cambridge: Harvard University Press, 1974.

Hwang, Mei-shu. "Allusions." In *An Encyclopedia of Translation*, edited by Chan Sin-wai and David Pollard, 14–21. Hong Kong: The Chinese University of Hong Kong Press, 1995.

"Introduction." In *China Centenary Missionary Conference Records*, 519–21. New York: American Tract Society, 1907.

Israel, John. *Student Nationalism in China: 1927–1937*. Stanford: Stanford University Press, 1966.

J., A. E. (surname unknown). "Review of *Short Stories for Chinese Students*, by J. H. McNair." *CR* 50 (August 1919) 569–70.

James, Fleming. *Jiuyue renwu zhi* (Personalities of the OT). Translated by Li Rongfang. Shanghai: Qingnian Xiehui Shuju, 1949. 詹辅民:《旧约人物志》, 李荣芳译

Jia, Yuming. "Yage" (The "Song of Songs"). *Lingguang* (Spiritual Light) 7.2 (August 1928) n.p. 贾玉铭:"雅歌",《灵光》

Jian, Youwen. "Shengjing lide qingju—jiuyue suoluomen yage zhi yanjiu" (A Love Drama in the Bible—a Study of Solomon's "Song of Songs" in the OT). *ZLYSM* 1.9 (October 15, 1926) 265–69. 简又文:"圣经里的情剧——旧约所罗门雅歌之研究",《真理与生命》

Jiang, Lianyuan. "He hankou jiaoyou shijie shi yi yuanyun" (Poems on the Ten Commandments as a Response to Those Composed by the Convert from Hankou). *WGGB* 13 (May 28, 1881) 369b. Continued in *WGGB* 13 (June 1881) 387b and *WGGB* 13 (July 1881) 396b. 蒋连元:"和汉口教友十诫诗依原韵",《万国公报》

Jiang, Yizhen. "Rensheng" (Human Voice). *ZLYSM* 7.2 (November 1932) 58–59. 蒋翼振:"人声",《真理与生命》

———. "Xiandai de lingxiu you ci jianxin ma" (Do Modern Chinese Leaders Have So Strong a Faith?). *ZJ* 7.1 (September 1934) 10–17. 蒋翼振:"现代的领袖有此坚信吗",《紫晶》

———. "Yu youren lun jidujiao wenzi shiye shu" (A Letter to a Friend on the Issue of Christian Literature). *ZLYSM* 7.1 (October 1932) 57–60. 蒋翼振:"与友人论基督教文字事业书",《真理与生命》

Jieyu zi. "Yesu jiaotiao yi" (Some Comments on Jesus' Doctrines). *JHXB* 2 (May 20, 1870) 201b–2a. 劫余子:"耶稣教条议",《教会新报》

J., J. (surname unknown) "Review of *Shipian shiyi*" (A Commentary on the Book of Psalms). *CR* 33 (July 1902) 361. 《诗篇释意》

Juemeng jushi. "Shangdi bushi qi yu li"(God is Neither Matter nor Principle). *WGGB* 13 (September 1880) 49b–50a. 觉梦居士:"上帝不是气与理",《万国公报》

Juvenis. "One Bible for China." *CR* 11 (May–June 1880) 222–25.

Kang, Youwei. *Changxing xueji* (Lecturing Notes in Changxing). Guangzhou: Wenge, 1896. 康有为:《长兴学记》

———. "Da zhongguoren si" (A Fourth Message to the Chinese). First published in 1915. In *Wanmu caotang yigao waibian-shang* (Additional Manuscripts of Wanmu Grass Hall), vol. 1, edited by Jiang Guilin, 103–6. Taipei: Chengwen Chubanshe, 1978. 康有为:"答中国人四",《万木草堂遗稿》

———. "Fu Kangchangru xiaolian" (A Reply to Kang Changru). First published around 1897. In *WMCYWB-S*, vol. 2, edited by Jiang Guilin, 831–34. Taipei: Chengwen Chubanshe, 1978. 康有为:"复康长孺孝廉",《万木草堂遗稿外编》(下)

———. "Kangnanhai zibian nianpu" (Chronological Biography of Kang Youwei). In *Wuxu bianfa* (The 1898 Reformation Movement), vol. 4, edited by Jian Bozan, et al., 107–69. Shanghai: Shenzhou Guoguangshe, 1953. 康有为:"康南海自编年谱",《戊戌变法》,翦伯赞等编

———. Untitled Essay. In *WMCYWB-S*, vol. 1, edited by Jiang Guilin, 343–47. Taipei: Chengwen Chubanshe, 1978. 《万木草堂遗稿外编》(上)

———. "Yelusaleng riwu nanfu kucheng gan fu bai yi yun" (Thoughts on Jews Wailing under the Wall at Noon in Jerusalem). *Buren zazhi* 1 (February 20, 1913) 9–11. 康有为:"耶路撒冷日午男妇哭城感赋百一韵",《不忍杂志》

———. "Zhi Zhurongsheng shu" (A Letter to Zhu Rongsheng). First published in 1891. In *Wanmu caotang yigao waibian-xia* (Supplementary Collection of Works by Kang Youwei in the Wanmu Cottage), vol. 2, edited by Jiang Guilin, 805–11. Taipei: Chengwen Chubanshe, 1978. 康有为:"致朱蓉生书",《万木草堂遗稿外编》(下),蒋贵麟编

Keedy, John L. "Movement toward Graded Sunday Schools." *The Biblical World* 24.1 (July 1904) 42–43.

Kinkley, J. C. *The Odyssey of Shen Congwen*. Stanford: Stanford University Press, 1987.

Kirk, Harris E. *A Man of Property*. New York: Harper, 1935.

Knowlton, M. J. "Bible Distribution in China, as a Means of Evangelization." *CR* 2 (January 1870) 209–11.

Kuriyagawa, Hakuson. "Kumen de xiangzheng" (The Symbol of Depression). Translated by Lu Xun. In *Luxun quanji* (Complete Works of Lu Xun), vol. 13, 95–104. Beijing: Renmin Wenxue Chubanshe, 1973. 厨川白村："苦闷的象征"，《鲁迅全集》

Kwok, D. W. Y. (Guo Yingyi). *Zhongguo xiandai sixiang zhong de wei kexue zhuyi, 1900–1950* (Scientism in Modern Chinese Thought, 1900–1950). Translated by Lei Yi. Nanjing: Jiangsu Renmin Chubanshe, 1989. 郭颖颐：《中国现代思想中的唯科学主义：1900–1950》，雷颐译

Lam, Wing Hung. "The Emergence of a Protestant Christian Apologetics in the Chinese Church during the Anti-Christian Movement in the 1920s." PhD diss., Princeton Theological Seminary, 1978.

———. *Zhonghua shenxue wushi nian 1900–1949* (Fifty Years of Chinese Theology 1900–1949). Hong Kong: China Graduate School of Theology, 1998. 林荣洪：《中华神学五十年1900–1949》

Latourette, Kenneth S. *A History of Christian Missions in China*. London: Society for Promoting Christian Knowledge, 1929.

Lay, George T. *The Chinese As They Are*. Albany: George Jones, 1843.

Lee, Leo Ou-fan. "Tradition and Modernity in the Writings of Lu Xun." In *Lu Xun and His Legacy*, edited by L. Lee, 3–31. Berkeley: University of California Press, 1985.

———. *Voices from the Iron House: A Study of Lu Xun*. Bloomington: Indiana University Press, 1987.

Lee, Mei-Yen. "An 'Aesthetic Education': The Role of 'Sentiments' in the Transition from Traditional Confucianism to Modern Aesthetics." *IIAS Newsletter* 47 (Spring 2008) 19–22.

Leonard, Jane Kate. "W. H. Medhurst: Rewriting the Missionary Message." In *Christianity in China: Early Protestant Missionary Writings*, edited by Suzanne Wilson Barnett and John King Fairbank, 50–53. Cambridge: Harvard University Press, 1985.

Levenson, Joseph R. *Liang Ch'i-ch'ao and the Mind of Modern China*. Cambridge: Harvard University Press, 1953.

Lew, T. T (Liu Tingfang). "Making the Christian Church in China Indigenous." *CR* 53 (May 1922) 297–306.

Li, Qianli. "Eryue renwu shi (you xu)" (Poems about Biblical Persons, with a Preface). *ZG* 27.9 (1928) 74–75. 李千里："二约人物诗（有序）"，《真光》

Li, Rongfang. *Amosi zhushi* (A Commentary on Amos). Shanghai: Christian Literature Society, 1933. 李荣芳：《阿摩司注释》

———. "Hongshui de shexun" (The Social Ethics of the Flood). *ZLYSM* 10.5 (October 1936) 281–87. 李荣芳："洪水的社训"，《真理与生命》

———. "Jiuyue daoyan" (Introduction to the OT). *SM* 6 (January 1921) 1–13. 李荣芳："旧约导言"，《生命》

———. "Jiuyue li de guoji guannian" (International Ideas in the OT). *ZLYSM* 2.16 (1927) 22. 李荣芳："旧约里的国际观念"，《真理与生命》

———. "Kouyin bianluan" (God Confused the Languages). *ZLYSM* 10.8 (January 1937) 489–96. 李荣芳："口音变乱"，《真理与生命》

———. "Minzu tongxibiao" (The Table of Nations). *ZLYSM* 10.7 (December 1936) 429–35. 李荣芳："民族统系表"，《真理与生命》

———. "Moxi de zongjiao" (The Religion of Moses). *ZLYSM* 8.8 (January 1935) 441–45. 李荣芳："摩西的宗教"，《真理与生命》

———. "Xu yi." (Preface I to "Aige," Li Rongfang's Chinese translation of Lamentations). *ZLYSM* 5.8 (June 1931) 48-49. For Li's serialized translation, see *ZLYSM* 4.12 (May 1930) 44-45; *ZLYSM* 5.1 (November 1930) 68-70; *ZLYSM* 5.2 (December 1930) 48-50; and *ZLYSM* 5.3 (January 1931) 67-69; or *Aige*. Translated by Li Rongfang. Beiping: Yenching University, 1931. 李荣芳：《哀歌》"序一"，《真理与生命》；《哀歌》，李荣芳译

———. "Rende laiyuan yu tade peiou" (The Origin of Man and his Wife). *ZLYSM* 9.1 (March 1935) 473-80. 李荣芳："人的来源与他的配偶"，《真理与生命》

———. "Shengjing de xiaoyong" (The Usefulness of the Bible). *ZLYSM* 8.2 (April 1934) 82-91. 李荣芳："圣经的效用"，《真理与生命》

———. "Shengjing gaiwei xuanke hou zai jidujiao daxue kecheng zhong yingyou hezhong diwei" (What is the Position of the Bible After it is Reduced to a Selected Course in Christian Colleges?). *ZLYSM* 2.3 (February 15, 1927) 60-63. 李荣芳："圣经改为选课后在基督教大学课程中应有何种地位"，《真理与生命》

———. *Xiandai qingnian jiuyue bidu* (OT Selections for Present-day Youth). Shanghai: Zhonghua Jidujiao Nüqingnianhui Quanguo Xiehui, 1933. 李荣芳：《现代青年旧约必读》

———. "Xibolai zaonian gushi zhong de shehuixun" (Social Ethics in Some Early Hebrew Stories). *ZLYSM* 5.1 (November 1930) 34-42. 李荣芳："希伯来早年故事中的社会训"，《真理与生命》

———. "Xiongfan gaiyin" (The Murderer Cain). *ZLYSM* 10.2 (April 1936) 75-82. 李荣芳："凶犯该隐"，《真理与生命》

———. "Yesu yu jidu" (Jesus and Christ). *SM* 6.3 (December 1925) 1-12. 李荣芳："耶稣与基督"，《生命》

———. "Yiselie de xianzhi-amosi" (The Israel Prophet Amos). *SM* 6.1 (October 1925) 39-46. 李荣芳："以色列的先知——阿摩司"，《生命》

———. "Zongjiao shenghuo de fazhan" (The Development of Religious Life). *ZJ* 7.2 (December 1934) 166-73. 李荣芳："宗教生活的发展"，《紫晶》

———. "Zuide laiyuan yu xiaoguo" (The Origin and Effect of Sin). *ZLYSM* 10.1 (March 1936) 7-14. 李荣芳："罪的来源与效果"，《真理与生命》

Liang, Junmo. "Rensheng yiyi yu yejiao shengjing" (The Meaning of Human Life and the Bible of Christianity). *Daguang bao* (Great Light) 2 (December 25, 1922) 1-8. 梁均默："人生意义与耶教圣经"，《大光报》

Liang, Qichao. "Dili yu niandai" (Geography and the Age). First published in 1922. In *Yinbing shi heji-zhuanji* (Collected Works and Essays of the Ice Drinker's Studio-Works), by Liang Qichao, vol. 12, no. 47, 1-10. Shanghai: Zhonghua Shuju, 1936. 梁启超："地理与年代"，《饮冰室合集——专集》

———. "Guodu shidai lun" (On the Transitional Period). First published in 1901. In *Yinbing shi heji-zhuangji* (Collected Works and Essays of the Ice Drinker's Studio-Essays), by Liang Qichao, vol. 3, no. 6, 27-32. Shanghai: Zhonghua Shuju, 1936. 梁启超："过渡时代论"，《饮冰室合集——文集》

———. "Guojua sixiang bianqian yitong lun" (On Changes in Thoughts about State). First published in 1901. In *YBSHJ-WJ*, by Liang Qichao, vol. 1, no. 6, 12-22. Shanghai: Zhonghua Shuju, 1936. 梁启超："国家思想变迁异同论"，《饮冰室合集——文集》

———. "Hongshui kao" (About the Flood). Publication year unknown. In *YBSHJ-ZJ*, by Liang Qichao, vol. 12, no. 43, 1-29. Shanghai: Zhonghua Shuju, 1936. 梁启超："洪水考"，《饮冰室合集——专集》

———. "Lun bu bianfa zhi hai" (On the Harmfulness of No Reforms). First published in 1897. In *Liang qichao siwen xuan* (Collected Poems and Essays by Liang Qichao), edited by Fang Zhiqin and Liu Sifen, 6-15. Guangzhou: Guangdong Renmin Chubanshe, 1983. 梁启超："论不变法之害"，《梁启超诗文选》，方志钦和刘斯奋编

———. "Lun hequn" (On Group Cohesion). First published in 1902. In *YBSHJ-ZJ*, by Liang Qichao, vol. 3, no. 4, 77-80. Shanghai: Zhonghua Shuju, 1936. 梁启超："论合群"，《饮冰室合集——专集》

———. "Lun jinbu" (On Progress). First published in 1902. In *YBSHJ-ZJ*, by Liang Qichao, vol. 3, no. 4, 67-68. Shanghai: Zhonghua Shuju, 1936. 梁启超："论进步"，《饮冰室合集——专集》

———. *Lun Li Hongzhang* (On Li Hongzhang). First published in 1901. Taiwan: Zhonghua Shuju, 1936. 梁启超：《论李鸿章》

———. "Lun youxue" (On Children's Education). First published in 1897. In *YBSHJ-WJ*, by Liang Qichao, vol. 1, no. 1, 44-60. Shanghai: Zhonghua Shuju, 1936. 梁启超："论幼学"，《饮冰室合集——文集》

———. "Kong zi" (Confucius). First published in 1920. In *YBSZJ-ZJ*, by Liang Qichao, vol. 10, no. 36, 1-69. Shanghai: Zhonghua Shuju, 1936. 梁启超："孔子"，《饮冰室合集——专集》

———. "Mengxue bao yanyi bao hexu" (A Preface for the Enlightenment School and the Historic Romance Newspapers). First published in 1897. In *YBSHJ-WJ*, by Liang Qichao, vol. 2, no. 2, 56. Shanghai: Zhonghua Shuju, 1936. 梁启超："蒙学报演义报合序"，《饮冰室合集——文集》

———. *Qingdai xueshu gailun* (General Introduction to the Learning of Qing Dynasty). First published in 1920. In *YBSHJ-ZJ*, by Liang Qichao, vol. 8, no. 34, 235-87. Shanghai: Zhonghua Shuju, 1936. 梁启超：《清代学术概论》

———. "Rujia zhexue" (Confucian Philosophy). First published in 1927. In *YBSHJ-ZJ*, by Liang Qichao, vol. 24, no. 103, 1-102. Shanghai: Zhonghua Shuju, 1936. 梁启超："儒家哲学"，《饮冰室合集——专集》

———. "Shenshi yinshu xu" (Preface to Mr. Shen's Book on Phonetics). First published in 1896. In *YBSHJ-WJ*, by Liang Qichao, vol. 1, no. 1,[1] 56-76. Shanghai: Zhonghua Shuju, 1936. 梁启超："沈氏音书序"，《饮冰室合集——文集》

———. "Shuo xiwang" (On Hope). First published in 1903. In *YBSHJ-WJ*, by Liang Qichao, vol. 5, no. 14, 18-22. Shanghai: Zhonghua Shuju, 1936. 梁启超："说希望"，《饮冰室合集——文集》

———. "Xianqin zhengzhi sixiang shi" (A History of the Political Thought in the Pre-Qin Period). First published in 1922. In *YBSHJ-ZJ*, by Liang Qichao, vol. 13, no. 50, 1-217. Shanghai: Zhonghua Shuju, 1936.梁启超："先秦政治思想史"，《饮冰室合集——专集》

———. "Xindalu youji jielu" (Selected Records of the Journey to the New Continent). First published in 1903. In *YBSHJ-ZJ*, by Liang Qichao, vol. 5, no. 22, 1-147. Shanghai: Zhonghua Shuju, 1936. 梁启超："新大陆游记节录"，《饮冰室合集——专集》

———. "Xinhai geming zhi yiyi yu shinian shuangshijie zhi leguan" (The significance of the 1911 Revolution and an Optimistic Speech at the Tenth Anniversary). First published in 1921. In *YBSHJ-WJ*, by Liang Qichao, vol. 13, no. 37, 1-12. Shanghai:

---

1. We have replaced "ce" and "juan" with "vol." and "no." in these references.

Zhonghua Shuju, 1936. 梁启超: "辛亥革命之意义与十年双十节之乐观", 《饮冰室合集——文集》

———. "Xinmin shuo" (On New Citizens). First published in 1902. In *YBSHJ-ZJ*, by Liang Qichao, vol. 3, no. 4, 1-162. Shanghai: Zhonghua Shuju, 1936. 梁启超: "新民说", 《饮冰室合集——专集》

———. "Xin shixue" (New Historiography). First published in 1902. In *YBSHJ-WJ*, by Liang Qichao, vol. 4, no. 9, 1-32. Shanghai: Zhonghua Shuju, 1936. 梁启超: "新史学", 《饮冰室合集——文集》

———. "Xin yingguo juren kelinweier zhuan" (Biography of the British Giant Cromwell). First published in 1903. In *YBSHJ-ZJ*, by Liang Qichao, vol. 4, no. 13, 1-20. Shanghai: Zhonghua Shuju, 1936. 梁启超: "新英国巨人克林威尔传", 《饮冰室合集——专集》

———. *Xixue shumubiao* (Book List of Western Learning). Shanghai: Shiwu Baoguan, 1896. 梁启超: 《西学书目表》

———. "Zhongguo falixue fadashi lun" (History of the Development of Law Studies in China). First published in 1904. In *YBSHJ-WJ*, by Liang Qichao, vol. 5, no. 15, 41-94. Shanghai: Zhonghua Shuju, 1936. 梁启超: "中国法理学发达史论", 《饮冰室合集——文集》

———. "Zhongguo lishi yanjiufa" (Method for Research of Chinese History). First published in 1922. In *YBSHJ-ZJ*, by Liang Qichao, vol. 16, no. 73, 1-128. Shanghai: Zhonghua Shuju, 1936. 梁启超: "中国历史研究法", 《饮冰室合集——专集》

———. "Zhongguo lishi yanjiufa bupian" (Method for Research of Chinese History, continued). First published in 1926. In *YBSHJ-ZJ*, by Liang Qichao, vol. 23, no. 99, 1-117. Shanghai: Zhonghua Shuju, 1936. 梁启超: "中国历史研究法补篇", 《饮冰室合集——专集》

———. "Zhongguo qiantu zhi xiwang yu guomin zeren" (The Promising Future of China and the Responsibility of Her Citizens). First published in 1911. In *YBSHJ-WJ*, by Liang Qichao, vol. 10, no. 26, 1-40. Shanghai: Zhonghua Shuju, 1936. 梁启超: "中国前途之希望与国民责任", 《饮冰室合集——文集》

———. "Zhongguo zhimin bada weiren zhuan" (Biographies of Eight Great Chinese of Colonization). First published in 1905. In *YBSHJ-ZJ*, by Liang Qichao, vol. 3, no. 8, 1-5. Shanghai: Zhonghua Shuju, 1936. 梁启超: "中国殖民八大伟人传", 《饮冰室合集——专集》

———. "Ziyou shu" (Notes on Freedom). First published in series between 1899 and 1905. In *YBSHJ-ZJ* by Liang Qichao, vol. 2, no. 2, 1-112. Shanghai: Zhonghua Shuju, 1936. 梁启超: "自由书", 《饮冰室合集——专集》

Liang, Fa. *Quanshi liangyan* (Good Words to Admonish the Age). First published in Guangzhou in 1832. Taipei: Xuesheng Shuju, 1985. 梁发: 《劝世良言》

Liang, Shuming. *Dongxi wenhua jiqi zhexue* (Eastern and Western Cultures and Their Philosophies). Shanghai: Commercial, 1922. 梁漱溟: 《东西文化及其哲学》

Lin, Yü-sheng. "The Morality of Mind and Immorality of Politics: Reflections on Lu Xun, the Intellectual." In *Lu Xun and His Legacy*, edited by Leo Ou-fan Lee, 107-28. Berkeley: University of California Press, 1985.

———. "Reflections on the 'Creative Transformation of Chinese Tradition.'" In *Chinese Thought in a Global Context: A Dialogue Between Chinese and Western Philosophical Approaches*, edited by Karl-Heinz Pohl, 74-99. Leiden: Brill, 1999.

Liu, Changxing. "Moxi shijie yu rudao xianghe lun" (The Ten Commandments of Moses Conform to the Confucian *dao*). *WGGB* 4 (March 1876) 405a. 刘常惺："摩西十诫与儒道相合论",《万国公报》

Liu, Guangzhi. "Liangpian xiaoju-xuyan" (Preface to Two Short Dramas). *ZLYSM* 6.7 (May 1932) 35. 刘广志："两篇小剧——序言",《真理与生命》

———. "Libaijia" (Rebecca). *ZLYSM* 6.7 (May 1932) 36-41. 刘广志："利百加",《真理与生命》

———. "Yage" (Jacob). *ZLYSM* 6.8 (June 1932) 46-57. 刘广志："雅歌",《真理与生命》

Liu, Qiang. "Cong shehui kexue shang guancha jidujiao" (A Look at Christianity from the Perspective of Social Science). *ZLYSM* 4.15 (July 1930) 14-22. 刘强："从社会科学上观察基督教",《真理与生命》

Liu, Shijing. "Xiangzheng tiandao qi" (Evidence for the Revelation of the Heavenly Way). *WGGB* 15 (September 16, 1882) 50a-b. 刘世镜："祥证天道启",《万国公报》

Liu, Songyun. "Lun yisaiyashu shangban zhi dazhi" (The Main Idea of the First Isaiah). *Shenxue zhi* (Theological Quarterly) 7.2 (June 1921) 19-22. 刘松筠："论以赛亚书上半之大旨",《神学志》

Liu, Tingfang. "Buxing zhi nian" (The Pedestrian Years). *ZJ* 12.2 (July 1937) 40-55. 刘廷芳和杨荫浏："步行之年",《紫晶》

———. "'Jiaohui wenzi shiye de wenti' xulun" (Preface to the "Issue of Christian Literature of the Church"). *SM* 3.2 (October 1922) 1-6. 刘廷芳："'教会文字事业的问题'绪论",《生命》

———. "Meng yu shengya" (The Dream and Business). *ZJ* 12.1 (March 1937) 70-85. 刘廷芳和杨荫浏："梦与生涯",《紫晶》

———. "'Sage' de kaichang" (How the "Saga" of Jacob Began). *ZJ* 10.2 (June 1936) 222-32. 刘廷芳："'萨格'的开场",《紫晶》

———. "Shende xingxiang" (The Image of God). *ZJ* 4.2 (April 1933) 174-87. 刘廷芳："神的形象",《紫晶》

———. "Xu san" (Preface III to "Aige," Li Rongfang's Chinese translation of Lamentations). *ZLYSM* 5.8 (June 1931) 50-52. 刘廷芳：《哀歌》"序三",《真理与生命》

———. "Yige daxue de zongjiao xueyuan de renwu yu biaozhun" (The Mission and Standard for the College of Religion of a University). *ZLYSM* 8.7 (December 15, 1934) 330-38. 刘廷芳："一个大学的宗教学院的任务与标准",《真理与生命》

———. "You le chanye" (Having Property). *ZJ* 11.1 (September 1936) 81-95. 刘廷芳："有了产业",《紫晶》

———. "Zhonghua jidutu yu sunzhongshan" (Chinese Christians and Sun Yat-sen). *SM* 5.6 (1925) 90-93. With two untitled poems attached to lament Sun Yat-sen's death on page 94, one by Liu and the other by Liu's wife Wu Zhuosheng. 刘廷芳："中华基督徒与孙中山",《生命》；吴卓生

Liu, Tingfang, and Yang Yinliu. "Buxing zhi nian" (The Pedestrian Years). *ZJ* 12.2 (July 1937) 40-55. 刘廷芳和杨荫浏："步行之年",《紫晶》

———. "Huoyan zhong de jingji" (The Bush on Fire). *ZJ* 6.2 (June 1934) 239-56. 刘廷芳和杨荫浏："火焰中的荆棘",《紫晶》

———. "Meng yu shengya" (The Dream and Business). *ZJ* 12.1 (March 1937) 70-85. 刘廷芳和杨荫浏："梦与生涯",《紫晶》

———. "Shen jinlai le" (Where God Breaks Through). *ZJ* 11.2 (December 1936) 254-68. 刘廷芳和杨荫浏："神进来了",《紫晶》

Liu, Yu. "Xinai shan (Mount Sinai)." *Xiandai* (Les Contemporains) 3.5 (September 1933) 632-38. 刘宇："西乃山"，《现代》

Liu, Yun. *Yuyan de shehuishi: jindai shengjing hanyi zhong de yuyan xuanze* (The Social History of Language: Language Styles in Modern Chinese Bibles). Shanghai: Shanghai Renmin Chubanshe, 2015. 刘云：《语言的社会史：近代圣经汉译中的语言选择1822-1919》

Lovell, Florence B. "Some Suggestions on Bible Teaching in Schools." *CR* 43 (May 1912) 289-94.

Lu, Xun. "Huran xiangdao" (Sudden Thoughts). In *LXQJ*, vol. 3, 19-25. Beijing: Renmin Wenxue Chubanshe, 1973. 鲁迅："忽然想到"，《鲁迅全集》

———. "Moluo shili shuo" (On the Power of Mara Poetry). Written in 1907. In *LXQJ*, vol. 1, 55-102. Beijing: Renmin Wenxue Chubanshe, 1973. 鲁迅："摩罗诗力说"，《鲁迅全集》

———. "Postscript to *Shuqin*." Written on September 10, 1932. In *LXQJ*, vol. 19, 241-46. Beijing: Renmin Wenxue Chubanshe, 1973. 鲁迅："《竖琴》后记"，《鲁迅全集》

———. "Preface to *Shuqin*" (The Harp). Written on September 9, 1932. In *LXQJ*, vol. 19, 7-11. Beijing: Renmin Wenxue Chubanshe, 1973. 鲁迅："《竖琴》序"，《鲁迅全集》

———. "Xiao zagan" (Mini-thoughts). Composed on September 24, 1927. In *LXQJ*, vol. 3, 508-13. Beijing: Renmin Wenxue Chubanshe, 1973. 鲁迅："小杂感"，《鲁迅全集》

Lu, Zhiwei, "Jidujiao yu meishu" (Christianity and Fine Arts). *ZLYSM* 2.7 (April 15, 1927) 175-78. 陆志韦："基督教与美术"，《真理与生命》

Luce, Henry W., "Some Characteristics of Curriculum Bible Study," *CR* 47 (May 1916) 306-8.

Lunačarskij, A. V. "Tuoersitai yu makesi" (Tolstoy and Marx). Translated by Lu Xun. In *LXQJ*, vol. 17, 277-98. 卢那卡尔斯基："托尔斯泰与马克斯"，鲁迅译，《鲁迅全集》

Lunz, Lev. "Zai shamo shang." Translated by Lu Xun. In *LXQJ*, vol. 19, 39-49. Beijing: Renmin Wenxue Chubanshe, 1973. 伦支："在沙漠上"，鲁迅译，《鲁迅全集》

Mak, George Kam Wah. *Protestant Bible Translation and Mandarin as the National Language of China*. Sinica Leidensia 131. Leiden: Brill, 2017.

Marty, Martin E. "Protestantism." In *The Encyclopedia of Religion*, edited by Mircea Eliade, 12:23b-38a. New York: Macmillan, 1987.

Mascarenhas, Sidney J. "The Bible as a Book of Memory." *Antonianum* 79 (2004) 412-13.

Mateer, Calvin W. "What is the Best Course of Study for Mission Schools?" In *Records of the Second Triennial Meeting of the Educational Association of China held at Shanghai, May 6-9, 1896*, 48-55. Shanghai: American Presbyterian Mission, 1896.

McDougall, Bonnie S., and Kam Louie. *The Literature of China in the Twentieth Century*. London: Hurst & Company, 1997.

McClatchie, Canon T. "The Jewish Nation." *CR* 9 (March–April 1878) 81-85.

McIlvaine, Jasper S. "Cushite Ethnology." *CR* 6 (September–October 1875) 344-62.

———. "The Garden of Eden." *CR* 6 (September–October 1875) 344-62.

———. "Noah in China." *CR* 11 (July–August 1880) 251-59.

McNeur, George Hunter. *Liangfa zhuan* (Life of Liang A-fa). 2nd ed. Hong Kong: The Council on Christian Literature for Overseas Chinese, 1968. 麦沾恩：《梁发传》

Medhurst, Walter H. *China: Its State and Prospects, with Especial Reference to the Spread of the Gospel, Containing Allusions to the Antiquity, Extent, Population, Civilization, Literature, and Religion of the Chinese*. Boston: Crocker and Brewster, 1838.

———. "Dongxi shiji hehe" (A Comparative Study of Eastern and Western History). *Dongxiyang kao meiyue tongji zhuan* (*Eastern and Western* monthly magazine, known also as the *Chinese Magazine*) (July 1833–June 1834) 4b–6b,14b–16b, 24a–25b, 34a–36a, 44a–45a, 54a–56a, 63b–64b, 73b–74b, 87a–90a, 100a–101a, 111b–114a, 123b–25b. 麦都思："东西史记和合",《东西洋考每月统计传》

Mei, Hua-Chuen. "The Returned Student in China." *CR* 48 (March 1917) 158–75.

Mencius. *Mencius*. Translated by D. C. Lau. Hong Kong: the Chinese University of Hong Kong Press, 2003.

Miluo xiangren. "Miluo xiangren xueyue jiumiu" (A Person from Miluo Redressing Errors). In *Yijiao congbian* (Collected Writings for Upholding Orthodoxy), prefaced by Su Yu, vol. 4, 333–39. Taipei: Wenhai Chubanshe, 1971. 汨罗乡人（叶德辉）："汨罗乡人学约纠谬",《翼教丛编》, 苏舆序

"Missionary News." *CR* 40 (December 1909) 727–28.

Montague, W. P. "Xinyang de jiefang" (Liberation of Faith). Translated by Xu Baoqian. *ZLYSM* 7.3 (December 1932) 25–30. 蒙达久："信仰的解放",徐宝谦译,《真理与生命》

"Moses." In *Xishi tongzhi*, vol. 118, 1–2. 《西史通志》

Moule, C. C. "Correspondence to Editorial." *CR* 9 (January–February 1878) 67.

Moule, W. S. "On Certain Characteristics of Three Versions of Holy Scripture Published by the British and Foreign Bible Society." *CR* 14 (September–October 1883) 410–13.

"Moxi wei zhongbao" (Moses as Intermediary). *SJB* 181 (1936) 1–9. "摩西为中保",《圣经报》

Muirhead, William. "The Style of the Mandarin Bible." *CR* 31 (July 1900) 311–36.

M., W. (surname unknown). "Review of *Jiuyue shipian jiuyue zhenyan*" (Old Testament Books of Psalms and Proverbs). *CR* 29 (June 1898) 301. 《旧约诗篇旧约箴言》

Nakamura, Masanao. "Preface." In *Wanguo shiji* (Historical Records of Ten Thousand Countries) by Okamoto Kansuke, 4a. Shanghai: Shenbao Guan, 1879. 中村正直："序",《万国史记》

Neave, James. "West China Evangelism." *CR* 47 (February 1916) 104–12.

Nord, Christiane. *Translating as a Purposeful Activity: Functionalist Approaches Explained*. Manchester: St. Jerome, 1997.

"Note on *Shengshi ji*" (An Account of Sacred History [in the Old and New Testaments]). *CR* 18 (July 1887) 287. 《圣史记》书讯

"Notes." *CR* 32 (December 1901) 623–25.

"Notes." *CR* 34 (June 1903) 301–3.

"Notes and Items." *CR* 29 (January 1898) 36–37.

Noth, Martin. *Exodus: A Commentary*. Old Testament Library. Philadelphia: Westminster, 1962.

Okamoto, Kansuke. *Wanguo shiji* (Historical Records of Ten Thousand Countries). Translator unknown. Shanghai: Shenbao Guan, 1879. 冈本监辅:《万国史记》

"Our Book Table." *CR* 48 (February 1917) 125.

Owen, George. "The Mosaic Account of the Creation Geologically Considered." *CR* 13 (January–February 1882) 1–17.

Palmer, Richard. *Hermeneutics: Interpretation Theory in Schleiermacher, Dilthey, Heidegger, and Gadamer*. Evanston: Northwestern University Press, 1969.

Pan, Wenhe. "Ningbo panwenhe jiaoyou jiuyue qilü bashou" (Eight Poems by Pan Wenhe from Ningbo in the Form of qilü on OT stories). *JHXB* 1 (May 15, 1869) 162a-b. 潘文鹤："宁波潘文鹤教友旧约七律八首"，《教会新报》

Patt-Shamir, Galia. "Confucianism and Judaism: a Dialogue in Spite of Differences." In *The Jewish-Chinese Nexus: A Meeting of Civilizations*, edited by M. Avrum Ehrlich, 61-4. London: Routledge, 2008.

Peake, A. S., ed. *Peake's Commentary on the Bible*. London: T. C. & E. C. Jack, 1920.

Peill, S. G. and E. J. "The Scriptures in Phonetic for North China." *CR* 47 (May 1916) 329-37.

Peng, Bide. "Ping Lishicen rensheng zhexue zhi yiduan" (A Book Review of Li Shicen's *Life Philosophy*). *ZLYSM* 2.11 (June 15,1927) 302-8. 彭彼得："评李石岑人生哲学之一端"，《真理与生命》

Peng, Changlin. "'Zhongguo jidujiao wenzi shiye de wenti' gailun" (Introduction of the "Issue of Chinese Christian literature"). *SM* 3.2 (October 1922) 1-11. 彭长琳："'中国基督教文字事业的问题'概论"，《生命》

Peters, Irma. "Die Ansichten Lu Hsün über das Verhältnis von Literatur und Revolution in der Zeit von 1927–1930." *International Congress of Orientalists* 5 (1960) 149-57.

"Pingfen jiayi" (The Appraisal). *WGGB* 13 (March 1881) 265a-b. "评分甲乙"，《万国公报》

Pitcher, P. W. "Vernacular Schools and Vernacular Education." *CR* 37 (December 1906) 681-89.

Pollard, David. "Introduction." In *Translation and Creation: Readings of Western Literature in Early Modern China, 1840-1918*, edited by David Pollard, 5-23. Philadelphia: Benjamins, 1998.

Porter, Frank C. "Lishide yesu yu baoluo de zhengci" (A Historical Jesus and Testimony of Paul). Translated by Taijian (Jian Youwen). *SM* 5.2 (December 1924) 15-22. 博富朗："历史的耶稣与保罗的证辞"，太简（简又文）译，《生命》

Porter, H. D. "The Missionary Invasion of China." *CR* 21 (July 1890) 293-300.

Porter, Lucius C. (Bo Chenguang). "Zhongguo de jiuyue" (China's OT). Translator unknown. *ZLYSM* 2.9-10 (May 1927) 240-44. 博晨光："中国的旧约"，《真理与生命》

Price, P. F. "The Place of Bible Study in Mission Schools." *CR* 47 (May 1916) 291-96.

———. "The Present Intellectual Awakening and its Bearing upon the Christian Church." *CR* 52 (June 1921) 411-21.

Qian, Xuantong et al. "Xinwenhua zhong jiwei xuezhe duiyu jidujiao de taidu" (The Attitude of Some Scholars to Christianity in the New Culture). *SM* 2.8 (April 1922) 1-4. 钱玄同等："新文化中几位学者对于基督教的态度"，《生命》

Qiu, Tingliang. "Lun baihua wei weixin zhi ben " (Vernacular as the Basis for Reforms). First published 1897. In *Zhongguo jindai wenlun xuan* (Collected Essays on Literarature and Art in Modern China), vol. 1., edited by Guo Shaoyu and Luo Gengze, 176-80. Beijing: Renmin Wenxue Chubanshe, 1959. 裘廷梁："论白话为维新之本"，《中国近代文论选》，郭绍虞和罗根泽编

Query (full name unknown). "Noah-Nüwa 女娲, Are They Identical?" *CR* 36 (July 1905) 297.

Rad, Gerhard von. *Genesis: A Commentary*. Old Testament Library. London: SCM, 1972.

Records of the General Conference of the Protestant Missionaries of China Held at Shanghai. Shanghai: American Presbyterian, 1877.

"Review of *The Harmony of the Bible with Science*." *CR* 14 (May–June 1883) 245.

"Review of *Jiuyue kelue*" (Lessons from the OT). *CR* 24 (March 1893) 140. 评《旧约课略》

"Review of *Notes on Genesis*." *CR* 36 (July 1905) 365.

"Review of *The Representative Men of the Bible*." *CR* 37 (September 1906) 513–14.

"Review of *The Scriptures in the Light of Modern Discovery and Knowledge*." *CR* 13 (March–April 1882) 158–60.

"Review of *Wansuo shengshi*" (Studies on the Sacred History [in the OT]), by Earnest Faber. *CR* 24 (February 1893) 90–91. 评《玩索圣史》

"Revision of the Chinese Version of the Bible; Remarks on the Words for God, Father, Son, Spirit, Soul, Prophet, Baptism and Sabbath." *CRP* 15.4 (April 1846) 161–65.

Richard, Timothy. *Forty-Five Years in China*. New York: Stokes, 1916.

———. "The Historical Evidences of Christianity—Present Benefits (continued)." *CR* 22 (November 1891) 491–98. Continued from *CR* 22 (October 1891) 443–51.

———. "Qingzuo shengshu liangqi" (Two Notices Inviting Contributions about Christianity). *WGGB* 11 (January 1880) 207a. 李提摩太："请作圣书两启"，《万国公报》

———. "Yingguo jiaoshi qingzuo sheng dawei shipian shici qi" (A Notice Inviting Poetic Contributions on the Psalms by Holy David). *WGGB* 11 (December 1879) 162b. 李提摩太："英国教士请作圣大卫诗篇诗词启"，《万国公报》

Robinson, Lewis S. *Double-edged Sword: Christianity and 20th Century Chinese Fiction*. Hong Kong: Tao Fong Shan Ecumenical Centre, 1986.

Rowe, Harry F. "Jiuyue de lijie" (Etiquette in the OT, continued). Narrated by Rowe and written down by Zhao Zongfu. *SXZ* 7.1 (March 1921) 24–27. 饶合理口述，赵宗福笔录："旧约的礼节"，《神学志》

Ruan, Yuan, ed. *Shisanjing zhushu* (Notes and Commentaries to the Thirteen Classics). Yangzhou: Jiangsu guangling guji keyinshe, 1995. 阮元：《十三经注疏》

Ruth, Arthur. "Chinese Students Abroad." *CR* 48 (March 1917) 156–57.

S., J. L. (surname unknown) "Review of *How to Study the Old Testament* by F. Sanders and H. Sherman." *CR* 50 (June 1919) 417–18.

Seymour, W. F. "Sunday School Work for Chinese Children. Difficulties and Suggestions." *CR* 40 (March 1909) 127–30.

Shan, Shili. "Moxijiao liuxing Zhongguo ji" (Note on Moses' Religion in China). In *Guiqianji* (Diary of Italy), edited by Yang Jian, 196–203. Changsha: Hunan Renmin Chubanshe, 1981. 钱单士厘："摩西教流行中国记"，《归潜记》，杨坚校点

Shen, Congwen. "Huangjun riji" (Diaries of Huang jun). In *Shencongwen wenji* (Collected Works by Shen Congwen), vol. 2, edited by Shen Congwen, 189–249. Guangzhou: Huacheng Chubanshe, 1982. 沈从文："篁君日记"，《沈从文文集》

———. "Mei yu ai" (Beauty and Love). In *Shencongwen wenji*, vol. 11, edited by Shen Congwen, 376–79. Guangzhou: Huacheng Chubanshe, 1984. 沈从文："美与爱"，《沈从文文集》

"Shengshu jiuyue yizheng" (Dating of the Five Books). *WGGB* 11 (January 1880) 210a–11b. "圣书旧约疑证"，《万国公报》

Shi, Qide. (original name unknown) "Fazhan yu fenhua" (Development and Breakup). Translated by Zhao Zichen. *ZLYSM* 4.12 (April 1930) 2–12. 施其德："发展与分化"，赵紫宸译，《真理与生命》

———. "Kexue yu zongjiaode chongtu" (The Conflict of Science and Religion). Translated by Zhao Zichen. *ZLYSM* 4.12 (April 1930) 12–20. 施其德："科学与宗教的冲突"，赵紫宸译，《真理与生命》

Shigeno, Yasutsune. "Preface." In *Wanguo shiji* (Historical Records of Ten Thousand Countries) by Okamoto Kansuke, 2a. Shanghai: Shenbao Guan, 1879. 重野安绎："序"，《万国史记》

Silsby, J. A. "The Spread of Vernacular Literature." Read at the Monthly Meeting of the Shanghai Missionary Association. *CR* 26 (November 1895) 508-9.

Sima, Qian. "Bao ren'an shu" (A Letter to Ren An). In Ban Gu, "Simaqian zhuan" (Sima Qian's Biography), *Hanshu* (A Historical Account of Han Dynasty), vol. 2, 1979-86. Beijing: Zhonghua shuju, 1962. 司马迁："报任安书"；班固："司马迁传"，《汉书》

Smith, G. B. "Shenxue lunli de gaizao" (Reform in Ethical Theology). Translated by Jian Youwen. *SM* 6.1 (September 1925) 47-55. 史美夫："神学伦理的改造"，简又文译，《生命》

———. *Social Idealism and the Changing Theology: A Study of the Ethical Aspects of Christian Doctrine*. New York: MacMillan, 1913.

———. "Zongjiaode quezheng zhi lunlide jichu" (Ethical Basis of Religious Assurance). Translated by Jian Youwen. *SM* 5.5 (January 1925) 42-56. 史美夫："宗教的确证之伦理的基础"，简又文译，《生命》

Smyth, Egbert. "Christianity and Missions." In *Progressive Orthodoxy: A Contribution to the Christian Interpretation of Christian Doctrines*, edited by Egbert Smyth et al., 153-90. Boston: Houghton Mifflin, 1885.

Song, Yuren. *Caifeng ji* (Records of Folk Collection). Shanghai: Xiuhai Shanfang, 1895. 宋育仁：《采风记》

———. "Public Law." In *Caifeng ji* (Records of Folk Collection) by Song Yuren, 1-4. Shanghai: Xiuhai Shanfang, 1895. 公法

———. "Religion." In *CFJ* by Song Yuren, 1-12. Shanghai: Xiuhai Shanfang, 1895. 教门

———. "School." In *CFJ* by Song Yuren, 1-9. Shanghai: Xiuhai Shanfang, 1895. 学校

———. "Secular Custom." In *CFJ* by Song Yuren, 1-7. Shanghai: Xiuhai Shanfang, 1895. 俗礼

Sperling, S. David. "Jeremiah." In *The Encyclopedia of Religion*, edited by Mircea Eliade, 8:1-6. New York: Macmillan, 1987.

Spillett, Hubert W., ed. *A Catalogue of Scriptures in the Languages of China and the Republic of China*. London: British and Foreign Bible Society, 1975.

Standaert, Nicholas. "The Bible in Seventeenth Century China." *Shijie hanxue* (World Sinology) 3 (April 2005) 64-86. 钟鸣旦，"《圣经》在十七世纪的中国"，《世界汉学》

Stauffer, Milton T. *The Christian Occupation of China*. Shanghai: China Continuation Committee, 1922.

"Summer Schools in China." *CR* 41 (June 1910) 432-33.

Sun, Yat-sen. "Mian zhongguo jidujiao qingnian shu" (A Letter to Encourage Chinese Christian Youth). First published in 1924. In *Guofu quanji* (Complete works by Sun Yat-sen), vol. 4b, edited by the Committee for Kuomingtang's History, 1448-49. Taipei: Zhongguo Guomindang Zhongyang Weiyuanhui, 1973. 孙逸仙："勉中国基督教青年书"，《国父全集》，中国国民党中央委员会党史委员会编

Sydenstricker, A. "Review of Schereschewsky's Plain *wenli* Rendering of the NT of 1898." *CR* 31 (June 1900) 317-18.

Tashan. "Jiuyue xiyi" (OT Commentary) *SXZ* 7.3 (October 1921) 1-12. 他山（许地山）："旧约析义"，《神学志》

Taijian. "Shengjing lide qingju" (A Drama of Love in the Bible). *ZLYSM* 1.9 (October 1926) 265-69. 太简（简又文）："圣经里的情剧"，《真理与生命》

Tang, Caichang. "Xiao yaxiya zhonglei kao" (A Study of Ethnic Groups in Asia Minor). In *Xinxue da congshu* (Great Series of New Learning), edited by Liang Rengong (Liang Qichao), 50, 11a-b. Shanghai: Jishan Qiaoji Shudian, 1903/4. 唐才常："小亚细亚种类考"，《新学大丛书》，梁任公（梁启超）编

Tang, Yin. "Xianzai xuyao gaoshuizhun de jidujiao zazhi ma—xiangei 1937 jidujiao wentan" (For the Christian Literature in 1937—Is There a Need for Christian Journals of High Quality?). *ZLYSM* 10.8 (January 1937) 521-27. 汤因："现在需要高水准的基督教杂志吗——献给1937基督教文坛"，《真理与生命》

Tang Chengbo and Ye Qifang. "Shengjing zhi wenxue de yanjiu" (A Literary Study of the Bible). Translation of "The Bible as Literature," by W. H. Hudson, in *Peake's Commentary on the Bible*, edited by Arthur Samuel Peake, 18-25. London: T. C. & E. C. Jack, 1920. "圣经之文学的研究"，汤澄波和叶启芳译

Tao, Chengqi. "Shijie shi" (Some Verses about the Ten Commandments). *WGGB* 14 (October 29, 1881) 108a, continued in *WGGB* 14 (November 5, 1881) 117b-18b. 陶澄祺："十诫诗"，《万国公报》

Tarumoto, Teruo. "A Statistical Survey of Translated Fiction 1840-1920." In *Translation and Creation: Readings of Western Literature in Early Modern China, 1840-1918*, edited by David Pollard, 37-42. Philadelphia: Benjamin, 1998.

Taylor, W. E. "Some Points in Work for the Educated Classes of China." *CR* 41 (May 1910) 336-43.

Teng, Ssu-yü, and John King Fairbank. *China's Response to the West: A Documentary Survey, 1830-1923*. Cambridge: Harvard University Press, 1961.

Tomlin, Jacob. *Missionary Journals and Letters: Written During Eleven Years' Residence and Travels Amongst the Chinese, Siamese, Javanese, Khassias, and other Eastern Nations*. London: James Nisbet, 1844.

Toyohiko, Kagawa. "Yesu de zhihui" (Wisdom of Jesus). Translated by Xiao Wenan. *ZLYSM* 7.6 (April 1933) 23-30. 贺川丰彦："耶稣的智慧"，萧文安译，《真理与生命》

Tu, Weiming. "Rooted in Humanity, Extended to Heaven." *Harvard Divinity Bulletin* (Spring 2008) 60-65.

Twelfth Annual Report of the Chinese Religious Tract Society 1890, *CR* 22 (May 1891) 234.

Tyson, Lois. *Critical Theory Today: A User-Friendly Guide*. 2nd ed. London: Routledge, 2006.

"The Union Version Bible." *CR* 50 (February 1919) 134-35.

Van Seters, John. "Moses." In *The Encyclopedia of Religion*, edited by Mircea Eliade, 10:115b-21b. New York: Macmillan, 1987.

"Vernacular Translations of the Bible." *CR* 32 (November 1901) 563-64.

Walker, J. E. Note in "Correspondence." *CR* 21 (May 1890) 235-36.

Wallace, Alfred. *The World of Life*. London: Chapman & Hall, 1910.

Wallace, Edward Wilson. "Bible Study in West China." *CR* 47 (May 1916) 296-300.

Wang, Benchao. *Ershi shiji zhongguo wenxue yu jidujiao wenhua* (Twentieth-century Chinese Literature and Christian Culture). Hefei: Anhui Jiaoyu Chubanshe, 2000. 王本朝：《二十世纪中国文学与基督教文化》

Wang, Chen-mian. "Moving toward a Mature, Balanced Stage of Studying Christianity in China." *International Institute for Asian Studies (IIAS) Newsletter* 27 (March 2002) 22.

Wang, Guowei. "Hongloumeng pinglun" (A Study of the *Dream of the Red Chamber*). In *Wangjing'an wenji*, 83–112. Tainan: Shengmian Chubanshe, 1978. 王国维："红楼梦评论",《王静庵文集》

———. "Shubenhua zhexue jiqi jiaoyu xueshuo" (The Philosophical and Educational Thoughts of Schopenhauer). In *Wangjing'an wenji* (Collected Works by Wang Jiang'an), 113–92. Tainan: Shengmian Chubanshe, 1978. 王国维："叔本华哲学及其教育学说",《王静庵文集》

Wang, Jingwei. "Minzu de guomin" (National Citizens). *Min bao* (People's Journal) 1 (1905) 1–31. 汪精卫："民族的国民",《民报》

Wang, Shanzhi. "Kaocha shengjing de xinde" (What I Have Learned in Bible Reading). *SM* 3.6 (March 1923) 1–10. 王善治："考察圣经的心得",《生命》

Wanguo tongjian (A General Record of Ten Thousand Countries).《万国通鉴》

Wanguo tongshi (A General History of Ten Thousand Countries).《万国通史》

Watts, John D. *Isaiah 34–66*. Word Biblical Commentary 25. Waco: Word, 1987.

Wei, Dongya, ed. *Hanying cidian* (Chinese-English Dictionary). Beijing: Waiyu Jiaoxue Yu Yanjiu Chubanshe, 1997. 危东亚等编:《汉英词典》

Wen, Qing et al., eds. *Chouban yiwu shimo* (Complete Account of Management of Barbarian Affairs: Daoguang Period [1821–1851]). Beiping: Forbidden City Museum, 1930. Original publication date unknown. 文庆等编:《筹办夷务始末》

Wenham, Gordon J. *Genesis 1–15*. Word Biblical Commentary 1. Waco, TX: Word, 1987.

Wheeler, L. N. "The Bible in China." *CR* 21 (December 1890) 541–45.

Wherry, John. "Historical Summary of the Different Versions of the Scriptures." In *Records of the General Conference of the Protestant Missionaries of China, Held at Shanghai, May 7–20, 1890*. Shanghai: Presbyterian Mission, 1890, 50–52.

White, William C. "The Sunday School Movement and Its Opportunities." *CR* 40 (March 1909) 130–33.

Willeke, Bernward. "Das Werden der Chinesischen Katholischen Bibel." *Neue Zeitschrift Für Missionswissenschaft XIV* (1960) 281–95.

Williamson, Alexander. "Jizhi diqiu kezhi shangdi zhi zhuzai" (God's Dominance Can be Known from [the Evolution of] the Earth). *WGGB* 13 (May 1881) 338b–39a. 韦廉臣："稽之地球可知上帝之主宰",《万国公报》

———. "A Uniform Version of the Sacred Scripture in Wenli." *CR* 9 (May–June 1878) 230–32.

Wu, Shuhui. "On Chinese Sacrificial Orations *chi wen*." *Monumenta Serica* 50 (2002) 1–33.

Wu, Zhenchun. "Guojiazhuyi yu jidujiao shifou chongtu" (Is Christianity in Conflict with Nationalism?). *SM* 5.4 (February 1925) 4–5. 吴震春："国家主义与基督教是否冲突",《生命》

———. "Jidujiao jing yu rujiao jing" (Christian and Confucian Classics). *SM* 3.6 (March 1923) 1–6. 吴震春（吴雷川）:"基督教经与儒家经",《生命》

Wylie, Alexander. "The Bible in China (to be continued)." *CR* 1 (November 1868) 121–28. Continued in *CR* 1 (December 1868) 145–50.

———, ed. *Catalogue of the Chinese Imperial Maritime Customs Collection at the International Exhibition, Philadelphia, 1876*. Shanghai: The Statistical Department of Inspectorate General of Customs, 1876.

———, ed. *Catalogue of Publications by Protestant Missionaries in China*. Shanghai: Statistical Department of the Inspectorate General of Customs, 1876.

Xie, Fuya. "Wode zongjiao jingyan zhi sanjieduan" (Three Stages of My Religious Experience). *ZLYSM* 5.6 (April 1931) 4–8. 谢扶雅："我的宗教经验之三阶段",《真理与生命》

Xie, Jingsheng. "Jidujiao yu shehui jinbu" (Christianity and Social Progress). *SM* 6.2 (November 1925) 17–23. 谢景升："基督教与社会进步",《生命》

Xie, Wanying. "Chenji" (Quietude). *SM* 2.3 (October 1921) 2. 谢婉莹："沉寂",《生命》

———, et al. "Yanjing daxue (xu)" (Yenching University, [continued]). *SM* 2.2 (September 1921) 1–8. 谢婉莹等:"燕京大学(续)",《生命》

Xing, Mei. *Shengjing guanhua heheben jufa yanjiu* (Syntactic Studies on the Chinese Mandarin Version). MA thesis. Shanghai: Fudan University, 2012. 邢梅:《圣经官话和合本句法研究》

Xiong, Yuezhi. "Degrees of Familiarity with the West in Late Qing Society." In *Translation and Creation: Readings of Western Literature in Early Modern China 1840–1918*, edited by David E. Pollard, 25–36. Philadelphia: Benjamins, 1998.

Xishi tongzhi (A General Account of Western History). Shanghai: Wensheng Tang, 1902.《西史通志》

Xu, Baoqian. "Jidujiao zai zhongguo de qiantu" (The Future of Christianity in China). *ZLYSM* 1.13 (December 15, 1926) 333–38. 徐宝谦："基督教在中国的前途",《真理与生命》

Xu, Dishan. "Women yao shenmeyang de zongjiao" (What Kind of Religion Do We Want?). *SM* 3.9 (May 1923) 1–4. 许地山："我们要什么样的宗教",《生命》

———. "Yage xinyi" (A New Translation of the "Song of Songs"). *SM* 2.5 (December 1921) 1–18. 许地山:"雅歌新译",《生命》

———. "Yage xinyi, xuyan" (Preface to the New translation of the "Song of Songs"). *SM* 2.4 (November 1921) 1–8. 许地山:"雅歌新译,绪言",《生命》

Xu, Jiyu. "Fanli" (Guide to the Use of the Book). *YHZL* 1, 2b. 徐继畬:"凡例",《瀛寰志略》

———. "Yindu yixi huibu siguo" (Four Countries to the West of India). *YHZL* 3, 30. "印度以西回部四国"

———. *Yinghuan zhilue* (Brief Description of the World). 4th ed. Aiyou:Taigakaku, 1861. 徐继畬:《瀛寰志略》

Xu, Ruomeng. *Gudai shengjing hanyi yu zhongxi wenhua jiaoliu* (Chinese Bible Translating in History and Sino-Western Cultural Exchanges). Beijing: Zhongguo Wenshi Chubanshe, 2014. 徐若梦:《古代圣经汉译与中西文化交流》

Xu, Zhimo. "Renzhong de youlai" (The Origin of Humankind). In *Xuzhimo quanji*, vol. 1, edited by Zhao Xiaqiu, et al., 351–54. Nanning: Guangxi Minzhu Chubanshe, 1991. 徐志摩:"人种的由来",《徐志摩全集》, 赵遐秋等编

———. "Youyici shiyan" (Another Experiment). In *Xuzhimo quanji* (Complete Works of Xu Zhimo), vol. 1, edited by Zhao Xiaqiu, et al., 162–63. Nanning: Guangxi Minzhu Chubanshe, 1991. 徐志摩:"又一次实验",《徐志摩全集》, 赵遐秋等编

Xue, Fucheng. *Chushi ying fa yi bi siguo riji: 1890–1894* (Diaries of Missions to Four Countries: England, France, Italy, and Belgium 1890–1894). Changsha: Yuelu Shushe, 1985. 薛福成:《出使英法意比四国日记:1890–1894》

Yampolsky, Philip B. *The Platform Sutra of the Sixth Patriarch: The Text of the Tun-Huang Manuscript*. New York: Columbia University Press, 1967.

Yan, Jiqing. "Eryue renwu shi—yuese" (Poems about Biblical Characters—Joseph). *ZG* 27.8 (1928) 76. 严霁青:"二约人物诗——约瑟",《真光》

Yan, Yutan. "Dujing xinde" (Inspirations from Reading the Scriptures). *ZG* 36.3 (1936) 48–52. 严玉谭：" 读经心得"，《真光》

Yang, Jianlong. *Kuangye de husheng: zhongguo xiandai zuojia yu jidujiao wenhua* (Crying in the Wilderness: Contemporary Chinese Writers and Christian Culture) Shanghai: Jiaoyu Chubanshe, 1998. 杨剑龙：《旷野的呼声：中国现代作家与基督教文化》

Yang, Jiantang. "Shangdi shijie jie" (A Commentary on God's Ten Commandments). *JHXB* 5 (February 22, 1873) 177b–78a. 杨鉴堂：" 上帝十诫解"，《教会新报》

Yao, Xingfu. "Jidulun yu yangming xinxue—yi *Jiaohui xinbao* (1868–1874) de wupian zhengwen weili " (Christology and Wang Yangming's Doctrine of Heart-Mind—a Case Study on the Five Prize Essays on *The Church News*, 1868–1874). In *Jidujiao sixiang pinglun* (Comments on Christian Thought), vol. 3, edited by Xu Zhiwei, 357–65. Shanghai: Shanghai renmin chubanshe, 2006. 姚兴富：" 基督论与阳明心学——以《教会新报》（1868–1874）的五篇征文为例"，《基督教思想评论》

Yariv-Laor, Lihi. "Linguistic Aspects of Translating the Bible into Chinese." In *Bible in Modern China: The Literary and Intellectual Impact*, edited by Irene Eber, et al., 101–20. Monumenta Serica Monograph Series 43. Sankt Augustin: Monumenta Serica Institute, 1999.

Ye, Dehui. "Xiangsheng xueyue" (Study Regulations for Hunan Province). In *YJCB*, vol. 5, prefaced by Su Yu, 367–76. Taipei: Wenhai Chubanshe, 1971. 叶德辉：" 湘省学约"，《翼教丛编》，苏舆序

———. "Yehuanbin (dehui) libu mingjiao" (Ye Dehui Expounding Confucianism). In *YJCB*, vol. 3, prefaced by Su Yu, 163–71. Taipei: Wenhai Chubanshe, 1971. 叶德辉：" 叶焕彬（德辉）吏部明教"，《翼教丛编》，苏舆序

———. "Yelibu *Changxing Xueji* boyi" (Ye Dehui's Criticism on *Research records made in Changxing*). In *YJCB*, vol. 4, prefaced by Su Yu, 241–300. Taipei: Wenhai Chubanshe, 1971. 叶德辉：" 叶吏部《长兴学记》驳议"，《翼教丛编》，苏舆序

———. "Yelibu yu daixuanqiao jiaoguan shu" (Ye's Letter to Dai Xuanqiao). In *YJCB*, vol. 6, prefaced by Su Yu, 431–44. Taipei: Wenhai Chubanshe, 1971. 叶德辉：" 叶吏部与戴宣翘校官书"，《翼教丛编》，苏舆序

———. "Yelibu yu nanxuehui pilumen xiaolian shu" (Ye's Letter to Pi Lumen with the Southern Learning Society). In *YJCB*, vol. 6, prefaced by Su Yu, 415–21. Taipei: Wenhai Chubanshe, 1971. 叶德辉：" 叶吏部与南学会皮鹿门孝廉书"，《翼教丛编》，苏舆序

———. "Yelibu yu yukeshi guancha shu" (Ye's Observatory Letter to Yu Keshi). In *YJCB*, vol. 6, prefaced by Su Yu, 441–46. Taipei: Wenhai Chubanshe, 1971. 叶德辉：" 叶吏部与俞恪士观察书"，《翼教丛编》，苏舆序

Yili shi. "Shangdi shijie shi" (A Poem on God's Ten Commandments). *WGGB* 11 (October 1879) 76b–77b. 一蠡氏：" 上帝十诫诗"，《万国公报》

Yiselie liewang zhuan (Biographies of the Kings of Israel). 《以色列列王传》

Yonekawa, Masao. *Laonong luxiya xiaoshuo ji* (Collection of Russian novelettes). Tokyo: Jinxin Tang, 1925. 米川正夫：《劳农露西亚小说集》

You, Rujie. "Shengjing fangyan yiben shumu kaolu" (A Study and Catalogue of Chinese Vernacular Versions of the Bible). In *Jidujiao yu zhongguo wenhua congkan*, vol. 3, edited by Zhang Kaiyuan and Ma Min, 80–131. Wuhan: Hubei Jiaoyu Chubanshe, 2000. 游汝杰：" 圣经方言译本书目考录"，《基督教与中国文化丛刊》，章开沅和马敏编

Youtai dizhi (Geography of Judea). 《犹太地志》

"Youtai guoren si guiguo" (Jews Wish to Return to their State). *JHXB* 4 (March 30, 1872) 149b. "犹太国人思归国"，《教会新报》

Youtai liewang zhuan (Biographies of the Kings of Judea). 《犹太列王传》

"Youtai mingshi zhuanlue" (Biographical Notes of Famous Jews). *Waijiao bao* 94 (Foreign Affairs Paper), n. d., 5a-6b. "犹太名士传略"，《外交报》

Yu, Muren. "Wenyi zai chuandao shigong shang de diwei yu gongyong" (The Status and Function of Art in the Missionary Work). *Jinling shenxue zhi* (The Nanking Theological Seminary quarterly) 14.1 (January 1932) 35-43. 余牧人："文艺在传道事工上的地位与功用"，《金陵神学志》

Yuan, Ding'an. *Jidujiao gailun* (Introduction to Christianity). Shanghai: Commercial, 1939. 袁定安：《基督教概论》

———. *Shende zhexue* (Philosophy of Theism). Shanghai: Christian Literature Society, 1924. 袁定安：《神的哲学》

———. *Xibolai de minzu yingxiong moxi* (Moses: the National Hero of the Hebrews). Shanghai: Commercial, 1935. 袁定安：《希伯来的民族英雄摩西》

———. *Youtaijiao gailun* (Introduction to Judaism). Shanghai: Commercial, 1935. 袁定安：《犹太教概论》

Zeng, Jize. *Chushi ying fa e riji* (Diaries of Missions to England, France, and Russia). Changsha: Yuelu Shushe, 1985. 曾纪泽：《出使英法俄日记》

Zeng, Yugen. "Zhongguo jidujiao wenzi shiye de wenti" (The Issue of Chinese Christian Literature). *SM* 4.9-10 (June 1924) 9-29. 曾郁根："中国基督教文字事业的问题"，《生命》

Zetzsche, Jost Oliver. *The Bible in China: The History of the Union Version or The Culmination of Protestant Missionary Bible Translation in China.* Sankt Augustin: Monumenta Serica Institute, 1999.

Zhang, Dongsun. *Lixing yu minzhu* (Rationality and Democracy). First published in 1946. Hong Kong: Longmeng Shudian, 1968. 张东荪：《理性与民主》

———. *Sixiang yu shehui* (Thought and Society). First published in 1946. Hong Kong: Longmeng Shudian, 1968. 张东荪：《思想与社会》

Zhang, Taiyan. "Bo shenwo xianzheng shuo" (Refuting the Idea of Constitutionalism). *Min bao* 21 (1908) 1-11. 章太炎："驳神我宪政说"，《民报》

———. "Shehui tongquan shangdui" (A Discussion on General Sociology). *Min bao* 12 (1907) 1-24. 章太炎："社会通诠商兑"，《民报》

Zhang, Yongxun. "Shengjing shifu kao" (On Biblical Poetry and Poetic Prose). *SXZ* 5.4 (December 1919), 19-33. 张永训："圣经诗赋考"，《神学志》

———. "Shijing jingyi" (Interpreting the True Meaning of the Canon). *SXZ* 5.4 (December 1919) 9-19. 张永训："释经精义"，《神学志》

Zhang, Zhidong. "A Letter to Xu Renzhu," April 11, 1898. In *Zhangwenxiang gong quanji* (Complete Works of Zhang Zhidong), vol. 155, edited by Wang Shunan, 21a-b. Taipei: Wenhai Chubanshe, 1970. 张之洞：致徐仁铸函，《张文襄公全集》，王树枏编

———. *Quanxue pian* (Exhortations to Study). Wuchang: Lianghu Shuyuan, 1898. 张之洞：《劝学篇》

"Zhansheng tongku" (Victory over Suffering). Translated by Zhao Zichen. *ZLYSM* 4.15-17 (May 1930) 27-33. "战胜痛苦"，赵紫宸译，《真理与生命》

Zhao, Liutang. "Moxi zhi dansheng jiqi shaonian" (Moses' Birth and Early Years). *Shengjing bao* (The Bible Newspaper) 177 (1936) 21-28. 赵柳塘："摩西之诞生及其少年"，《圣经报》

———. "Moxi zhi mengzhao" (Moses' Being Called). *SJB* 178 (1936) 1–8. 赵柳塘:"摩西之蒙召",《圣经报》

———. "Moxi zhi wannian" (The Last Years of Moses). *SJB* 183 (1936) 1–7. 赵柳塘:"摩西之晚年",《圣经报》

———. "Moxi zhi wei lingxiu" (Moses as a Leader). *SJB* 179 (1936) 6–15. 赵柳塘:"摩西之为领袖",《圣经报》

Zhao, Weiben. *Yijing suyuan—xiandai wuda zhongwen shengjing fanyi shi* (Tracing the Origin of Bible Translating—History of the Production of the Five Major Chinese Bible Versions). Hong Kong: Zhongguo Shenxue Yuanjiuyuan, 1993. 赵维本:《译经溯源——现代五大中文圣经翻译史》

Zhao, Xiaqiu. "Preface." In *Xuzhimo quanji*, vol. 1, edited by Zhao Xiaqiu, et al., 20. Nanning: Guangxi Minzhu Chubanshe, 1991. 赵遐秋:"序言",《徐志摩全集》, 赵遐秋等编

Zhao Zichen. "Shengjing zai jinshi wenhua zhongde diwei" (The Place of the Bible in Modern Civilization). *SM* 6 (January 1921) 1–22. 赵紫宸:"圣经在近世文化中的地位",《生命》

———. "Wo dui zhongguo gaodeng shenxue jiaoyu de mengxiang" (My Dream about Higher Theological Education in China). *ZLYSM* 8.7 (December 15, 1934) 343–53. 赵紫宸:"我对中国高等神学教育的梦想",《真理与生命》

———. "Xu er" (Preface II to "Aige," Li Rongfang's Chinese translation of Lamentations). *ZLYSM* 5.8 (June 1931) 49–50. 赵紫宸:哀歌"序二",《真理与生命》

———. "Yiye de yu" (A Night of Rain). *ZLYSM* 8.4 (June 15, 1934) 185–90. 赵紫宸:"一夜的雨",《真理与生命》

Zheng, Yuren. "Qingzuo shengshu gaobai" (A Notice Inviting Contributions on the Bible). *WGGB* 11 (December 1879) 171a. 郑雨人:"请作圣书告白",《万国公报》

Zhou, Dunyi. *Zhouzi quanshu* (Complete Works of Zhou Dunyi). Taipei: Commercial, 1978. 周敦颐:《周子全书》

Zhou, Weihan. *Xishi gangmu* (Outline of Western History). Shanghai: Jingshi Wenshe, 1902. 周维翰:《西史纲目》

Zhou, Weitong. "Shengshu renwu zhuan" (Biographical Notes about Biblical Characters). *Anzhong zhi guang* (Light in Darkness) 1.3 (January 1930) 18–21. 周维同:"圣书人物传",《暗中之光》

Zhou, Xun. *Chinese Perceptions of the "Jews" and Judaism: A History of the Youtai*. Richmond: Curzon, 2001.

Zhou, Zuoren. "Shengshu yu zhongguo wenxue" (The Bible and Chinese Literature). In *Yage* (The "Song of Songs"), translated by Wu Shutian. Shanghai: Beixin Shuju, 1930, appendix, 1–19. 周作人:"圣书与中国文学",《雅歌》, 吴曙天译

Zhu, Baohui. "Yueboshu xiaoyin" (A Brief Introduction to the Book of Job). *SXZ* 5.4 (December 1919) 19–30. 朱宝会: "约伯书小引",《神学志》

Zhu, Weizhi. "Amosi—renmin de xianzhi" (Amos—the People's Prophet). First published in 1949. In *Wenyi zongjiao lunji* (Essays on Literature and Religion), by Zhu Weizhi, 112–33. Shanghai: Qingnian Xiehui Shuju, 1951. 朱维之编译:"阿摩司——人民的先知",《文艺宗教论集》

Zhu, Weizhi. *Jidujiao yu wenxue* (Christianity and Literature). Shanghai: Shanghai Shudian, 1992. First published in 1940. 朱维之:《基督教与文学》

———. "Wen yiduo lun zongjiao" (Wenyiduo's Comments on Religion). First published in 1949. In *Wenyi zongjiao lunji* (Essays on Literature and Religion), by Zhu Weizhi,

12–16. Shanghai: Qingnian Xiehui Shuju, 1951. 朱维之："闻一多论宗教"，《文艺宗教论集》

———. "Yage yu jiuge" (The "Song of Songs" and The "Nine Songs"). First published in 1947. In *Wenyi zongjiao lunji* (Essays on Literature and Religion), by Zhu Weizhi, 102–11. Shanghai: Qingnian Xiehui Shuju, 1951. 朱维之："雅歌与九歌"，《文艺宗教论集》

———. "Zhongguo wenxue de zongjiao beijing" (The Religious Background of Chinese Literature). First published in 1940. In *Wenyi zongjiao lunji* (Essays on Literature and Religion), by Zhu Weizhi, 42–57. Shanghai: Qingnian Xiehui Shuju, 1951. 朱维之："中国文学的宗教背景"，《文艺宗教论集》

Zhu, Xi. *Sishu zhangju jizhu* (Collected Commentaries to the Four Books). Beijing: Zhonghua Shuju, 1983. 朱熹：《四书章句集注》

Zhuo, Xuezhi. "Shangdiguan de yanjin" (The Evolution of the Idea of God). *XWYK* 6.8 (August 1929) 7–11. 卓学之："上帝观的演进"，《希望月刊》

Zürcher, Erik. "Aliens and Respected Guests: The Role of Foreign Monks in Early Chinese Buddhism." *Transactions of the International Conference of Eastern Studies* [Kokusai Tôhô Gakusha Kaigi kiyô] 40 (1995) 91–92.

Author Index

Adams, Marie, 122n46, 141
Adler, Joseph, 99n63, 141
Ai, Silan, 126n57n59, 141
Allen, Young John, 1, 1n2, 7, 7n34, 18–20, 19n81, 20n83, 25, 48, 141
Álvarez, Román, 40n50, 141
Ashmore, William, 4, 4n16, 7n33, 66n44, 66–67, 141

Bakeman, P. R., 65n40, 141
Baldwin, C. C., 60n17, 61n23, 141
Bangu yongren, 19–20, 19n78n81, 141
Barnett, Suzanne Wilson, 141–42, 144–45, 149
Barton, George, 85n6, 112, 112n13, 116, 116n23–24, 132n86, 141
Bary, William Theodore de, 92n32, 141, 144
Bays, Daniel, xin1, 45n75, 141
Bjornson, Bjornstjerne, 67
Blodget, Henry, 11, 59
Bloom, Irene, 92n32, 141, 144
Bohr, P. Richard, 14n65, 15n69, 142
Bridgman, Elijah, 5, 9–10, 29, 144
Boone, William J., 59n10
Burdon, John S., 7, 7n36, 11
Butcher, Dean, 66n43, 142
Buwang, 19n79, 25, 25n101, 142

Cai, Hongzhang, 17, 142
Cai, Lianfu, 69
Cai, Yuanpei, xxi, xxiv, 76, 84, 84n1–4, 86, 86n14, 101–3, 102n72–73, 117, 117n27–28, 125n52, 134, 142, 146
Camps, Arnulf, 8n41, 143

Cao, Jian, xv, 143
Cao, Xinming, 78–79, 143
Cary-Elwes, Columba, viiin6, 143
Cha, Shih-chieh, 141
Chan, Sin-wai, 147
Chen, Chi-yun, 48n84n87, 143
Chen, Duxiu, 104, 104n82, 143
Chen, Juemin, 40, 146
Chen, Shenxiu, 22, 22n90, 143
Chen, Xuming, 80, 80n102, 143
Chen, Yinke, 70
Cheng, Zhiyi, 72, 72n74, 75, 75n85, 85n9, 143
Chiang, Tsong Hai, 65n40
Chiping sou, 19, 19n78–79, 143
Cohen, Alexander, 103n77, 107n95, 115n21, 144
Cohen, Paul A., xiii, xviin13, 16n73, 33n26, 144
Collins, W. H., 6n32, 144
Connery, Christopher Leigh, 78n94, 144
Cornaby, Arthur, 61, 61n22, 144
Crawford, T. P., 144
Culbertson, Michael, 10

D'Elia, Pasquale M., xiiin6, 144
Dampier, W. C., 1n1, 144
Dean, William, 10
Dong, Jiangyang, 71n70, 144
Drake, Fred W., 5n24, 29n5, 30n12, 31n15n17n19, 32n20n25, 33n25, 36n39, 144
DuBose, Hampden C., 62n29, 144
Duiker, William J., 103n73, 144

Eber, Irene, viii–ix, xin2, xiin3, xiiin5, xvn10, 9n42, 11n54–55, 16n71, 18n77, 41n56, 59n12, 70n68, 92n34, 95n42, 130n72, 143, 145, 162
Edkins, Joseph, 11, 58n9
Ehrlich, M. Avrum, 156
Eliade, Mircea, 34n33, 145, 154, 158–59
Espey, J. M., 66n45, 145
Evans, R. K., 67n51, 145, 155

Faber, Ernest, 4n19, 68, 157
Fairbank, John King, 1n3–4, 2n5n8, 8n39–40, 12, 12n58, 16n70–72, 28n3, 33n27, 141–42, 144–45, 147, 149, 159
Fang, Zhiqin, 151
Feng, Youlan, 90–91, 91n30, 99, 145
Findeisen, Raoul, ix, 82n109, 131n78
Fokkema, Douwe, 111n7, 145

Gálik, Marián, ix, xiin3, 70n68, 145
Gamsa, Mark, 110n6, 145
Gao, Pingshu, 142–43
Garnier, Albert J., 8n41, 145
Garritt, J.C., 65n40, 68n56, 145
Glazebrook, Michael George, 7
Goddard, Josiah, 10
Goldman, Merle, 145
Goodrich, Chauncey, 61–62, 61n25–26, 62n27n31, 146
Goodspeed, E.J., 87, 87n18, 146
Graves, Rosswell Hobart, 4n18, 40, 40n53, 146
Gulick, John, 3, 3n11, 146
Guo, Bendao, 80n102, 97n50, 98n57, 146
Guo, Moruo, 70, 93n36, 146
Guo, Shaoyu, 156
Guo, Xiaoxia, xii, 146
Guo, Yingyi, 149
Guo, Zhanbo, 125n52, 146
Gützlaff, Karl Friedrich A., xv, 5–6, 6n28–31, 9–10, 29, 29n7–8, 146

Haishang shanren, 19–20, 19n79, 20n82n84, 146
Hanan, Patrick, 111n7, 146

He, Yuquan, 17, 17n75, 146
Hoare, J.C., 68
Horatii, Carlo, 11, 11n56
Hu, Shi. *Also* Hu Shih, 12n4, 67n47, 70, 86, 87n17, 88–89, 89n24, 128, 128n66, 133, 143, 146–47
Hu, Weiqing, 147
Huang, Ciyuan, 80–81, 80n104, 81n106, 147
Huang, Pinsan, 17, 147
Huang, Sungk'ang, 112n9, 147
Hudson, W.H., 125n54, 147, 159
Hutchinson, William R., 2n9, 25n103, 147
Hwang, Mei-shu, xivn9, 147

Israel, John, 110n1, 147

James, Fleming, 115n20, 117n31, 118n34–35, 119n37, 124n49, 132n83n86, 133n88, 147
Jia, Yuming, 73n76, 147
Jian, Bozan, 148
Jian, Youwen. *Also* Taijian, 72n76, 105n89, 131n79, 133n88, 134, 147, 156, 158
Jiang, Guilin, 148
Jiang, Lianyuan, 24, 24n98, 148
Jiang, Yizhen, 72n73, 120, 120n41–42, 121n44, 148
Jieyu zi, 19n79, 20, 20n82, 148
Juemeng jushi, 19n79, 21n89, 148
Juvenis, 59n15, 61n23, 148

Kang, Youwei, xvii, 28, 28n3, 43–44, 44n68–72, 47, 104, 148
Keith, C., 59n10
Keedy, John L., 69n58, 148
Kipling, Rudyard, 67
Kinkley, J.C., xiin3, 148
Kirk, Harris Elliot, 74–75, 74n82, 148
Knowlton, M.J., 58n8, 149
Kuruyagawa/Kuriyagawa, Hakuson, 87, 129, 149
Kwok, D.W.Y. *Also* Guo Yingyi, xxn19, 2n7, 149

AUTHOR INDEX

Lam, Wing Hung, xixn18, 71n69, 149
Latourette, Kenneth Scott, xiiin6, xviiin15, 69n62-63, 149
Lau, D. C., 144, 155
Lay, George T., 29, 29n10, 30n10, 149
Lee, Leo Ou-fan, 111n7-8, 112, 112n9-10, 145, 149, 152
Lee, Mei-yen, xxin22, 149
Leonard, Jane Kate, 2n5-6, 149
Levenson, Joseph R., 28n3, 149
Li, Qianli, 80n101, 149
Li, Rongfang, 70, 73, 73n77n79, 74n80, 75, 81, 85, 85n8n12, 97n51, 99, 99n61-62, 100n66-67, 103n76, 104n79, 105n84n86, 106, 106n93-94, 107n96-99, 112, 112n13, 115-18, 115n20, 116n23n26, 118n32-35, 125, 125n56, 126n57-58, 132, 132n82-86, 133n87, 134, 141, 147, 149-50, 153, 164
Lianfeng jushi, 19, 19n80
Liang, A-fa. *Also* Liang Fa, 14-16, 14n64-66, 15n67-69, 23, 28n4, 142, 152, 154
Liang, Qichao. *Also* Liang Ch'i-ch'ao, xvii, 27-28, 28n3, 45-60, 47n80, 48n84n86-87, 49n88-90, 50n91-94, 51n95-99, 52n100-3, 53n104-6n108, 54n109-11, 55n111, 57n4, 93-96, 94n38-41, 95n42-45, 96n46-48, 98n54, 110, 110n2-4, 113, 113n14, 117, 134, 136, 143, 149-52, 158-59
Liang, Junmo, 105n85, 150
Liang, Shuming, 86n15, 152
Lianxi yishi, 19
Lin, Yǔ-sheng, 130, 130n71, 152
Liu, Changxing, 22, 23n92, 152
Liu, Guangzhi, 80-81, 80n103, 81n107-8, 153
Liu, Qiang, 96n49, 153
Liu, Shijing, 3n14, 153
Liu, Sifen, 151
Liu, Songyun, 127n61, 153
Liu, Tingfang. *Also* T.T. Lew, 68n55, 73-74, 74n80n82, 85n8, 103,
103n77-78, 114-15, 114n17-18, 115n22, 117n29, 118n35, 119n38, 122, 122n46, 143, 149, 153
Liu, Yu, 121-22, 122n45, 153
Liu, Yun, xiin3, 154
Lord, Edward C., 10
Louie, Kam, xiiin8, 154
Lovell, Florence B., 65n41, 154
Lu, Xun, xxi, 110-12, 110n5n7, 111n7-8, 124, 128-30, 130n72, 132, 134, 145-46, 149, 152, 154
Lu, Zhiwei, 103n74, 154
Luce, Henry W., 69n60, 154
Lunačarskij, Anatolij V., 129-30, 129n70, 154
Lunz, Lev, 110-12, 110n5, 124, 154

Mair, Victor H., 144
Mak, George Kam Wah, xiin3, 154
Malek, Roman, ix
Marshman, Joshua, 9
Martin, W. A. P., 11
Marty, Martin E., 15n11, 154
Mascarenhas, Sidney J., 15n12, 154
Mateer, Calvin W., 3n12, 68, 154
McClatchie, Canon T., 4n20, 154
McDougall, Bonnie S., xiii8, 154
McIlvaine, Jasper S., 4n17, 5n25, 154
McNair, George Hunter, 147
Medhurst, Walter H., xv, 2n5-6, 5, 5n26, 9-10, 10n47-48, 29, 29n7, 59n10, 149, 154
Mei, Hua-Chuen, xviiin16, 155
Milne, William, 9-10, 14, 14n64
Miluo xiangren, 47n82, 155
Montague, W. P., 85n11, 128n65, 155
Morrison, John Robert, 9
Morrison, Robert, 9, 9n46, 14, 14n64
Moule, C. C., 61n23, 155
Moule, W. S., 60n17, 144, 155
Moulton, R. G., 72
Muirhead, William, 19, 61, 61n24, 155
Mutch, William J., 68, 68n58

Nakamura, Masanao, 38n46, 155
Neave, James, 67n46, 155
Nevius, J. L., 68

AUTHOR INDEX

Nord, Christiane, 39n50, 155
Noth, Martin, 88n20, 155

Okamoto, Kansuke, 38, 38n45, 43n65, 155, 157
Owen, George, 4n17, 155

Pan, Wenhe, 24, 24n100, 155
Patt-Shamir, Galia, xxn20, xxiin25, 156
Peake, A. S., 147, 156, 159
Peill, S. G., 58n10, 156
Peng, Bide, 86n13, 156
Peng, Changlin, 72n73, 156
Peters, Irma, 112n9, 156
Pitcher, P. W., 63n32, 156
Plaks, Andrew, 144
Pohl, Karl-Heinz, 152
Pollard, David, 27, 27n1, 41n55, 147, 156, 159, 161
Porter, Frank C., 112n12, 156
Porter, H. D., 60n20, 156
Porter, Lucius C. *Also* Bo Chenguang, 118n33, 127, 127n63, 156
Price, P. F., 58, 58n6, 67, 67n48, 156

Qian, Xuantong, 81n109, 156
Qianbao zi, 19–20, 19n79–80
Qiu, Tingliang, 57–58, 57n5, 156

Richard, Timothy, 3, 3n13, 20–21, 21n85–86, 25, 48, 48n87, 54n109, 157
Robinson, Lewis S., xiin3, 70n68, 157
Rowe, Harry F., 113n15, 157
Ruan, Yuan, 97n52, 107n99, 157
Ruth, Arthur, xix, xixn17, 157

Sanders, Frank K., 68, 157
Schereschewsky, Samuel I. J., xv, 7, 11, 59, 59n13n15, 71n71, 145, 158
Seymour, W. F., 63n34, 157
Shan, Shili, 17, 42, 42n58–59, 157
Shen, Congwen, xii, 101–2, 101n70, 102n71, 148, 157
Sherman, Henry A., 68, 157

Shi, Qide, 85n7, 89n26, 90n27, 132n85, 157
Shigeno, Yasutsune, 39n47, 157
Silsby, J. A., 60, 60n18–19, 61n21, 158
Sima, Qian, 120n43, 158
Smith, G. B. *Also* Shi Meifu, 85n10, 131n79, 133n88, 158
Smyth, Egbert, 26n104, 158
Song, Yuren, xvi, 33–36, 33n30, 34n31–34, 35n35–37, 36n38–41, 37n42, 39, 46, 46n77, 158
Sperling, S. David, 134n94, 158
Spillett, Hubert W., 9n43, 158
Standaert, Nicholas, 8n41, 158
Stauffer, Milton T., 63n33, 71n71–72, 158
Stronach, John, 10
Sun, Changwei, 142–43, 146
Sun, Yat-sen, xxi, 64, 64n37, 112, 112n11, 114, 114n17, 130, 153, 158
Sydenstricker, A., 59n15, 158

Tang, Caichang, xvii, 42, 42n60, 158
Tang, Chengbo, 125n54, 131, 159
Tang, Degang, 146
Tang, Yin, 79n97, 159
Tao, Chengqi, 23–24, 23n93n97, 24n99, 159
Tarumoto, Teruo, 39n50, 159
Tashan, *see* Xu Dishan.
Taylor, W.E., 63n35, 159
Teng, Ssu-yü, 28n3, 159
Tokutomi, Soho, 53
Tomlin, Jacob, 6n28, 159
Toyohiko, Kagawa, 128n65, 159
Tu, Weiming, xxn21, 159
Tyson, Lois, 82n110, 159

Van Seters, John, 118n36, 124n51, 159
Vidal, M. Carmen-África, 40n50, 141

Rad, Gerhard von, 104n83, 156

Wallace, Alfred, 89, 89n24, 159
Wallace, Edward Wilson, 65n42, 159
Walker, J.E., 60n17, 159
Wang, Benchao, xiin3, 71n68, 159
Wang, Chen-mian, xiiin7, 159

Wang, Guowei. *Also* Wang Jing'an, xxi, 75, 90, 90n28, 98n54, 101, 101n69, 159
Wang, Jingwei, 42, 42n62, 160
Wang, Shanzhi, 98n60, 105n87, 160
Wang, Shunan, 163
Wang, Wandai, 68n55
Wang, Yuande, 68, 68n58
Watts, John D., 90n29, 160
Wheeler, L. N., 66n43, 160
Wei, Dongya, 73n78, 160
Wei, Yuan, 28, 34, 39, 46, 46n77
Wen, Qing, 29n10, 160
Wenham, Gordon J., 107n95, 160
Wherry, John, 9, 9n44, 160
White, William. C., 64n36, 160
Willeke, Bernward, 11n56, 160
Williamson, Alexander, 3, 3n10, 43n65, 48, 59, 59n14, 160
Wylie, Alexander, 9n43, 15n70, 58n7, 59n13, 160
Wu, Leichuan. *Also* Wu Zhenchun, 91–92, 91n31, 131, 131n80, 160
Wu, Shuhui, 77n89, 160
Wu, Shutian, 164
Wu, Zhuosheng, 114n17, 153

Xiao, Wenan, 159
Xie, Fuya, 86n13, 160
Xie, Jingsheng, 69n65, 161
Xie, Wanying, 80n102, 161
Xing, Mei, xiin3, 161
Xiong, Yuezhi, 39n48–49, 40n51, 161
Xu, Baoqian, 85, 105n88, 155, 161
Xu, Dishan. *Also* Tashan, 72, 72n75–76, 98n58, 106n93, 158, 161
Xu, Jiyu, xvi, 28–35, 28n2n4, 29n6–7n10, 30n11–12n14, 31n16–19, 32n21–25, 33n25, 38n44, 39, 43n65, 48, 48n84, 161
Xu, Kai, 92
Xu, Renzhu, 45, 45n73, 163
Xu, Ruomeng, xiin3, 161
Xu, Shen, 92
Xu, Zhiwei, 154, 162
Xu, Zhimo, 99, 99n64–65, 100n65, 161, 164

Xue, Fucheng, 33, 33n29, 161

Yampolsky, Philip B., 23n93, 161
Yan, Jiqing, 79, 79n100, 161
Yan, Yutan, 98n58, 161
Yang, Jianlong, 71n68, 162
Yang, Jiantang, 23, 23n92n95, 162
Yang, Vi En, 65n40
Yang, Yinliu, 74n82, 115n22, 117n29, 118n35, 119n38, 122, 122n46, 153
Yao, Xingfu, 16n74, 20n83, 162
Yariv-Laor, Lihi, xvn10, 59n13, 162
Ye, Dehui, xvii, 45–47, 46n76–80, 47n81–83, 162
Ye, Qifang, 125n54, 131, 132n81, 147, 159
Yili shi, 19n79, 23, 23n96, 162
Yonekawa, Masao, 110, 110n5, 162
You, Rujie, 58n10, 162
Yu, Muren, 74–75, 74n81, 76n86, 79n98, 163
Yuan, Ding'an, xxi, 85n8, 87, 88n21–22, 89n23–24n26, 90, 90n26, 92, 92n33, 93n35, 95n45, 97n52–53, 98n55n59, 99, 99n63, 101n68, 104–5, 104n80–81, 105n88, 106n91–92, 113n16, 114, 115n20, 117, 117n29, 118n35, 119n38, 122, 123n48–49, 127, 127n62n64, 128n65, 133, 133n90, 163

Zeng, Guofan, 28, 28n3
Zeng, Jize, 33, 33n28, 163
Zeng, Yugen, 72n73, 163
Zetzsche, Jost Oliver, xiin3, xvn10, 8n41, 9n45–46, 10n47–50n52, 70n67, 163
Zhang, Dongsun, 86, 86n15, 128, 129n67, 130n70, 163
Zhang, Gengsheng, 16
Zhang, Kaiyuan, 147, 162
Zhang, Taiyan, 42, 42n63–64
Zhang, Xisan, 126n57, 141
Zhang, Yongxun, 76–78, 77n87–88, 78n91n93–94
Zhang, Zhidong, 45, 45n73–74

Zhao, Liutang, 116n26, 119, 119n39–40, 120n40, 122n47, 124n50, 163–64
Zhao, Weiben, xiin3, 164
Zhao, Xiaqiu, 161, 164
Zhao, Zichen. *Also* T. C. Chao, 73, 73n79, 85, 85n5–6, 89–90, 89n25, 100, 100n65, 105, 126, 126n60, 132n85, 134, 144, 157, 163
Zhao, Zongfu, 113, 113n16, 157
Zheng, Yuren, 21, 21n88, 164
Zhou, Dunyi, 99, 99n63, 141, 164
Zhou, Weihan, 42–43, 42n61, 43n65–67, 164
Zhou, Weitong, 106n93, 164
Zhou, Xun, xviin14, 29n8–9, 37n43, 164
Zhou, Zuoren, 75, 86, 86n16, 131n77, 164
Zhu, Baohui, 113n15, 164
Zhu, Weizhi, 87, 87n18–19, 93, 93n36–37, 117, 117n30, 118n35, 122n46–47, 127, 127n64, 130–31, 130n73–75, 131n78–19, 164–65
Zhuo, Xuezhi, 125n53, 133n89, 165
Zuijing sheng, 19–20, 19n79
Zürcher, Erik, xxiin24, 165

Subject Index

Aaron, 36, 66, 110–11, 114, 121
Abel, 18, 66, 80
Abraham, 6, 24, 29, 31–32, 66–67, 81, 99n61, 133
Achan, 100
Adam, 5, 24, 80, 88, 90, 97–99, 106n93, 117, 132
Ahriman, 90
Amorites, 118
Amos, 65n40, 105, 125, 125n56, 128, 130, 130n73, 132, 132n83n85, 134, 137, 149–50, 164
Aristotle, 88

Babel, 5, 42, 106
Babylon(ian), 32, 43, 100, 104, 117
Balzac, Honoré de, 67
Ban, Gu, 120n43, 141
benevolence. Also ren, 15, 52, 54, 85, 127, 138
Bible class, xviii, 64, 64n40, 67
Bible society/societies, 11, 59, 62, 64n37, 67, 144, 155, 158
Bible version, iv, xii, xiin3, xv, xvii, 7, 8n41, 9–11, 10n51, 13n60–62, 46n76, 58n10, 59–62, 59n13–14, 60n16–17, 61n23, 62n30, 69–72, 69n61, 71n71, 74, 115n19, 141–45, 155, 157, 159–64
Bilhah, 79, 79n95, 143
bush, 115, 115n25, 117n29, 118n35, 119n38, 121, 153
Byron, George G., 131

Cain, 18, 42, 80, 97, 150

Canaan, 31, 51–52, 111–12, 114, 118–19, 120n40, 121–23, 129
Carlyle, Thomas, 129–30
Cheng, Yi, 97n53
Chiang, Kai-shek, 111
chosen people, 8, 65, 116, 123
civil rights, 45–46
colloquial, 11, 14n64, 57, 58n9, 59n13, 61–62
Commandment, xvi, 14–15, 21–24, 22n90, 23n92–93n95–97, 24n98–99, 35–37, 35n37, 44–46, 84, 94–95, 103, 114, 116–17, 120–21, 143, 148, 152, 159, 162
Confucianism, xvi–xvii, xxn20, xxii, xxiin25, 15, 17, 22–23, 27, 33–34, 37, 41, 43–47, 46n76–77, 55, 90–92, 94, 108, 136–38, 149, 156, 162
Confucius, xx, 15, 31–32, 33n25, 45, 47, 47n81, 52n101, 81n109, 93–94, 98n60, 99n62, 107, 110, 110n3, 113, 118, 122, 127, 130, 133–34, 134n92–93, 144, 151
conscience, 20, 63, 84, 96–98, 132
covenant, 90, 98, 116–17, 116n23
creation, xxii, 2, 4n17, 5n26, 18, 46, 89, 106n93, 117, 142, 155
creator, xxii, 14, 20–21, 23, 51, 54, 84, 90–92, 101
Cromwell, Oliver, 55n111, 122, 152

Darwin, Charles, 88, 105
Darwinism, 2, 49n89, 84
Darwinian theory, 40, 89

SUBJECT INDEX

dao. Also the Way, xx, xxii, 3n14, 6, 16, 18n77, 20, 21n86, 22, 47, 82, 88, 92–93, 93n36, 102, 107, 146–47, 152–53
Daoism, 92–93, 102
Daoist ideas, 108, 137
David, vii, 29, 31, 44, 67, 76–77, 132n83, 157
Decalogue, the, xvi, 6n29
deity, 88, 92, 94, 97, 102, 105n88
Deluge/Flood, the, 95n44–45, 100n66, 105n86, 142, 149–50
Deuteronomy, 18, 127, 141
Diaspora, xvii, 39, 41, 42n57, 48, 55, 84n3, 96, 104, 122, 136, 139
Dong, Zhongshu, 94

Ecclesiastes, 14, 89
Eden, 4n17, 24, 80, 154
Egypt, 31, 35, 40–43, 51–53, 79, 100, 110, 112, 114, 116–17, 119, 121–24
Elisha, 29
Enoch, 80
Enosh, 80
Esau, 24–25, 142
Eve, 24, 80, 90, 98, 106n93, 117, 132
exile, 27, 37–38, 38n44, 47, 50, 52, 55, 65, 100, 104, 119, 123
exodus, xvii, 36, 41–43, 51, 65, 88n20, 100, 112, 114, 123, 155
Ezekiel, 100
Ezra, 65

Fall, the, 88, 90, 97
Freud, Sigmund, 67

Gadamer, Hans-Georg, 145, 155
Gadites, 119–120n40
Genesis, 4, 8n38, 14, 18, 24, 34, 42, 65, 68, 84, 101, 101n70, 103, 104n83, 107n95, 144, 156, 160
ghost, 36n41, 46, 88
Gideon, 88
Golden Calf, 35, 118n34, 120, 122
Great Harmony, 157
Gu, Yanwu, 29

Hadrian, 38
Ham, 31
Hammurabi, 117
Han, Fei, 47
Han, Yu, 76–77, 76n87, 82
Hawthorne, Nathaniel, 67
heart. Also heart-mind *or xin*, 16n74, 20, 22, 89, 97, 162
Hebrew, viii, xiii, xx, 10, 38, 40, 41n54, 51, 70, 73, 75, 77–78, 86, 86n12–13n15, 103, 103n77, 105n88, 115, 117, 122, 124, 125n55, 127, 133, 144, 150, 163
Hegel, Georg, 88
Higher Criticism, xviii, 4, 71n70, 85–86
holiness, 99, 105, 115
Horeb, 114, 116, 120
Huang, Zunxian, 57–58, 57n3, 147
Hui Neng, 23n94
Huxley, Thomas, 88

idol, 43, 121, 132
idolatry, 14, 43
Isaac, 6n29, 24, 67
Isaiah, 14, 64n40, 65n40, 89, 90n29, 132, 153, 160
Ishmaelites, 81
Israel, 28–31, 43, 43n65, 64n40, 65–66, 85n6, 86, 88n20, 103, 111, 115–16, 116n23–24, 123–24, 129, 132n84–86, 141, 145, 150, 162
Israelites, 35, 28, 41n54, 42–43, 48, 48n86, 53–54, 72, 77–78, 81n109, 89, 89n26, 93, 98, 100, 104, 110–18, 115n20, 116n23, 118n34, 121–23, 129

Jacob, 6n29, 24–25, 31, 67, 74, 74n82, 76–79, 81, 81n108, 95n45, 100, 153
James, William, 88
Japheth, 31
Jeremiah, 64n40, 100, 125, 129–34, 131n78, 132n86, 133n88, 134n94, 137, 141, 158
Jerusalem, viii, ix, xin2, 38n44, 44, 44n71, 68, 148

SUBJECT INDEX

Jesuit, xi, xin1, 134
Jesus, 3, 19, 20, 20n82, 25, 29, 31–32, 32n25, 37, 46, 49, 71, 112n12, 117n27, 124, 127–28, 128n65, 130, 132–33, 132n85–86, 134n93, 137, 148, 150, 156, 159
Jethro, 113n16, 123
Jew, xiin4, xvii, 27–30, 37–38, 38n44, 41–44, 41n54, 42n57, 44n71, 47–53, 50n94, 55, 84, 84n3, 93, 94n38, 95–96, 105, 123n49, 131, 133, 136, 145, 148, 162–64
Job, 36, 89, 100, 113n15, 164
Jonah, 132
Jordan, 118, 119n40
Joseph, 24, 31, 67, 76, 79–81, 79n100, 81n106, 100, 147, 161
Joshua, 18, 31, 41, 112, 121–22
Judah, 78
Judaism. Also *youtaijiao*, xxn20, xxii, xxiin25, 29, 31–32, 49, 84, 89–90n26, 95n45, 98n59, 104–5, 104n80–81, 105n88, 113n16, 115n20, 117, 117n29, 123, 123n49, 127, 127n62n64, 133, 133n90, 138, 156, 163–64
Judas, 66
Judea, 4n17, 28, 30, 32, 38–39, 41, 43–44, 43n65, 110, 142, 162–63
Judges, 34, 133

Kant, Immanuel, 75, 88, 97–98, 97n50, 102n73, 146
kingdom, 91, 93, 104–5, 133, 139
Kings, 18, 43n65, 162–63
Kropotkin, Peter, 106, 106n91

Laban, 24, 78
Lamech, 80
Lamentations, 73, 73n77, 130–31, 131n76, 150, 153, 164
Lao Zi, 47, 88, 92–93
Lassar, Joannes, 9, 13

law, 1, 4, 6, 6n29, 32, 35–37, 35n37, 37n42, 39, 49n89, 50, 54, 54n109, 64, 74, 89, 94–95, 104–5, 115, 117–18, 117n29, 121, 127–28, 152, 158
Learning, 2, 44–45, 47, 51, 57n4, 63, 87, 99, 105, 110, 113, 126, 162
Learning, New, 39–40, 67, 113
Learning, Western, 1, 4, 26, 35, 39–40, 39n48, 48, 48n86, 113, 135, 152
Legge, James, 10
Leviticus, 18, 127
Levites, 35, 110–11
Li, Hua, 76, 76n87
Liu, Tui, 76–77
Lu, Xiangshan, 90n28
Luther, Martin, 130

Maccabean period, 68
Mandarin. Also *guan hua*, vii, xiin3, xv, xvn10, 7–9, 10, 59–62, 59n11n13, 60n16, 61n24–25, 62n27–28n31, 68–71, 143, 146, 154–55, 161
mandate, 93–94, 103, 117
Manichean controversy, 5
Marx, Karl, 129, 129n67n70, 154
Matthew, 18
Masoretic Text, the, 77
Maupassant, Guy de, 67
Mencius. Also Meng zi, xx, 18n77, 22n91, 47, 53, 53n108, 90n28, 97, 97n53, 99–100, 99n61, 101n68, 127, 127n61, 133n91, 155
messiah, 20, 133, 134n93
Micah, 132
Midian, 115
Milton, John, 75
Mizraim, 31–32
Mo zi, 36n41, 47, 93–94, 94n40, 106, 106n91
monotheism/monotheist(ic), vii, xix–xxii, 14–15, 22, 32, 82–84, 88–89, 92–93, 100, 102, 132, 132n85, 136–37

SUBJECT INDEX

Moses. *Also* Moxi, v, vii–viii, xvii,
    xxi, 5–6, 6n29n31, 22, 23n92,
    27–29, 31–32, 32n25, 34–38,
    35n37, 36n41, 40–41, 41n54,
    42n58, 44–47, 49, 49n89, 51–55,
    54n111, 65–66, 70, 88, 88n20,
    94, 96, 99, 109–25, 110n2,
    112n12, 113n15–16, 114n17,
    115n20, 116n23n26, 117n27n30,
    118n34–36, 119n38–40, 120n40,
    122n46–47, 123n49, 128, 130,
    136, 144, 146, 149, 152, 155, 157,
    159, 163–64
myth(ical), 18, 30, 37n41, 84, 94–95, 103,
    117, 117n27, 121
mythology, xiv, 4, 4n22

Nachmanides, 115n21
narrative, xv, 6, 24, 26, 65–66, 137
nationalism, xvi–xvii, xix–xx, 42, 68,
    83, 103–7, 109, 110n1, 122–23,
    123n49, 130–31, 133, 136, 147,
    160
nature. *Also xing*, xxii, 7, 14–15, 20, 23,
    23n94, 44, 54, 66, 75, 83, 90n28,
    91–92, 91n32, 97, 99, 129, 134,
    137–39
nature. *Also ziran*, 2, 54n109, 76, 88, 91,
    94–95, 95n45, 97, 102, 115, 117,
    137
Nebo, 114
Nebuchadnezzar, 43
Nehemiah, 65
Newton, Isaac, 2
Noah, 4n22, 5, 5n25, 30, 66, 80, 85, 105,
    154, 156
Numbers, 118–19, 127

Ormuzd, 90
Ouyang, Xiu, 76–77, 77n87

Pangu, 5, 5n26, 117
pantheism/pantheistic, 84, 102, 123
paradise, 14, 90–91
patriarch, 6, 6n29, 66, 69, 146
Pharaoh, 113, 118–19, 122–23

Plato, 88–89, 97
Poe, Allen, 67
polytheism/polytheist(ic), 84, 88, 92–93,
    100, 123
precepts (of Buddhism), 17, 17n76, 31, 44
priest, 36, 104, 111, 113n16, 116–18
Promised Land, the, 110
prophet. *Also Xianzhi*, viii, xiii, xxi, 43,
    54n111, 64n40, 65–66, 70, 77,
    90, 103–5, 109, 116–18, 125–34,
    125n52n55, 126n57, 130n70,
    131n79, 132n83–86, 137, 150,
    157, 164
Proverbs, 8, 18, 75, 155
Psalms, xi, 7n35, 8n37, 18, 20, 75, 104,
    132n83, 148, 155, 157
punishment, xx, 100, 132, 148

Qi, 36n41
qi, 21n89, 90n28
Qu, Yuan, 73, 78n94, 131, 131n78

Rahab, 79, 79n96, 143
Rashbam, 115n21
Rashi, 106, 115n21
Rebecca/Rebekah, 24, 81, 81n108, 153
Red Sea, 100
redemption, 75, 96, 101, 131
retribution, 74, 100, 127
Reubenite, 119n40
revelation, 3, 3n14, 66, 71, 85, 106, 125,
    153
revolution, xvii, 42, 44, 50n94, 57, 59n11,
    63, 67, 104, 110–11, 111n8, 114,
    117n27, 122–24, 130, 151, 156
righteousness, 15, 54, 127, 132
ritual, 17, 36, 132
ritualistic piety, 14
Roman, 5, 29, 32, 36–38, 65
Rousseau, Jean Jacques, 88, 129–30

Sabbath, 18, 117, 157
sacrifice, 14, 18, 46, 53, 77n89, 117, 120,
    160

SUBJECT INDEX

sage, viii, xxi, 6, 40, 46, 54–55, 99, 99n61n63, 113, 116, 118, 126–27, 133, 138, 141
salvation, xx–xxi, 23, 57, 71n70, 133
Samson, 34, 38
Samuel, 65–66
Satan, 90
Saul, 66, 100
Schmidt, N., 79
Scriptures. Also *jing*, xi, xviii, 4n21, 9n43–44, 11, 13n61, 17, 21–22, 22n91, 36, 56, 58–59n10, 60–61, 64, 87, 98n58, 136, 142–43, 156–58, 160–61
Semites, 49–50
serpent, 80, 80n102, 99, 143
Seth, 66
Sforno, 115n21
shangdi, 3n10, 21, 21n89, 22n90, 23n92n95–96, 92–93, 97n52, 101–2, 125n53, 133n89, 143, 146, 148, 160, 162, 165
Shakespeare, William, 7, 66, 75
Shem, 31
shen, 31, 53, 74n82, 85n8, 88–89n21–24, 90n28, 92, 92n33–34, 93n35, 94n38, 97n52–53, 98n55, 99n63, 101–2, 101n68, 103n77, 106n91, 114n18, 153, 163
Shen Xiu, 23, 23n90
Shun, 36, 37n41
sin, 14, 26, 66, 88, 91, 97n51, 99–100, 99n61–62, 106, 118n32, 133n87, 150
Sinai, 22, 32, 88n20, 114, 117, 119–21, 122n45, 153
Socrates, 88, 122
Solomon, 44, 65, 147
Song of Songs, the, 18, 72, 72n75–76, 73n76, 75, 86–87, 87n18–19, 101n70, 147, 161, 164–65
soul. Also *ling, hun, linghun*, 13n62, 15, 20, 43, 45, 76, 97n50, 98n57, 99, 111, 146, 157
Spencer, Herbert, 88–89

spirit. Also *ling*, 3, 10, 14, 90, 94, 98, 103, 111, 147, 157
storytelling, vii, 6, 6n29, 24, 76n86, 79–80, 81n106, 95
Sunday School, 64, 64n36n40, 69n58, 148, 157, 160

tabernacle, 36, 117
Tent of Congregation, 113n16
theism / theistic, 2, 87
theocracy, 113n16
theology, 70–71, 76, 103, 117, 124
theology, biblical, 67, 104
theology, Christian, 19, 67, 78, 81, 112n12
theology, liberal, xviii, 23, 25, 139
theology, natural, 1, 3
theology, scholastic, 89
tian. Also heaven, xxii, 6–7, 14, 16, 18, 21n86, 22, 31, 34, 36n41, 46–47, 47n81, 54, 73, 91n32, 92–97, 93n36, 94n38n40, 97n53, 99, 99n63, 101, 103, 105, 113, 117, 123, 125, 127, 130, 132, 132n83, 139, 146, 153, 159
Tolstoy, Lev, 129–30, 129n70, 154
Torah, 54
tract, 1–2, 12, 24, 45, 45n75, 58n9, 141, 147, 159

Wang, Yangming, 16n74, 20, 20n83, 90n28, 162
Washington, George, 122
Wellington, Duke, 35
Western learning, 1, 4, 26, 35, 39–40, 39n48, 48, 48n86, 113, 135, 152
will, 2, 6, 35, 45, 52–54, 81, 85, 89, 91, 93–94, 94n40, 96–101, 114, 126, 146
wisdom, 3, 6, 35, 37, 51, 54, 64–65, 64n40, 91, 119n38, 128, 128n65, 138, 159

Xun zi, 22, 97

Yahweh, 43, 88n20, 90, 93, 114–16, 115n20, 116n23, 123
Yang, Guangxian, 34
Yang, Zhu, 47
Youtai, 4n17, 38n44, 40, 40n53, 42n57, 43n65, 50, 90n26, 95n45, 98n59, 104n80–81, 105n88, 113n16, 115n20, 117n29, 123n49, 127n62n64, 133n90, 142, 145–46, 162–64
Yu, 94

Zedekiah, 43
Zeng zi, 52
Zhang, Zhongcheng, 22
Zhou, Duke, 33n25
Zhu, Xi, 20, 47, 68, 91, 91n32, 92n32, 130, 165
Zhuan Xu, 36, 37n41
Zilpah, 79, 79n95, 143
Zoroastrianism, 90

Scripture Index

Old Testament/Hebrew Bible

Genesis

1–2	18
1	89
1:3	100n65
2–3	90
2:7	90–91
2:18–24	106
6:4	105
9:5–6	104, 106
10	107
11:1–9	106
24	81
25:29–34	24
31:26–32	78
31:36–53	78
37–46	79–80
37:33–35	76–77
49:8–12	78

Exodus

2:11–15	124
3:14–15	115n20
3:14	114
9:15	124n49
19–20	121
20:3	116
20:4	103, 103n77
24	121
32	118n34, 121
33:8–13	88
33:12	88n20
33:13	88n20
34	121
34:14	116n23

Numbers

11:14	119
11:17	119
11:29	119
27:13	119
27:14	119

Deuteronomy

18:15	117

Joshua

7	100

Judges

6:36–40	88
14:8	77n90

1 Samuel

	65

2 Samuel

18:33	76–77
19:4	76–77
21:1–14	100

Psalms

25	77n90
27:1	78
34	77n90
35:26–27	78
72:10	77n90
122	104
145	77n90

Proverbs

3:11–13	100

Song of Songs

1:1–2:7	72
2:8–3:5	72
3:6–5:1	72
5:2–6:3	72
6:4–7:10	72
7:11–8:4	72
8:5–8:14	72

Isaiah

1:9	77n90
10:6	77n90
14:9–20	77
45:67	90

Jeremiah

10:15	132
14:22	132

Amos

9:7	105

New Testament

Matthew

16:15	18

www.ingramcontent.com/pod-product-compliance
Lightning Source LLC
Chambersburg PA
CBHW051739230426
43670CB00012B/2080